MARINE ART & ANTIQUES

JACK TAR

A SAILOR'S LIFE

1750-1910

Dancing the Hornpipe.

Painted in 1878 by English painter George Green, this watercolor captures a sailor dancing the hornpipe, to the amusement of his fellow sailors and their lady friend. (For a fuller description see page 149)

MARINE ART & ANTIQUES
JACK TAR
A SAILOR'S LIFE
1750-1910

Smooth Sailing?
Welles Hen

J. Welles Henderson
and
Rodney P. Carlisle

ANTIQUE COLLECTORS' CLUB

Contents

Dedication

To My Family

To my wife, Hannah, some of whose ancestors went to sea,
for her understanding and patience, helpful advice and steadfast support

to

My children – Joe, Cabot, David, Lisa and Sy,
with apologies for the hours spent
gunk holing for marine art and antiques instead of getting to know them better

and to their progenies

Lulu, Welles, Davina, Consuelo, Cabot, Alessandra, Hannah and Eliza

all in all, an enthusiastic and ship-shape crew.

Acknowledgements

This book is the culmination of many years of collecting, observation, assimilation and research. Many people from various countries have contributed in multiple ways.

In our collaboration for over two years in writing this book, I am indebted to my co-author, Rodney P. Carlisle, for his cooperation in fleshing out the structure of the book and conveying my insights as a collector.

Over three and a half years ago, Mary Sinclair came on board as my Administrative Assistant. In addition to computer and organization skills, she broadened the definition of Assistant in many helpful ways. Her son, John, also aided the project.

Support of the Independence Seaport Museum (ISM, formerly the Philadelphia Maritime Museum) through its Board of Port Wardens, Walter D'Alessio (Chairman), and John S. Carter (President), as co-publisher of this book, is deeply appreciated. ISM is also to be thanked for the exhibit it is mounting simultaneously with the publication of this book on 'Life of a Sailor: A Collector's Vision' primarily of material of my Collection illustrated in, and following the general outline of, the book. The exhibit is to be open for approximately a year and then may travel. Many are to thanked at ISM through the years, especially the present Curator, Ed Lynch, his Volunteer wife, Nancy, and his staff, including Craig Bruns. In various ways, Carol Burkert (Assistant to the President), has been a continuing source of invaluable help. The present Librarian, Michael Angelo, and former Librarian, Ann Wilcox, willingly provided meaningful information. Chad Smith, former Curator, has also made suggestions.

The quality of the illustrations in the book is of primary importance and I wish to express my deep appreciation to Will Brown for his splendid photography.

Over the years, a series of graduate students at the University of Pennsylvania worked at cataloging my Collection. The one who deserves special credit is Sue Popkin who acted as my Curator for about four years.

For his enthusiasm, helpful observations in many ways, and supportive friendship through many years, I wish to thank warmly fellow huntsman on many fruitful forays, collector Bob Teitelman.

Dan Finamore, Curator of Maritime Art & History at Peabody Essex Museum, has been very helpful. Also to be thanked from that institution are Lyles Forbes, Assistant Curator, Geraldine Ayers, Managing Editor of the *American Neptune*, and John Koza, a former Librarian.

Two outstanding dealers, Charles Childs and Harry Shaw Newman, and collector, Francis B. Lothrop, who, unfortunately, are no longer with us, were unstinting with their knowledge and advice to a fledgling collector.

Ron Bourgeault, Alan and Janice Granby, and John Rinaldi have made significant contributions on many occasions. Jack Freas has supplied knowledgeable advice concerning books and prints. Those who found treasures have included: Diana Bittel, Carl Crossman, Norm Flayderman, Greg Gibson, David Good, Eleanor Gordon, Lew Howland, Mimi and Paul Ingersoll, Joel Kopp, Ken Newman and Richard York. In England, Martyn Gregory, Hugh Bett and Glenn Mitchell of Maggs, as well as Brian Newbury of Parker Gallery, have kept their acquisitive eyes open for me.

In the way of research and information, I am indebted to many including: Charles Burden; James Cheevers (Curator) of the Naval Academy Museum; Dr William S. Dudley (Director), Mark J. Wertheimer (Curator), and Jesse R. Rankin (Specialist) of the Naval Historical Center; Stuart Frank (Director) Kendall Whaling Museum; Fritz Gold; Paul Johnston (Curator of Maritime History) Smithsonian Institution; Pat Halfpenny (Director of Museum Collections) Wintertur Museum; John Lastavica; Innis Shoemaker (Curator of Prints) Philadelphia Museum of Art; Lita Solis-Cohen (Senior Editor) *Maine Antique Digest*; James Tanis (former Librarian) Bryn Mawr College; Herbert W. Warden, III, and John Wilmerding. In England, Rina Prentice (a Senior Curator) and Brian Lavery (Head of Display) at the National Maritime Museum in London; Anthony Tibbles (Curator of Maritime History) at Merseyside Maritime Museum, Liverpool; and Marc Loost.

For model restoration work, I am thankful for George Dukes; for imaginative conservation of textiles, my warm appreciation is given to Virginia Whelan; and for his expertise in paper conservation, I wish to thank Terry Harvey.

I am most enthusiastic with my gratitude to my publisher Diana Steel (Antique Collectors' Club), for her understanding of what I wished to accomplish and for making the dream come true. To my editor, Peter Robertson, I am indebted for his taking the manuscript and assorted illustrations and weaving them together; also Sandra Pond for her vital contribution towards the lay-out and design of this handsome book.

There have been many people, certainly not limited to those included here, who have given generously of their time and expertise as part of this endeavor. My thanks to each of them is sincere.

Foreword

Welles Henderson has dedicated himself over the past half century to assembling an extensive collection of art and artifacts that visually tells the life of a sailor from the mid-eighteenth to the early twentieth century. Over twenty-five years ago I became aware of Welles' interest in the sea and those who sailed on it when he was the head of the US World's Fair on the Environment (Expo '74) and I was the American Ambassador to Great Britain. We had a mutual interest in maritime history as I served in the US Naval Reserve from 1950 to 1966 with the rank of Commander.

Through the ensuing years I have watched with admiration as Welles' collection grew and hoped he would write a book. With his innovative approach to collecting objects pertaining to the ordinary life of a sailor, Welles' interests are broader than those of the traditional museum focused on ship paintings, ship models, navigational instruments, figureheads and weaponry.

Through this book based on his collection he has brought to our attention the importance of the sailor without whom no ships would have sailed. The contemporaneous illustrations bring to life the fears and joys, loneliness and hearty gatherings, perils and triumphs, female relationships, and handicrafts, from crude to magnificent, born of boredom or inspiration.

Education is the key to our future. His collection is unique and through the illustrations and text, the reader will have the opportunity to learn about sailors from a different and meaningful viewpoint.

Walter H. Annenberg

Preface

The Independence Seaport Museum is proud to co-publish this book devoted to the life of the sailor, with the museum's founder, J. Welles Henderson. Over the years, Welles Henderson has gathered one of the finest private collections of maritime art, artifacts, and manuscripts in the world relating to the life of a sailor. The museum will be exhibiting a significant portion of that collection in this book. The materials in the collection offer an unusual opportunity to gain insight into the lives of both ordinary sailing men and women as well as officers.

J. Welles Henderson has written this richly illustrated book which offers many insights and anecdotes to help explain the significance of the collection. Through the book we learn what impelled men and women to put their lives at risk on the high seas. We gain a feel for the daily life aboard merchant and naval ships of Britain, the United States, and some of the other maritime countries of the world between 1750 to 1910. We view their handicrafts, see the tools they used, examine the fine needlework and embroidery they produced, and, through some of the art made by sailors themselves, we look through their eyes at the world around them. The crimes and punishments aboard ship, the separation from loved ones, the cavorting and carousing of sailors in port and on ship, the perils of the sea, and some of the sailors' inmost thoughts about romance, religion, death, and the afterlife are all here.

Museums and historians alike are moving away from representing only the life of the 'social elite', such as the political and military leadership of the past, in an attempt to penetrate the lives of the poor, the illiterate, and ordinary working people. Such study is not easy, for often those at the bottom of the social structure left no written record, and only rarely did they attain skill in the visual and related arts. Even the well-read sea-captain, naval officer, or merchant-trader was usually too busy to record his thoughts and experiences for posterity.

By thoughtful and selective collecting over half a century, Welles Henderson has put together a magnificent assemblage of items that achieves the near-impossible. Through the materials he has gathered, one glimpses the elusive – the daily life, the boredom and the heartache – sensed and felt not only by the officers, but especially by those men and women whose story has rarely been told: the seamen, their loved ones, the whalers, and the naval sailors of a bygone era.

Did you know that US sailors skipped rope aboard ship in the 1890s for exercise? Did you know that teenage boys were punished by being mastheaded – sent high aloft? Did you realize that peg-legs, eyepatches, and hooks in place of hands were not mythical or fictional attributes of pirates, but were the frequent result of accidents or battle among sailors on sailing ships? Did you know that prior to 1815, British sailors were often forcibly dragged into service by press gangs, or that merchant crews were often put together by paid 'crimps' who tricked sailors into signing aboard? These and a thousand other facts are portrayed and described here.

We recommend this book as an informative and handsome addition to any maritime or nautical collection or library. It is such a powerful vision of the past that we believe its appeal will reach far beyond those with a special interest in the sea. Look through these images, and you find yourself transported back to an era that was harder, tougher, sometimes more painful, yet often more beautiful than our own. Imagine the life of Jack Tar, if you will, through the materials he has left us and that J. Welles Henderson has put before us in this magnificent volume. The experience is enriching. The book offers a fresh view into the period 1750-1910. We are pleased to be associated with the effort that has gone into bringing these materials to the attention of the public.

John S. Carter, President
Independence Seaport Museum
Philadelphia, Pennsylvania USA 1999

Author's Note

How did I become a collector in the first place? As a seven-year old in 1927, I gave fifty cents to save America's most historic ship, the USS *Constitution* – 'Old Ironsides.' For that donation, I received a small anchor made of metal and wood salvaged from the ship. This event changed my life – it was as if I had become transfused with salt water. My quest as a collector had begun for all things relating to the sea.

By the early 1950s I had developed four guiding principles for my collecting: 1) I had to like the object; 2) it had to be the best of its category that I could afford; 3) was it genuine?; 4) I would not buy it for investment. I was interested in material relating to my hometown, the Port of Philadelphia and the Bay and River Delaware and on the life of the sailor, 'Jack Tar' – the universal sailor of all nations, seas and periods.

Philadelphia had a rich maritime history but no dedicated showcase for it. In 1960 I founded the Philadelphia Maritime Museum (now the Independence Seaport Museum). With the museum in place I had found a home for my nautical objects relevant to its mission statement. For many years my principal efforts were to build the regional importance of the Philadelphia Maritime Museum. At the same time, at a lesser pace, I continued to acquire objects relating to the life of a sailor. Recently I made a serious decision to write a book about that life; and, with this goal in mind, I made a full-fledged effort to enlarge greatly the scope and depth of the collection. My personal collection of the 'Life of the Sailor' took on all manner of material, especially visual, pertaining to this theme – an area long overlooked by a number of maritime museums and scholars. The guidelines for my sailor's life project were: 1) the personnel covered were 'deep water' officers and seamen; 2) they served in the merchant marine or navy; 3) they were multinational, but mostly British and American; 4) the period covered was *c.*1750 to *c.*1910.

In looking for material to collect, one found that artists in the early days of sail were not generally interested in the life of the common sailor – the important admirals and naval battles commanded their attention. Expeditions to exotic and remote regions of the world had artists accompany them, but little of the everyday life aboard ship was portrayed. So began a hunt – one piece at a time. From top dealers and great auction houses to house sales and flea markets – anywhere with a glimmer of a chance of yielding something interesting was fair game.

I cultivated dealers assiduously, hoping for first crack at anything in my field. Through the years I built up a reference library to round out the picture of Jack Tar's life, from the time he decided to go to sea, until he swallowed the anchor (retired on shore) or died.

The serendipitous connections between various items in my collection became an absorbing game – the fitting of pieces into this ever-expanding and meaningful mosaic. For example, a watercolor, probably by a crew member of a British sloop that eluded capture in an 1813 naval engagement paired with the entries in the log of a participating and disappointed American frigate, the USS *President*. A 1779 print of naval hero, John Paul Jones, was enriched by a letter of Robert Morris in 1777 to John Hancock, President of the Continental Congress imploring that something should be done to find a job for Jones. A chronometer used aboard HMS *Challenger* on its historic oceanographic voyage around the world (1872-1876) was made more meaningful by a series of thirty-one watercolors painted on the cruise by a cooper aboard the vessel.

Contemporary eye-witness accounts and original source material are of supreme importance to me and, whenever possible, I have tried to show examples in color throughout the book. However, sometimes the only rendition I could find of something relevant was in black and white. An area that one would think rich in written commentary and visual references would be eroticism or sex since sailors spent so much time at sea without the companionship of women. I have found very little. Perhaps the keepers of diaries and journals or letter writers were concerned lest their mothers, wives or sisters read their deeply personal comments. Perhaps it was the tenor of the times – of Victorian inhibitions. The one place, however, where sex is mentioned, sometimes very graphically, is in Court Martial reports.

Collecting is not just a matter of going to a speciality shop and pointing out what you want. You need to develop your want list. Sometimes the chase gives more satisfaction than the actual ownership of the desired item. Sometimes patience and determination yield rich rewards. Years ago I went to a newly-opened prestigious folk art gallery. Upon entering one of the galleries, a magnificent, towering sailor figure joyfully waving his sailor's hat in the air took my breath away. He was the embodiment of my quest – here was the ultimate expression of Jack Tar. I had to have it. Well, that is until I learned the price! It was light years away from what I could afford. Years later I heard that it had sold at auction and was now owned by one of America's leading nautical antique dealers. Applying my guidelines, I found I certainly liked it, it said something, it spoke to me. Secondly, as far as I was concerned, it was, to my knowledge, the best of its category. As to the genuineness test, I enlisted the professional help of a leading museum to check the type of wood (American pine), the painting layers and other characteristics. We then had an X-ray machine check the inner structure and this confirmed the presence of an old rod inside. Fortunately, the price of the piece was now considerably less than that asked all those years ago. I bit the bullet and Jack Tar became my prized possession. He became my logo. Many months later, the dealer told me he had just learned that Jack Tar was listed as one of one hundred American folk art masterpieces in a book written by leading folk art experts in 1990. It is a most rewarding feeling to have one's judgment confirmed by the leading authorities in that particular field.

Sometimes small sums can make you happy. Decades ago, while in a general antique shop, I found a book on American navigation. The price was five dollars, the dealer informed me, because it was a later edition. I gladly gave him the money and brought home a copy of Nathaniel Bowditch's first edition, 1802, of his *The New American Practical Navigator*, published by Blunt, one of the top scientific books published in America.

Although well worn and somewhat damaged by hard usage at sea, I had acquired a real treasure at a fraction of its real value. This does not happen very often to most collectors but it is a wonderful feeling when it does. Usually, you get what you pay for.

Sometimes an acquisition is given added value by a quirk of fate. Shortly after John F. Kennedy was inaugurated, a newspaper story stated that the first thing the President wanted his wife to do was to find him a painting of a naval engagement for the Oval Office. My wife brought the article to my attention and I sent a telegram to the President and his wife offering to lend him a painting of the US Frigate *Constitution* defeating HMS *Guerriere* on 19 August, 1812, or of the US Frigate *United States* defeating HMS *Macedonian* on 25 October, 1812. Several days later a US Navy station wagon carried the latter oil painting by Thomas Birch to the White House. The painting was given a place of honor to the left of the President's desk as one faced it in the Oval Office. I received a gracious letter from the President, thanking me for the loan and a photograph of the Oval Office showing its location.★ During his presidency we had a family game of seeing which photographs we could find of VIPs from around the world in the Oval Office with my ship painting in the background.

Connections make history much more interesting and meaningful. In the 1950s and early 1960s, many so-called art experts did not say much in favor of American art. It was not English, French or Italian. Undaunted, I tried to acquire some maritime scenes by those I considered top American artists. High on my list was Thomas Eakins of Philadelphia. As fate would have it, in a leading New York gallery, I found an oil painting of an American Rear Admiral in a gilded oak frame made by Eakins with nautical symbols attached to it. The sitter was identified as Rear Admiral Charles Dwight Sigsbee who in 1903, the year he was portrayed, was Commandant of the Philadelphia Navy Yard.

In 1898 he was the Captain of the USS *Maine* when it blew up in Havana Harbor. The explosion precipitated the Spanish-American War. I checked for authenticity with top experts and everyone agreed that the painting was by Eakins. Several years later in a Boston nautical antique shop, I found a journal of a US Naval Academy midshipman in the early 1860s filled with pen and ink and pencil sketches of a midshipman's life, initialed by a 'CDS' and in one drawing 'Sigsbee'. Here were actual drawings by a naval man who became a very well-known Rear Admiral in later years. In addition, I found out that he taught drawing at the Naval Academy in the 1870s. The overall picture was much richer in detail when all the pieces were fitted together. The portrait and various of the Sigsbee sketches are illustrated in this book. Today, Eakins is considered by many as one of the top artists of all time in the United States.

I have cast my net as broadly and deeply as possible in acquiring items to explore the life of Jack Tar. The themes that run through the materials range over the emotional, physical and spiritual life of seamen. Scenes of sailors ashore and at sea echo and re-echo themes and ideas: loneliness, wild celebration, hilarity, hard work and drudgery, stern discipline,

perils and crises, and solemn moments of grief.

The works selected give diverse insights, characterizations and episodes from different periods and from merchant and naval ships but what was true in one time and place was not necessarily so in another. Yet a reader of this book, like a visitor to a museum, may gain much from such diversity.

This book is not meant to be encyclopedic or a learned tome. The emphasis is on contemporary source material. I hope it will inform, enlighten and excite the curiosity of the general reader and also be of interest to the maritime specialist and those who love the sea.

J. Welles Henderson
Haverford, PA
1999

A Collector's Vision

This book presents a collector's vision of the life of the deep-water seaman in the age of sail and early steam-powered ships, as seen through his collection. The Collection is ranked by experts as the largest, most broad-based, and highest quality private collection of artifacts and pictorial images relating to the sailor's life ever assembled in the United States.

To assemble this material was a labor of over four decades, for prints, pictures, and craft products which show aspects of daily life of sailors are difficult to find, and must be tracked down not only in the great auction houses, but in obscure shops scattered all over Europe and America, and in private sales, and even, from time to time, in unlikely second-hand rummage sales. Searching, evaluating, identifying, and in some cases preserving and conserving the finds took thousands of hours. Although some of the prints have been reproduced in other books, some are so rare that they have not appeared in any recently published works and will be seen by modern viewers here for the first time.

Paintings, prints, craft work, and rare manuscripts find their way into public display at museums through many different pathways. Some valuable possessions are kept by participants as mementos or souvenirs of their own lives, passed on as heirlooms to their descendants, and thence often flow into the market via shops or auctions. Traces of the past move gradually from contemporary usage through sometimes countless hands to private display cases and, perhaps decades or centuries later, to public exhibit or into the obscurity of a museum vault. In the long span of the life of a such an image or object, ownership is only a temporary state, a caretaking responsibility in one generation.

Yet the role of private buyers can be crucial to artifacts and art as they pass through time. Collectors develop a special relationship with the treasures they momentarily possess. Often an item will fill a gap in an assemblage thought out by the collector, fitting into groupings or fields. Such a series may represent varied examples of a particular form, period, motif, medium, or content. The gathering of items to fill gaps in such groups can become an obsession, to fill out subcategories, categories, and themes, taking long hours of challenging detective work and intelligent study. From the collector's desire to bring together items that belong in certain groups, many basic functions important to the process of understanding human history are served. Unnoticed parallels can be traced, influences detected, and cultural connections uncovered. As the collecting community sets prices on rare items through auction houses, it helps ensure the preservation of the physical past.

As collectors look at this book, they may see patterns and connections to items they themselves have gathered. The Collection, and this book, have the theme of the search for Jack Tar himself – what motivated him, how he lived his ordinary daily life, and what extremes of risk and condition he faced. The themes that run through the materials range over the emotional, physical, and spiritual life of seamen.

This book is an effort to capture the vision of the Henderson Collection and to offer some insights gained from studying and living with the Collection to a wider audience. In pictorial representation, and through quotation from rare manuscripts and books, the book presents to the public many of the sources of the vision, from physical traces, from rare art, and from never-before published documentary evidence. Quotations used in the body of the text are primarily from the assembled rare editions of printed and manuscript materials.

The sense of the life of the seaman which emerges from close viewing of this gathering of art, object, and unique written document, parallels a new focus of interest among professional historians in the daily life of ordinary people of the past. In recent decades, historians have sought to uncover the history of people, including both those from the literate class, which in the late eighteenth century and in the nineteenth century, included most merchant and nearly all naval officers, as well as many who only rarely left any written or printed record of their lives, such as whalers, naval, and merchant sailors. This new social history is unlike traditional political history in both subject matter and method. For the majority of ordinary persons, most surviving traces of their lives are things and illustrations, with only an occasional letter, diary, notebook, or a handwritten account to flesh out the tale. The public record can give only one side, sometimes, very dry and impersonal, of what happened to the real individuals of the past.

In recent years, several social historians have studied the ordinary seamen and officers of the eighteenth and nineteenth century through statistics and through fugitive documentary sources such as rare diaries, journals, and travel accounts. Scholars have culled through archives and libraries to locate and publish whole journals and accounts written by ordinary seamen and ships' officers. The body of historical work reflecting this new emphasis continues to grow.[1]

Tangible and visual relics can be more compelling than the written record. The daily life of past generations is seen and touched through their equipment, tools, utensils, and clothing. Artists often caught details of costume, behavior, and even attitude or thought in paintings, prints, and other media. In the eighteenth and nineteenth century, a professional painter or sketch artist would capture the portrait of a captain, with either his wife by his side or with his ship visible in the distance, and sometimes, very rarely, with both. In such rare paintings, there are many examples where the name of the officer has not survived with his portrait but the modern viewer may imagine the lives of the anonymous couple as they stare from their mute, painted eyes (see page 43).

Many naval officers, like young Pownel Fleetwood Pellew (1823-1850) of Portsmouth, England, were trained to sketch and paint, because their depictions of ports, headlands, and coasts could serve as navigation aids. Pellew studied under John Christian Schetky, a well-known maritime artist of Portsmouth, sketching and painting both from life and by copying professional paintings of famous sea battles, of ships in storms, and vessels at anchor. Young officers like Pellew sometimes turned their skills to depicting a ship and life aboard it, or tried to represent some elusive detail of daily life. These well-executed sketches, like the formal portraits by professional artists, may speak to the modern viewer more poignantly than whole pages of carefully crafted prose.[2]

1. Citations in this work are generally restricted to unpublished manuscript journals or rare books in the J. Welles Henderson Collection (hereafter, JWHC). The reader seeking more general background on maritime art, crafts, and the life of the seaman, is directed to the bibliography.
2. This sketchbook begins with Pellew's work as a student under the artist Schetky, at Portsmouth, England. The beginning sketches and paintings are extremely fine for a thirteen year old student, depicting ships, shipwrecks, and noted naval engagements. While some of the sketches are drawn from life, many appear to be student copies of professional painters' works.

In other cases, sketches or watercolours done by untrained ordinary seamen or by passengers in their diaries or logbooks can show life as it was lived. Illustrations and text from these unique and rare journals are presented here to the public for the first time. The French Admiral Leon Paris, in his 'Voyage de la Bellone', captured innumerable details, some extremely rare, such as the scenes of punishment by being seized in the rigging or recreational moments like playing with pigs on deck during a smoke-break.[3]

Selecting artifacts and images from several thousand, and narrowing that selection down to several hundred which might be depicted in this book, was a difficult and laborious task. Henderson chose those which show some rarely-shown aspect of life, or are excellent and well-preserved, or through their intrinsic aesthetic value, speak to the imagination. The variety of locale, type of vessel and work, and span of time itself is diverse, and the reader should be forewarned that what was true in one time and place was not necessarily so in another.

Over the more than 150 years and over the far-flung regions represented here, much in the life of sailors varied greatly. Abominable conditions of food, work, and daily duties for British merchant sailors in the eighteenth century gradually improved. For the Royal Navy, press gangs forced sailors into service during the Napoleonic era, but the practice virtually ended with the conclusion of hostilities. In the United States in the early nineteenth century, whalers and merchant sailors faced quite different conditions, and the US Navy never relied on impressment to find its able-bodied seamen.

Reform movements directed at changing the forms of punishment, at alcoholism and at the exploitation of the sailor ashore had gradual success in both the United States and Britain in the nineteenth century. Preachers and moral reformers worked to bring sailors under their influence and to convert them to their faiths. The articles of agreement that merchant sailors entered into when they shipped out evolved over time. Such change meant that conditions that prevailed in 1810 might be quite different by the 1850s or 1880s. So generalization from hundreds of illustrations and objects, no matter how well-chosen and representative, is to be undertaken very cautiously.

The works selected give diverse insights, hints, cross-sections, characterizations and episodes from different periods and from merchant and naval ships, that help convey a vivid sense of the past, not a defined or rigorous analysis of conditions in one setting, in one period, or across time and space. Yet a reader of this book, like a visitor to a museum, may gain much from such diversity. Through the pictures and artifacts that survive to our time, it is sometimes easier to get a feeling for the past than it is through strictly chronological and neatly divided topical categories of study. Often the viewer is surprised to see some parallel or similarity between the events and customs of one era and another. Sailors, for example, enjoying tobacco or a drink or the company of young women, or engaging in practical jokes, or dancing as they whiled away the hours aboard ship can be seen in the eighteenth, the nineteenth, and the twentieth century. Shipwreck, collision, storm, and fire at sea were all to be feared and prevented, no matter the era, the type of ship, or the

3. Leon Paris (de Leon de Veyran et Admiral Paris), 'Souvenir de la Bellone' (1871-73). This sketch book of the voyage of the *Bellone* contains numerous labelled pictures depicting life aboard and ashore on a French naval voyage.

nationality of the seaman. Daydreaming of a girl left behind was not limited to one time or place. Across the diversity, the universals of the human condition speak out. The result is a flavor of the past, not an analysis of that past. The viewer may sense how the circumstances of the sailor evolved, and at the same time, may take away some vivid images of what the sailing life was about over a century and half of the great era of sailing and the transition to steam power.

The goal of this book is to share publicly some rare visual material which presents a vision of the past. The work does not aspire to present a comprehensive synthesis of scholarship in the areas of maritime history and material culture. The text and the captions provide context, but not a thesis. Together, the illustrations are here because they give access to the life of Jack Tar over a long span of time and in different types of ships. For all these reasons, this book is very different in purpose and approach from many other works on nautical subjects. Published work ranges from popular presentations to more serious, scholarly, and beautifully designed art books. There exist many shelves of volumes which treat material culture and the life of the seaman with purposes like these:

> to provide guides to purchasing artifacts and art
> to present a history of nautical architecture and shipping
> to describe a particular craft
> to capture the life of one class of sailors, such as whalers
> to depict one type of ship and its history
> to provide accounts of maritime warfare
> to depict great naval and merchant shipping disasters
> to show the role of sailors of African ancestry
> to trace the careers of women sailors

Other works have filled in particular aspects of the story and provide different ways of examining overlapping or tangential features of what is covered here. More scholarly works provide insights and background, helping to put in a broader historical setting several of the themes and connections found among pictures, documents, and three-dimensional objects, or showing detailed material about a particular era or social condition.

Academic monographs published in recent years dealing with the ordinary seaman can be valuable resources for background. Among many others, W. Jeffrey Bolster, *Black Jacks: African American Seamen in the Age of Sail*, (Harvard University Press, 1997), and Marcus Rediker, *Between the Devil and the Deep Blue Sea: Merchant Seamen, Pirates, and the Anglo American Maritime World, 1700-1750*, (Cambridge University Press, 1987), give solid background. The Bibliography reflects these and other modern and older works.

To pursue insights into the life of Jack Tar, the story begins with where sailors began, on shore, motivated to sail, but reluctant to depart from their loved ones.

A Lesson in Boat-Building.
Hand-colored wood engraving.

A sailor carves a boat model while two boys look on in this 1877 print. The boys appear to be catching the romantic lure of the sea, implied by their intensity, and by the distant vista through the window. While art and literature gave great emphasis to boyhood daydreams and thoughts of distant adventure, boys and men frequently went to sea from economic necessity or through being tricked or compelled.

Reading Robinson Crusoe. (Opposite)
Lithograph, hand-colored, based on a painting by R. Gollinson.

Here a motivation for going to sea is depicted: the Romance of the sea. A knicker-clad boy lies in a field, his jacket and straw hat beside him, reading *Robinson Crusoe.* He is absorbed, at least one-third of the way through the book, and oblivious to the beauty of the sea-scape behind him. But the scene, like the book, would draw one to the sea, as two sloops sail in, while three others lie pulled up on shore. The scene behind him echoes the book, for he is alone on the land in view of the ocean, like Robinson Crusoe himself. In journals and memoirs seamen and officers often acknowledged that their early readings and childhood imaginations beckoned them to the sea.

CHAPTER ONE

Going to Sea

Why did boys and men, and a few women, go to sea? The art, books, and documents in the Henderson Collection present a surprisingly wide number of motives. Reasons to go to sea in the eighteenth and nineteenth century in Britain and the United States ran from simple inclination, romantic search for adventure, pursuit of income or career, patriotism, through necessity, crimping, to impressment, and other forms of compulsion. A few even thought that life at sea would improve their health.

Early in the history of the English novel, with Tobias Smollett (1721-1771), a one-time surgeon's mate on HMS *Cumberland* in 1741, an account of a voyage would begin with an exploration of motives that drew or pushed a man to the sea.[1] Daniel Defoe (1660-1731), Jonathan Swift (1667-1745), Herman Melville (1819-1891), who had served as both a merchant and naval sailor, all repeated the theme, and Richard Henry Dana, Jr. (1815-1882) in his own non-fiction account of his two years before the mast, echoed the question. Almost every story of the sailor at sea had to begin with at least a few paragraphs, as an explanation of the reasons that drew the sailor to the sea.

By dwelling on why men went to sea, early novelists had not simply established a literary convention, but had captured a question naturally asked by many sailors. The authors of privately kept journals and diaries frequently explored their own motives, speculating on the lure of nautical life.

A seaman in the eighteenth or nineteenth century who volunteered to go into either the merchant or naval service of Britain or the United States had good reason to ask himself why he chose such torments. After a few months or years at sea, he might indeed wonder what had moved him to leave behind the secure and predictable life ashore for the isolation from family, the enforced celibacy, the drudgery, short rations, intense discomfort, risk to life, and sometimes abusive discipline of the sailing vessel. As Samuel Johnson said, 'No man will be a sailor who has the contrivance to get himself in jail, for being in a ship is being in jail, with a chance of

1. Smollett, as one of the first novelists in English, established many 'stock' characters, including several nautical types. An excellent treatment of this issue is Nathan Comfort Starr, 'Smollett's Sailors', *American Neptune* 82, 1972, pp.81-99.

'The Sailors Farewell', 1785.
Mezzotint, hand-colored. Artist: T.H. Ramberg. Engraved by H. Hudson London.

A British warship is nearby, two others are at sea in the distance. In the foreground, a crimp is paid off for furnishing a sailor. The title of this print itself contained an irony because by contrast with the more sentimental and gentle departures often depicted in farewell scenes, here we see a sordid money exchange which drags the sailor away from domestic bliss. As the sailor takes leave of his wife, one child reaches for the mother, a teenage daughter holds the smaller child. In the background, another boat is pushed away from the dock, leaving behind mother, two children, and a dog, suggesting what will happen in the foreground in a few moments. The moment of transition is captured in that both the crimp and the sailor himself have one foot in the boat, one ashore.

being drowned…A man in jail has more room, better food, and commonly better company.'[2]

Nineteenth century Romantic artists and writers frequently depicted the motivation to go to sea as springing from some inner longing or mystical attraction. But many early written sources, both factual and fictional, represented the issue of motive in much colder, and to twentieth century eyes, more realistic, terms. Economic conditions in the seventeenth and eighteenth century in Europe created a system which needed seamen to move commerce and to fight the wars of empire. These hard political, social and economic realities led to a wide variety of ways of supplying the merchant and naval fleets with manpower, documented in diaries, journals, and in the art of the period.

The creation of fenced in estates in eighteenth century Britain provided a basic supply of workers, as farm workers were driven off the land. The growing merchant shipping of Britain drew upon this landless and uprooted mass for labor, offering the alternative of set wages (some paid in advance) which would help fill the seemingly insatiable need to man merchant ships. In the mid-eighteenth century, some eighteen to twenty men would be needed to man a vessel of 200 to 300 tons. As ships modernized and could carry larger cargoes, the ton-man ratio increased to closer to twenty tons per man, with 500 ton ships and somewhat smaller crews. With the increasing size of the British and colonial American

2. Samuel Johnson, as quoted in Robert Debs Heinl, jun., *Dictionary of Military and Naval Quotations* (Annapolis: US Naval Institute Press, 1966), p.284.

'The Idle Prentice Turned Away and Sent to Sea'.
Artist: William Hogarth, 18th century. Engraving, hand-colored.

This oft-reproduced picture contains many details showing how a young man, a failure at his apprenticed task, is sent off to sea. His mother is crying as he departs. In the rowboat, two men sadistically suggest to the somewhat apprehensive lad what awaits him in the ship at anchor, especially the cat-o'-nine-tails for punishment. Floating in the water is the discarded indenture of his apprenticeship; in the boat is his sea chest, marked, 'Tho Idle, his chest.' The legend from Proverbs, chapter X, verse 1 reads: 'A Foolish Son is the heaviness of his mother.' The seaman who will row the apprentice to the waiting ship is oblivious to all around him, smoking his pipe, while the mother is distraught. A gallows looms in the distance, perhaps a symbol of punishment for wanton behavior.

merchant marine, the need for seamen created manpower shortages that were often met through compulsion or trickery.

The Crimp

When the labor supply tightened, the merchant service in Britain made use of recruiters, men who would deliver seamen to ships. A recruiter, or crimp, would lure a man by buying him cheap liquor and getting him to spend all his money. Then, stripped of his meager savings, he would be obliged to pay back the debt. The crimp would deliver the drunken seaman to a waiting ship and take an advance on his wages. The crimp would collect his debt and might receive a bonus or fee from the captain. The seaman would now be obliged to work for the ship to earn back the advance, enforceable at law. Befuddled by drink and signed up for work, the victim of the crimp could offer no resistance. For many seamen, such a form of debt peonage was their first introduction to the sea.

As artists captured elements of the life of the sailor, the poignant moments of going off to sea, whether freely, sadly, in pursuit of a career, in anticipation of adventure and fortune, or under the pressure of debt, are repeatedly represented through the decades and in British art. Departure and leave-taking became themes, recurring in print, painting, sketch, and cartoon. In this moment, the forces, both inward and external, that push and pull the man to sea were depicted through symbolic representation in a struggle against the forces that held him back.

William Hogarth (1697-1764) in a well-known print, 'The Idle Prentice', captured several of these themes. There is a distraught mother, hoping to keep the sailor ashore. Sailors point out the perils and discipline to be faced. But the idle apprentice is forced to go, and a crimp apparently receives a payment.[3]

3. Hogarth print in the Henderson Collection, hereafter, WH Collection. NOTE: all illustrations in this book are from the WH Collection.

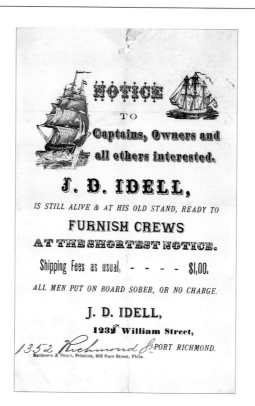

Idell broadside.
19th century.

This original broadside presented the practice of crimping as a respectable business. Interestingly, J. Idell guaranteed that men put aboard ship in Port Richmond, a part of Philadelphia, by him would be sober or he would not charge his fee of one dollar. Crimps frequently delivered sailors drunk after tricking them out of part of the advance wages they would receive on signing aboard ship. Such recruiting services remained a major means by which seamen were lured to sea despite the more romantic suggestions present in art and literature.

Crimping was common in the United States as well as Britain. A passenger escaping from the draft during the American Civil War, who apparently did not believe in forced compulsion to service, observed what appeared to be a crimp at work on his own packet ship. He assumed the sailors were subject to 'a system of pressing', but the episode puzzled him.

> We are to lie where we stay until we get our complement of men, which I believe should be thirty-six, but which can in this season be reduced to eighteen. We have but very few yet, but every now and then a little boat pulls up and a sailor is shoved aboard with a sack of clothes or his chest so that in the course of the day we may have our complement of men. In one or two cases I noticed the sailors to come aboard very unwillingly, but they were authoritatively ordered forward by the officers of the ship which they unhesitatingly obeyed. This seemed very strange to me, but I suppose it was a system of pressing in use in the merchant service.[4]

Impressment

The 1863 diarist used the word 'pressing', assuming that merchant sailors were subject to impressment. Strictly speaking, however, impressment was a British practice, not used in the United States. The British Royal Navy needed seamen as the Navy expanded during time of war, especially during the wars of the late eighteenth and early nineteenth centuries.

To meet manning needs impressment had its origins as early as the feudal days. However, the wars for empire in the eighteenth century and the Napoleonic wars, required vast increases in naval personnel who would be laid off suddenly in peacetime. The manpower needed could not be made up by volunteers, and under the practice of impressment the Royal Navy forcibly removed seamen from aboard British merchant

4. Ms. *Journal of Voyage on Plymouth Rock, Bound from New York to London, 1863*, WH Collection, pp.19-20. While not a seaman, this astute observer captured many elements of life at sea.

'The Use of a Gentleman, or, Patronage for the Admiralty'.
Engraving, hand-colored. Publisher: T. Tegg, Cheapside, London.
Early 19th century.

In this cartoon, a whole story is being acted out. The press gang to the left wear distinctive blue coats, red vests, black hats, and carry cudgels. Their sheathed swords are ready in case of forceful resistance. They and their companions have brought in two men, one a ruffian in his work clothes, who the press gang are suggesting will soon be made a gentleman by their other impressed man. 'D...d Jack, we'll constitute a Bond Street lounge upon deck, won't we?' The dandy, dressed in green, insists the gang have no right to press him into service, as he is 'Wastly well known in Bond Street.' The Captain turns this bit of information on its head, however, suggested that he is just the sort of person needed to teach others good manners. But off to the side a young girl tells her mother that the effete recruit is not a true gentleman, but none other than Tom Treacle, the gingerbread maker. Her mother agrees, 'They'll soon take the gold of [*sic*] his gingerbread...' All the ironic overtones and undertones of this scene conveyed by the dialogue and dress hint at the social tensions of late 18th century Britain. At the same time, however, the scene provides a comment on the difficulty of finding sufficient experienced men to serve in the British Navy during the many naval wars of the era.

ships anywhere in the world, or seized British seamen employed aboard foreign ships. Often a Royal Navy ship would replenish their crew by impressing sailors from merchant ships approaching their home ports in Britain. The naval officers would replace the healthy seamen taken from the merchant crews by transferring sick or injured naval seamen to the homeward-bound merchant ships.[5]

The impressment of sailors from aboard American merchant ships to serve in the British navy during the Napoleonic Wars angered not only the seamen, but the owners of the ships, and Americans generally who saw it as one of many examples of British infringement on their sovereignty. Many of the sailors claimed to be American citizens, but British naval officers disregarded such claims, especially if the sailor was known to have once been a British subject. Impressment became one of the principal causes of the War of 1812

5. Brian Lavery, *Nelson's Navy: The Ships, Men and Organisation, 1793-1815*, (Annapolis: US Naval Institute Press, 1994).

'The Waterman's Reluctance on Going to War'.
Mezzotint, hand-colored.
Painted by G. Morland. Engraved by W. Ward. Late 18th century.

Three members of a press gang seize a waterman, who was engaged in ferrying a young couple and their spaniel across the harbor. Two of the press gang have cudgels and wear characteristic blue coats and black hats. One has lost his hat into the water, while another is about to strike the reluctant waterman. With his hands crossed, he pleads with them, while his passengers look on, aghast at the proceedings. One of the press gang grasps the waterman by his jacket, and it is clear he will not be able to escape their clutches. Impressment into the British navy was a recurrent risk until the end of the Napoleonic Wars.

Recruiting Poster, US Navy, c. 1861.

This Civil War recruiting poster for the Union Navy is rare by contrast to more plentiful Army recruiting posters. Depicted is a three masted ship, with a steam-sail rig to the right in the background. The text reveals the locations of recruitment for Union sailors and the 'terms' of recruitment, in great financial detail. The pay of landsman would be $12 a month and that of the ordinary seaman would be $14 a month. The sailors would pay for their own uniforms, with the most expensive item being a pea jacket at $11.00. If accepted, the sailors would be reimbursed for travel from home to the post of enlistment at the rate of 3 cents per mile. The total kit would cost over $31.00, the equivalent of nearly three months' wages for a landsman. There is little appeal to patriotism, but rather, a sense that the prospective sailor will weigh the pros and cons from a financial point of view. Some men might go to sea to avoid the draft after thinking over their options.

Examining Recruits for the Navy.
Hand-colored wood engraving. 19th century.

A prospective volunteer demonstrates his skill with knots, while other recruits and officers look on, with expressions of sympathy, boredom, or disdain. In times of peace the US Navy relied heavily on volunteers.

between the US and Britain, although other British policies, such as holding forts on the western frontier and the British Orders in Council blockading trade to Europe also angered American politicians and citizens.

The British ceased impressment with the end of the Napoleonic wars in 1815, although the law remained available for possible use. The United States had never resorted to impressment, but had recruited volunteers, with appeals to patriotism, the likelihood of adventure, and the possibility of monetary gain.

Condemned to service

In Britain, impressment was supplemented by other means of obtaining sailors. The courts would co-operate by condemning men who had committed minor offences for service aboard ships. One scholar estimated that some six or seven per cent of the men of the British Navy were obtained in this fashion during the Seven Years War (1756-1763). During wars, the vast numbers of sailors required could only be made up by impressment and condemnation. So aboard a Royal Navy ship during the Napoleonic Wars, the sailors would include some volunteers, many impressed seamen and a few condemned to service.[6]

6. Brian Lavery, *Nelson's Navy: The Ships, Men and Organisation, 1793-1815,* (Annapolis: US Naval Institute Press, 1994) pp. 118-128.

Privateers

During time of war in Britain, men would prefer working for a percentage of prize-money aboard privateers, over service with the Royal Navy, or as regular merchantmen, but often such seamen would be subject to impressment at sea. Although the risk was high, the financial rewards could also be high. For American sailors and officers aboard privateers, the hope of sharing in prize money supplemented patriotism as a motive. American privateers played a major role in the American Revolution and the War of 1812, although the practice of awarding prize money to officers and crews of naval ships blurred the distinction between privateering and naval service.[7]

Apprenticeship

In Britain, and later in the United States, a young gentleman might be granted a berth as a midshipman, or a young man might serve a term as an apprentice aboard a merchant ship, learning the trade. Later, as schools were established, he might be trained for the sea, or by virtue of his preferment and the influence of the family, obtain a post. In a handsome and quite unique, cloth-bound manuscript diary which he illustrated with watercolors, George Hodge explained how his father got him two positions in 1790, first aboard the *Margerey*, then aboard the *Margreat*. Despite his seasickness aboard the first vessel, his father sent him back again:[8]

> My enclunation was for the sea but not my fairthers which...I was bent for it so he aQuainted with Capt Edgar he commanded the brig *Margerey*...I went up to London with coals but on the passage I was very sea sick in the going up...I went home which my parints was very happey to see me but at that time I would not go anymore on that brig *Margerey*. But my knoshen was still for the sea and winter coming on my fairther got a nother ship for which I went onboard of the Ship *Margreat* Capt Wilson which we saild from shields bound to London...

After a sea-sick adventure at age thirteen and return to happy parents, he went to sea again, through his father's connections, in a second ship. The diary is rich with adventures as Hodge was impressed, became a prisoner of war, was released, witnessed flogging and was himself punished. In retrospect, he had good reason to wonder what turn of fate took him to sea in the first place. George Hodge seemed to remember two motives mixed together: preferment via his father's influence, and his own personal inclination for the sea.

Patriotism

During and after the eighteenth century wars for empire and the Napoleonic Wars, recruiting posters would seek volunteers for the British Navy through exhortation, often reaching heights of patriotic hyperbole. In one privately-printed sheet, an older seaman urges on a promising volunteer, recounting a long list of British naval victories and heroes:

7. The state moved in to replace privateering with official naval use of force against the enemy, a subject of extensive research in recent years. An excellent exploration of this issue is presented by David J. Starkey, in the Introduction to *Pirates and Privateers: New Perspectives on the War on Trade in the Eighteenth and Nineteenth Centuries* (Exeter, Bristol (GB): University of Exeter Press, 1997).
8. George Hodge Diary, *c.*1790-*c.*1833, WH Collection.

Hodge Diary.

A manuscript diary of a British sailor from about 1790 to about 1833 includes numerous excellent small watercolors believed to have been painted by George Hodge showing a naïve self-portrait, ships he served aboard, ports of call and naval engagements. Hodge, a native of Tynemouth, wrote in his diary that at age thirteen in 1790 'my enclunation was for the sea' against his father's wishes 'for I was bent for it'. He took note of ordinary and extraordinary events, including his own impressment, capture, prisoner exchange, floggings, the effects of scurvy, sea battles with French ships, and foraging for food on isolated islands. An inventive and original speller, Hodge's references range over the whole experience of the common sailor, from shore side visits with ladies of the evening through hazards of the sea, to the ordinary and sometimes uneventful day-to-day life as they 'warterd the ship' or loaded 'provisions' on bord.' Never reprinted, this rare journal offers many insights into the life of seamen during the period of the Napoleonic wars.

You are now, young Man, entering on a scene of life the most glorious and enterprising – that of an ENGLISH SAILOR: to you is, in part, delegated the care of the British empire: be mindful of the sacred trust you have in charge...The deeds of mighty DRAKE, when SPAIN'S ARMADA shrunk beneath his valor; let HOWARD, BLAKE and POCOCK, (deathless names!) make the Invader tremble; RUSSELL, BOSCAWEN, and a train of Heroes fill the glorious list. Be these your great examples in the hour of battle; or if more modern deeds excite your ardour, think on the fearless DUNCAN, brave CORNWALLIS, HOWE, WARREN, HOOD, the famed ST. VINCENT, and the undaunted HERO OF THE NILE! names that will ever live in Time's eternal calendar! With such examples, GLORY must attend you, and your grateful Country shall reward your gallant prowess. Farewell! be vigilant, be bold – true to your GOD, your COUNTRY, and your KING![9]

9. Print, '– THE VETERAN'S ADDRESS TO A YOUNG SAILOR – 1803,' WH Collection (catalogue H119) includes this text.

Ambrotype.
Mid-19th century.

This ambrotype of sailors hints at the passage of the tradition of seafaring from father to son. Nautical families abounded, both among officers and seamen. Following a father's footsteps to sea represented a motive found in the Royal Navy, among merchant seamen, and as here, in the US Navy of the mid-nineteenth century.

Appeals to patriotism, the chance of adventure, and the promise of regular employment attracted volunteers to both the British and American navies. However, for the ordinary Jack Tar in both navies, the mix of financial, psychological, patriotic, and emotional pressures varied from individual to individual, and it remains impossible to generalize from period to period or group to group. Instead, we see in art and document a scattering of examples of parental influence, romance, financial hardship, and the promise of duty, fame and fortune.

The Veteran's Address to a Young Sailor.
Engraving, hand-colored, 1803.

In this print from the era of the Napoleonic Wars, a veteran recalls the exploits of British naval heroes, encouraging the lad on the right to go to sea voluntarily. 'You are now a young man, entering on a scene of life most glorious and enterprising – that of an English sailor'. As in much of the art through the era, a man encourages, rather than discourages another to go to sea, in contrast to scenes between sailors and their wives or sweethearts in which the woman dreads the removal of her man from domesticity. In this scene the sailor is ready to depart, already decked out in striped pants, double-breasted jacket, his walking stick and sailor's hat in hand. His older companion sends him on his way, 'true to your God, your country and your king.'

Captain with Child in Green Dress, c.1835.

This watercolor portrait has echoes of the sea throughout, and gives hints of one more set of motives as to why one might take up the sailing life. The gentleman holds a telescope, indicative of his rank as a merchant ship master. The picture on the wall has a symbolic illustration of Neptune. Through the window of this domestic scene are two ships under sail. Despite the feminine nature of the outfit, the child, who bears a strong resemblance to the gentleman, may be a boy, as young boys were often dressed in this fashion in the 1830s. Perhaps the father expected his son to someday follow his career at sea, a strong motive for many who went to sea.

Portrait of John Williams Finch.
Oil painting, artist unknown. Early 19th century.

This oil portrait of John W. Finch as a midshipman captures some of his boyish enthusiasm. Boys went off to sea, like young Finch, their eyes ablaze with anticipation and their fingers itching to draw their sword in battle, and sometimes returned much wiser young men after several years at sea. Finch in later years became a captain in the Royal Navy. He was born in 1800 and died in 1871.

Naval Career

In the early years of the American republic, officers in the Navy were drawn from the ranks of merchant officers and promoted from within from young boys who joined as midshipmen. A few schools turned out midshipmen candidates in the early nineteenth century, but a more formal system emerged. After the establishment of the Naval School in 1845 (renamed the US Naval Academy in 1850) on the Severn River in Maryland, a steady stream of career officers flowed into the Navy. The Henderson Collection contains many US naval officers' journals and diaries which provide, through sketches and text, details of their voyages. One young man left a rare and unique sketch book record of his trip to the Academy, his travails and studies there, and his transformation into a naval officer. Charles Dwight Sigsbee little knew when he penned his humorous sketches in the early 1860s, that in the 1870s, he would become an instructor in drawing at the Academy.

Sigsbee went on to greater fame, as his career brought him command of the battleship *Maine* when, in 1898, it steamed into Havana harbor, Cuba. While in his cabin the night of

1. Departeth from the home of his childhood.

2. Goeth aboard ye steamboate.

7. He is examined by ye Medical boarde.

8. And also by ye Academic boarde.

9. Ye superintendent lectureth him.

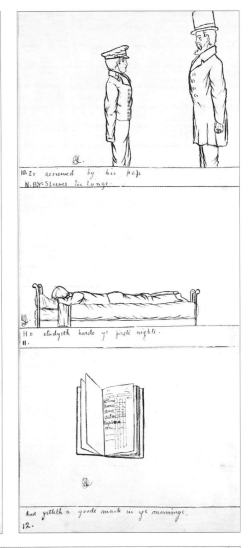

10. Is reviewed by his pap. N. B. ye Sleeves too longe.

He studyeth harde ye firste nighte. 11.

And getteth a goode marke in ye morninge. 12.

Sigsbee Sketchbook.

This collection of cartoon-like drawings from the Sigsbee sketchbook narrates the travails of a young civilian becoming a midshipman at the US Naval Academy from 1859-1863. For well-connected and bright young American gentlemen, the pathway to the sea sometimes led through the Academy into the US naval officer corps.

Journal sketch: 'HMS Lacedaemonian – Acteon *and* St Lawrence *lying in Hampton Roads blockading* Constellation *September 12, 1814'.* Watercolor.

This watercolor was done by Horatio Nelson Head, midshipman. Future naval officers were taught to use watercolors since there were no cameras in those days to record important information.

15 February, a mysterious explosion ripped through the vessel. As a result of the sinking, 253 of her 358 officers and men were killed, but Sigsbee escaped with his life. Five years later, when serving as Commandant of the Philadelphia Navy Yard, his portrait was painted by one of America's greatest artists, Thomas Eakins. Both a collection of drawings showing the route into the Navy by way of the Academy and Eakins' portrait are in the collection.[10]

In Britain and the United States, famous naval families passed on the tradition from generation to generation, some by father to son or elder brother to younger brother. The names echo through US naval history: Biddle, Decatur, Perry and Porter. Numerous lesser known merchant shipping families carried on the sailing tradition. A rare author's copy of the younger Porter's biography of the elder is in the collection, along with items from other naval and merchant families.[11]

Children were often named after naval heroes, implanting a compulsion from the moment of baptism. Horatio Nelson Head, who studied art under Edward Riddle at the Greenwich Naval School, perhaps knew his destiny as soon as he learned the origin of his name.[12]

10. The Bartlett/Sigsbee Journal; the Eakins portrait is on p.45.
11. Admiral David D. Porter, *Memoir of Commodore David Porter,* (Albany, 1875), WH Collection. This edition in the collection includes not only the printed text, but a rich collection of original manuscripts and prints gathered by Admiral Porter and bound into this copy of the book. The father, Commodore David Porter and the son, Admiral David D. Porter were only one of many father-son, and father-son-grandson officer families in the nineteenth century US Navy. The elder Porter commanded the *Essex* in the War of 1812; the younger David Porter commanded the Mississippi Squadron for the Union Navy in the Civil War. Stephen Decatur, sen. cruised during the Quasi War with France, Stephen Decatur, jun. was a hero of both the Barbary Wars and the War of 1812. Oliver Hazard Perry, at age twenty-seven was the hero of the Battle of Lake Erie in 1813; his younger brother, Matthew Calbraith Perry commanded the anti-slavery African Squadron in the early 1840s, led a fleet of steamers at Tabasco in the Mexican War in 1846, and negotiated the opening of Japan to American trade in 1853-54. The Porter *Memoir* is unique in that the son documents the activity of the father, and further, in that this particular copy is the only one of its kind, the personal copy of Admiral Porter in which he included original documents (not copies) at appropriate points in the text.
12. Horatio Nelson Head, *The Lacedaemonian, A Journal* (Two volumes, 1813-1814; 1814-1815), WH Collection.

'Sailor's Farewell'.
Reverse painting on glass.

Another departure scene plays on the standard pose of ship, sailor, and weeping girl. This Chinese reverse painting on glass is based on a British print of about 1785 and is in a Chinese frame. Artists in a wide variety of media repeated the themes of such departure scenes, often matching them with a poignant return scene.

Sailor's Farewell ceramic figure.

This Staffordshire pearlware figure with enamel decoration, *c.*1815-25, inscribed 'Departure' shows a sailor tenderly bidding farewell to his sweetheart or wife. At his foot is a small bundle of his belongings.

Health

For a very few, such reasons as improving one's health might motivate one to become a sailor. Richard Henry Dana, Jr., who later published his account in 1840 hoping that it might improve the lot of the seaman, originally went to sea as a young Harvard student believing that an affliction of his eyesight might be improved by the sea air.

Departures

The heart-rending moment of departure as well as the issue of motive, became embedded in art and literature by the end of the eighteenth century and flourished in the Romantic era, as the artist sought to evoke emotions of sadness, a sense of mortality, point of change,

La Vie D'un Navire-La Sortie du Port.
Lithograph.
Artist: Garneray. Engraved by A. Durand, Paris 1844.

An American sailing vessel loads and gets ready to depart the port of Havre, France, as a French coastal sail/steam packet moves out of the harbor on a nearly windless day. The entrance to the harbor is protected by a fort. Friends and relatives wave at departing passengers on deck, while final passengers arrive at the ship by sailboat. Aboard, the bustle of departure can be detected: an officer holds a speaking trumpet, while crew members hoist anchor. This realistic print gives a sense of an ordinary departure from a busy harbor, uncluttered with overly sentimental symbols.

'Sailor's Farewell'.
Liverpool painted ceramic tile.
Mid–18th century.

In this variation on a farewell or departure scene, the sailor leaves behind two women as well as home and, incidentally a cartload of fruit – all symbolic of the delights he leaves behind as he goes to sea. His mother and wife are both tearful as he moves to join his comrades in the waiting boat.

'Getting under weigh From Spithead'.
Lithograph, hand-colored.
Artist: O.W. Brierly. Lithographed by T.G. Dutton, 1853.

In the center, HMS *Agamemnon* is preparing for departure, with men climbing the rigging and loosening the sails from the bowsprit and yardarms. In the distance are two other ships and a schooner to the center and right. Three armed ships' boats are on the left. The 91-gunship is squarely in the era of combined sail and steam. The rather businesslike arrangements to get under weigh in this naval ship contrast with the festive atmosphere surrounding the American passenger packet in the picture on page 34.

separation from love and anticipation of excitement. Depicting the moment when a man or a whole ship is leaving, the artist can hint at the call of duty or the pressures at work. Torn from girlfriend or wife and children, the sailor carries his sea bag, or steps into a skiff, or stands so that, in the background, against the sea horizon, his sailing vessel can be seen awaiting, beckoning silently with its promise of risk, adventure, and an entirely unfamiliar way of life.

With maudlin and sentimental eighteenth and nineteenth century art, these symbols and conventions became so established that they served as simple restated clues or signals, whose intent was to call forth emotions automatically. Everyone would immediately understand what should be felt when viewing a picture showing a sailor stepping away from a young woman who holds a handkerchief to her eyes, and to whose skirts a young crying child clings, as a sailing vessel rocks at its anchorage beyond. The visual text was sufficient; it needed no explanation.

The simple act of leave-taking as a ship gets ready to leave harbor catches the eye of artists. Seamen take leave of their mothers, wives, girlfriends and daughters, but they also

'Industry and Oeconomy'.
Stipple engraving, 1800.

A young boy, with hat in hand, is being signed up at Bele Wharf by a gentleman in a high hat who writes with a quill. Behind the boy, a porter carries his sea bag. We may infer the lad's departure is entirely voluntary. There are hints throughout the picture of the world he is leaving and the world he is entering. In a window to the rear is a mother and child, while another slightly older child plays with a dog in the foreground. The world of longshoremen, ships, and echoes of international trade is about to welcome him, as one man pushes a barrel and chats with another who holds an oar against a backdrop of ships at the dock. Here we see a young man going to sea fully of his own accord, to make his fortune in the world.

'Sailor's Farewell' Plaque.

This pink lustreware wall plaque with enamelled decorations, Sunderland, *c.*1830-50, has a verse entitled 'The Sailor's Farewell'. The scene is unusual as it shows the sailor leaving behind three generations of women, presumably his mother, wife and daughter.

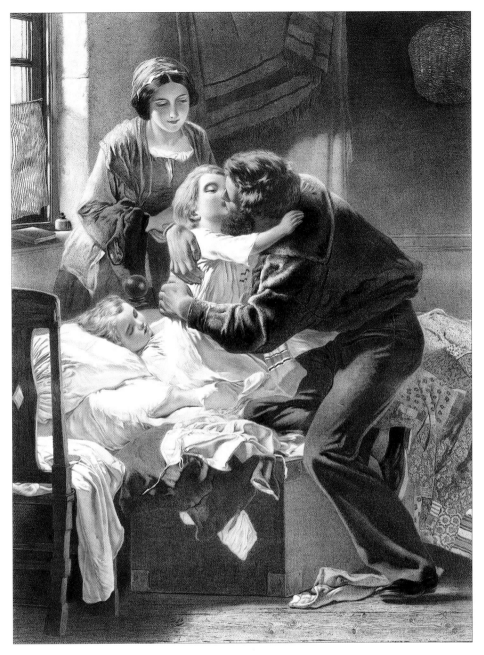

'Home and Its Treasures'.
Hand-colored engraving. 19th century.

In this touchingly romantic print, the sailor has a beautiful wife and two beautiful children. The message is a bit ambiguous. Does he kneel on his sea-chest after returning from sea, or is he about to depart in the early morning, taking leave of the children before they are fully awake? For romantic artists and writers, the separation of sailor from wife and children was a poignant moment. Direct evidence from journals, letters, and diaries suggests that the reality of separation was as heart-wrenching as the artists depicted.

take sage advice from their fathers and from knowledgeable Old Salts. Some are entrapped by crimps, some are forcefully impressed into service, while others dream of the sea, lured by an inner longing, in the Romantic tradition. For whatever the reason, all kinds of boys and men and a few women found themselves sailing out of a safe harbor on a merchant or naval vessel, bound for a voyage on the trackless sea.

Ann Jane Thornton.
Wood engraving, hand-colored. 19th century.

Like a few other cross-dressing women, Ann Jane passed herself off as a male in *c.*1833 to take up the sea-faring life. The caption on the broadside tells the story of her three year adventure which took her by way of several ships from Britain to the United States and back. Several such young women later made some earnings from their notoriety by going on stage to narrate their adventures, and this document may have served to promote such a presentation.

(Opposite) *Hannah Snell.*
Copperplate engraving. 18th century.

Among several cross-dressing women who joined the service, Hannah Snell became quite famous for her stints as a marine and a sailor in *c.*1748-1749. On her return, she told her story to a journalist, and highly fictionalized accounts of her adventures soon became the stuff of legend. She went on stage, where she attracted enthusiastic crowds as she sang the story of her service. In retirement, she collected a pension and was reported to have married and to have had a child.

CHAPTER TWO
Boys, Men and Women at Sea

Working from a collection of art and artifact in the search for the real life of seamen and officers takes us naturally to the question of what sorts of boys, men, and women went to sea. What did they look like and what roles did they play aboard ship? Paintings, drawings, prints, representations in ceramic, carving, sculpture, metal work, and, from the middle of the nineteenth century onwards, in photographs, should surely yield at least a visual depiction of the appearance of men from Admirals to the lowliest sailors.

The rich legacy of maritime pictorial art tends to leave a much better vision of ships, than of the people aboard them. Yet as we study these visual materials, we must seek constantly to sort out the messages of artists or photographers, and to look past their purposes in a search for the elusive reality that lay somewhere behind the depictions.

Some early paintings and prints might show an officer leaning on an anchor, or in the foreground with a stylized naval battle in the background. Over and over, artists would show an officer seated in the foreground with a view through a window of his ship in the background. To provide a visual clue to inform the viewer of the man's occupation, the artist might show him holding some instrument of the trade, just as medieval portraits of saints would show them with some identifying tool or artifact. A merchant officer clutches a telescope or a sextant; a boatswain (often shortened and pronounced as 'bosun') holds his

American Sea Captain.
Watercolor. Mid-19th century.

This watercolour by J. Wass, of Liverpool, shows the sea captain with tools of the trade, including dividers, a chart of the Atlantic Ocean and a sextant. Through the window, a full-rigged ship with American flag sails off. Captains' portraits often included a few stock emblems of office such as those shown here.

Captain Thompson with high hat, spyglass and sextant.
Oil Painting. Mid-19th century.

This magnificent portrait depicts a captain with two instruments of his trade, a spyglass and a sextant. Portraits with telescopes to show that the gentleman is a captain are common, but it is rare to find an instrument of navigation as well. The high hat and cravat hint that the picture was painted in *c.*1820.

whistle, so his signals could be heard above the sound of storm or battle; an ordinary seaman grasps a length of line or a marlinspike. Refinements and variations on such pictures became wonderfully diverse. We find gunners holding a rammer for a cannon, cooks with ladles, stewards with trays of food, a sailmaker with his needle and palm, a caulker with mallet and an iron, and a helmsman with his hands on the wheel. Naval officers have their uniforms to identify their calling and position.

In one sense, we can learn much from these pictures, yet surely a man would rarely sit with a tool of his trade in his hands, with his ship in the distance. Such posed or contrived pictures do not provide literal windows on a past reality, but capture only elements of the life of the seaman, symbolic parts of the whole. We constantly have to remind ourselves that most pictures are not actual views of the way things were, but *representations*, usually stylized and heavy with the mental outlook of artist, engraver, or photographer.

Over the period from the 1700s through the 1800s, a democratization of art gradually took place. In earlier pictures, whether rendered by accomplished portrait-painters or by amateurs, the body of surviving marine art seems largely limited to naval battles, famous vessels, harbor scenes of ships at anchor, Admirals and Captains of the naval service, and

Portrait of American sea captain, his wife and his ship.
Oil painting. Mid-19th century.

A spyglass is present in many prints or paintings in the collection indicating as a symbol that the holder is a captain. In portraits of naval officers their rank and profession was shown by their uniforms. A merchant marine officer had no such uniform indicators in his portrait; therefore, he generally resorted to holding a spyglass or sometimes a sextant or some other appropriate instrument to indicate his position as a captain. Here you have an ages old composition tradition of the captain, a window and, in the distance, his ship. In addition, we have his wife and a Victorian interior. This painting is unusual in that it includes four elements: captain, vessel, wife and an interior.

Captain William Farnsworth.
Oil Painting. Mid-19th century.

This oil painting of American merchant Captain William Farnsworth shows him with the badge of office, a telescope. Through a window his bark, the *J.W. Paige*, is shown in front of a towering peak. Often being financially successful at sea, many a captain had his portrait painted for posterity.

Portrait of William M. Hunter, USN.
Oil painting. Mid-19th century.

This handsome portrait, by Pennsylvania artist Jacob Eichholz, is of William M. Hunter. Hunter commenced sailing in the US Navy as a midshipman in 1809. By 1813 he was a lieutenant, by 1826 a commander, and in 1837 became a captain. From 1821 to 1824 he sailed on board the *Franklin* of 74 guns as First Lieutenant on her cruise to the Pacific Ocean under Commodore Charles Stewart. Various Hunter items including epaulets, coat, journals, nautical books, etc. are in the Collection.

famous naval heroes. In portraits, pictures of ships were frequently used as background definition elements to help the viewer associate the person in the foreground with a ship.

A collection of eighteenth century maritime fine art cuts across the social spectrum, giving a largely spotty, selected section of the elite of the sailing world, many pictures of ships themselves, but only rarely a view of day-to-day life aboard. Prints from the mid eighteenth century by Hogarth, and from the late eighteenth and early nineteenth century by Rowlandson, Cruikshank, and others present stylized cartoon views of the lower social orders, which provide hints, but not a realistic depiction of the ordinary sailor. A series of prints by Hogarth presents severe conditions of poverty. So as we look through nautical art, we must keep in mind that we are always seeing only a fraction of the past, through the eyes of many artists with messages to convey, giving scattered hints in the search for Jack Tar, and spread over time and place.

In many pictures, the ship itself would be the subject with no person visible, or only suggested to give a sense of proportion. Very rarely would a ship picture emphasize the crew

British naval officer and his wife.
Oil painting, *c.*1780.

This oil painting of a British naval officer with his wife, from around the time of the American Revolution, tells the whole story as he holds orders marked 'On His Majesty's Service Portsmouth' and points to a painting of a ship.

in detail working on deck or aloft. One category of document, the station bill, does show exactly the position of each individual sailor by name and number for manning the yards, handling the sails, dropping anchor and other maneuvers. A quarter bill would be for a warship and give the battle stations for every man aboard when the vessel went into action. Some of the station bills and quarter bills were handsomely executed with detailed pictures of the ship and the positions of crew members. Such drawings are rare prizes today, although when originally rendered, they had a simple and practical purpose.

Over and over in engravings and popular art from the late eighteenth century and early nineteenth century, Rowlandson and others showed an emerging standard clothing outfit of the merchant sailor, well before a standard uniform had been adopted in either the merchant or naval services. Between 1800 and 1840, the typical clothing depicted in such prints was rather elegant, and, like the wooden carving of Jack Tar on page 16, showed what a British or American sailor might wear as he came ashore. The broad brimmed black hat was waterproofed with tar or paint, supposedly the origin of the term for all sailors as 'tars'.

US Naval Lieutenant.
Hand–colored lithograph, *c.*1840.

This lithograph of a US naval lieutenant in full dress uniform aboard ship shows him with a speaking trumpet. Note the single epaulet on his right shoulder. The dress of the enlisted man at the wheel is typical of the period. The print is from the 'U.S. Military Magazine' by Huddy & Duval. The magazine has been described as one of the rarest of the nineteenth century periodical publications esteemed for its costume plates in brilliant colored lithographs.

Jack Tar, wooden carving, American.
86½in. high including deck, *c.*1845.

One of the outstanding objects in the Collection, this impressive wooden carving of 'Jack Tar' has been ranked as one of the 100 top masterpieces of American folk art by outstanding folk art experts. The beard, style of work, and clothing suggest a fairly accurate rendition of the typical American merchant seaman of about 1845. The carving may have served as a ship chandler's sign. He is attributed to the work of Jeremiah Dodge, a New York City ship figurehead carver. The jaunty wave of the hat captures the spirit of adventure that came to be associated with the sea.

Portrait of Rear Admiral Charles Dwight Sigsbee.
Oil Painting by Thomas Eakins, 1903.

As a captain, Charles Dwight Sigsbee commanded the battleship *Maine* when it suffered an explosion, 15 February, 1898 in Havana harbor. The cause of the explosion is still a mystery. Sigsbee was uninjured and was the last of 88 survivors out of a crew of 328 enlisted men and 26 officers to leave the ship. Although Sigsbee cautioned about rushing to judgment as to the cause of the explosion, the incident ignited popular and political passions in the US and led to the Spanish American War, 1898.

An open jacket, striped shirt, wind-swept neckerchief, white duck pants, and black shoes completed the outfit. In print after print, the elements of dress are repeated; many land-bound artists who had only seen Jack Tar ashore in his finery may have assumed he wore the same outfit when working in the rigging. In fact, a few depictions by sailor-artists in their journals suggest that, while the black hat was common on board ship, the rest of the outfit was rarely so elegant for day to day life.

The popular artist, however, wanted viewers to recognize the subject easily so that the social commentary in these cartoon-like pictures would be obvious. For that reason, whatever had become the customary image of a particular subject would be repeated, constantly reinforcing an image which in fact always varied somewhat from the reality, but which all viewers would instantly understand. Seeing a black hat, striped shirt, short jacket, flowing neckerchief and white pants, the viewer would know the artist meant that figure to be a sailor. If a further clue were needed, a ship might appear on the horizon. American print makers like N. Currier shamelessly copied British prints, providing new caption lines that suggested his work was drawn from the life of American sailors.

Heroes and Famous Ships

In a sort of hierarchy of fame, art depicting sailors and ships in the eighteenth and nineteenth century shows us men like Admiral Horatio Nelson aboard HMS *Victory* at Aboukir Bay (Egypt) or Trafalgar, Captain Farragut during the battle of Mobile Bay, or Captain Sigsbee of the *Maine*. One print based on a Gilbert Stuart painting of Isaac Hull places him with the historic battle between the USS *Constitution* and HMS *Guerriere*. A whole category of mid-nineteenth century Currier prints depict naval heroes in a cluster, with miniature pictures of their ships or battles. Often it is the outstanding, the unusual, the famous, rather than the ordinary man who is of interest to the early nineteenth century artist and art publisher. The visual art provides clues, but no rich feel for the fabric of everyday living.

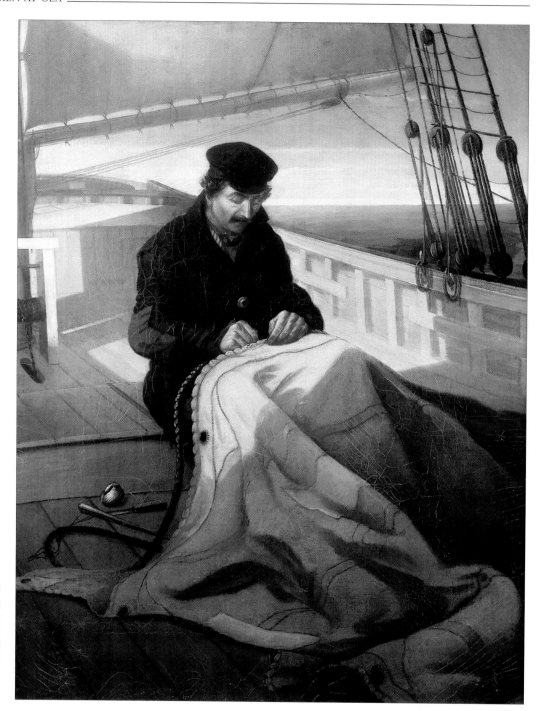

Sailmaker.
Oil painting, 19th century.

A sailmaker quietly attaches a bolt-rope to a sail working sail twine through the canvas with a needle and probably a hand-protecting 'palm'. On the deck, next to him, lie a ball of sail twine, a knife, and a fid for doing rope work.

Later in the nineteenth century, however, with illustrated periodicals such as *Harper's Weekly* and the *Illustrated London News*, artists became increasingly interested in more democratic elements. A few sketch books left by officers showed men working aboard ships, and now and then artists chose to depict seamen, petty officers, helmsmen, sailmakers, cooks and stewards, deckhands, midshipmen and boys, all at work, some below deck, some on deck, and some in the rigging. R.F. Zogbaum, who produced many illustrations for *Harper's Weekly* in the 1890s, depicted everyday situations aboard US naval vessels, often writing an extensive description to portray customs and habits. Like the naturalist novelists and the popular journalists of his era, Zogbaum strove to convey what he really saw aboard ship.

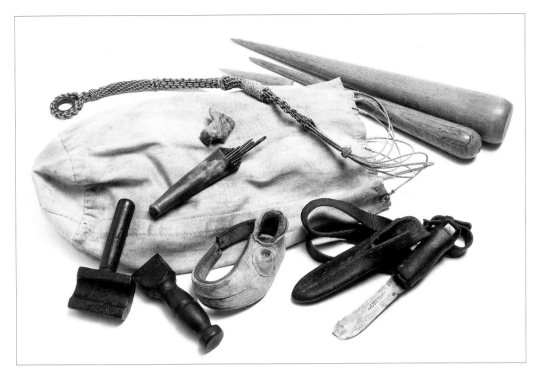

Sailmaker's bag and equipment.
American. 19th century.

A sailmaker's bag held many tools of his trade: three wooden fids for rope work, needles held in beeswax in a cow horn container, seam rubber, parcelling mallet, roping palm for ease of sewing, hand-made sheath knife and sheath attached to a leather belt. Note the fine rope work of different types of knots on the drawstring that closes the top of the bag.

Sailmaker.
Watercolor.

On a large sailing vessel, the sailmaker usually had plenty of work to do repairing or making new sails. This watercolor shows a sailmaker at work aboard a vessel in 1869.

If we study pictures from both the romantic and the more realistic periods, we gain insights of all kinds by looking closely at what clues the artist provides in order to define the rank or position of particular seamen or to catch them at their daily tasks. About 1800, Rowlandson or others often showed a cook with a wooden peg leg, capturing the concept that injured sailors would get the job of cook, since it did not require working in the rigging. A member of a press gang ashore would be shown with a cudgel or sword, or both. A bosun holds a bosun's whistle to his lips to give commands.

Other clues and signals of rank, position, task, or occupation aboard ship which artists used in their depictions of officers and sailors include many items that survive as artifacts into the modern collection. Telescopes, sextants, fids, bosuns' whistles, chests, navigation equipment, ditty boxes, and rope work, sometimes found in such paintings and engravings to define the man, survive today as artifacts. The collector experiences a special sense of discovery when a particular three-dimensional artifact turns out to be identical with one shown in a painting or engraving; such connections and linkages come up over and over again.

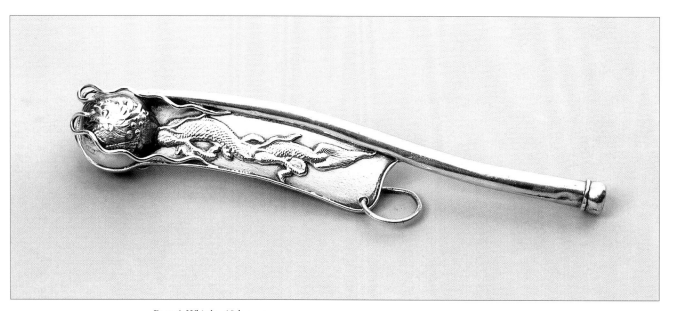

Bosun's Whistle. 19th century.

A rather elegant bosun's whistle could serve not only as a means of issuing commands but also as a badge of office. The high pitch could be heard through the tumult of battle or the roar of a storm. This silver example is Chinese and is decorated with a raised dragon.

Purser.
Thomas Rowlandson. Aquatint engraving, hand-colored.

One of a 1799 series of ten prints depicting British naval types, this one of a purser implies some observations. Pursers often had a reputation for cheating the sailors by short and poor quality rations, over-pricing items from the slop chest and selling naval stores. Hence the greedy expression, the tally of goods, and the nearby supplies.

La France Maritime.
Panorama (23 panels, 5x4in)
Folded lithograph, hand-
colored. Mid-19th century.

This selection of 12 cards
from a uniform-card book,
La France Maritime, shows
some of the same ranks in
the British selection of
1834, including captain,
lieutenant, and junior
ranking officers as well as
various seamen by rating.
Among the group are an
Almonier (cleric and
teacher), and a Matelot de
Commerce, shown working
on the docks.

Uniform books

Depictions of uniforms worn by the officers and men of the British, French, and American
navies can be found in well-printed uniform books. As each of these navies regularized
dress, detailed pictures showing the exact elements of uniform would be presented in such
booklets. Print publishers would sometimes show ranks and ratings in pictures that could
be laid out separately, like oversized playing-cards. The first instructions for dress of enlisted
men in the US Navy was by regulation approved 19 February, 1841. The first regulation
for an official uniform for British sailors was in 1857.

Pictures of naval officers' uniforms had several practical purposes. Perhaps an officer who
went to a tailor would be able to consult such a book to ensure that he would be properly
fitted out. Furthermore, such a book could allow men to recognize, learn, and memorize
the ranks of officers of their own and other navies. Uniforms had the psychological effect
of establishing order and discipline; by instantly recognizing an outfit and what service,

Costumes of the British Navy, 1834. Lithograph, hand-colored.

This 1834 print shows 12 costumes of officers ranging from Admiral through to Mid-shipmen, of several warrant officers, and of ordinary seamen. Such illustrations, together with detailed books, would permit the rapid identification of the rank of an officer at a distance.

standing, and power the individual possessed, proper deference or obedience could be obtained instantly. Uniforms were part of the whole process of establishing a complex system of discipline and mental control. The illustrated guides to uniforms were thus very accurate, because they served practical purposes. It is no accident that the word for such clothing and the concept of identical performance and identical behavior is 'uniform'. Both the clothing and the behavior were to fit a single form.[1]

Early American naval uniforms are difficult to come by. Some in the Collection can be traced to particular individuals, such as a shirt once belonging to John Lord, a gunner aboard the USS *Constitution*, a coat owned by Captain Hunter from the 1830s and a blouse belonging to George Dove from the Civil War. Others cannot be tracked to a specific person, but still leave interesting hints about their times. In a matching set from the 1890s, a five year old boy's uniform picks up the trim and decorations of the father's uniform.

1. Michel Foucault, *Discipline and Punish: The Birth of the Prison*. Translated from the French by Alan Sheridan (New York: Vintage, 1977), 166-169.

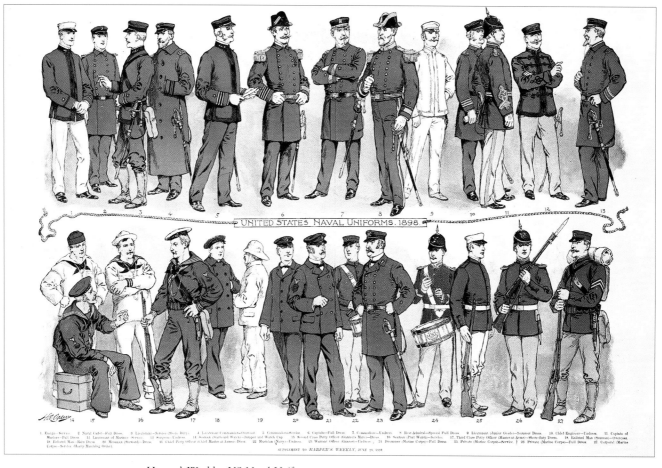

Harper's Weekly: *US Naval Uniforms.*
Chromolithograph.

This depiction of US Naval Uniforms in 1898 serves the same purpose as the older cards and printed uniform sheets; the two groups are divided between officers on the top of the page and petty officers and enlisted men on the bottom.

When a ship met another or entered a port, officers and men would often size up the strangers with a comment on their clothing, assuming, rightly or wrongly, that the quality of the outfit gave insights into character, rank, and other qualities. When Dr August Beers, aboard the USS *South Carolina* entered a Spanish port in 1824, he noted:

> I soon had an opportunity of viewing the Spanish exterior for we had no sooner dropt anchor than a boat with quarantine officers came off. They all made a shabby appearance ill dressed with swarthy complexions. The principal officers wore a chapeau which seems to have undergone the abrasion of some centuries. The rowers wore hats similar to those of the Quakers of our country, some of them having a cockade.[2]

Later, when civilians came aboard, Beers again took note of their clothing, linking his observations about exterior appearance to an assessment of character:

> The citizens of all denominations are flocking on board…The dress of the men as well as of the women is full of finery. Some of the latter may be called handsome but most of them are the reverse. What strikes a stranger most is their confidence and indifference.[3]

Keepers of some journals noted that the appearance of an outfit was a matter of pride and

2. Ms. *Journal of a Voyage to the Mediterranean in the US Ship North Carolina, 1824-1827*, by Dr Aug. P. Beers, Surgeon's Mate, entry for 29 April, 1824, in the WH Collection.

3. 'Beers Journal', entry for 1 May, 1824.

Father and Son Uniforms. Late 19th century.

The proud father, apparently at one time a member of the crew of the USS *Texas*, was instrumental in the creation of his young son's miniature-size uniform based on his father's but with more embellishment. For comparison, see the two photographs. The *Texas* was commissioned in 1895 and played an important role in the annihilation of the Spanish fleet at Santiago de Cuba, 3 July, 1898, during the Spanish-American War.

identity among the merchant sailors. In the naval service, maintaining one's clothing in good condition was a matter of regulation, strictly enforced. In the US Navy, before flogging was abolished, offenses by a sailor against his own outfit of clothing could merit severe punishment. It was clear from official and unofficial documents, that appearance and proper outfit was essential in the naval service.[4]

The nineteenth century elaboration and detailing of uniforms in the navies of Europe and America found echoes in popular culture, as children were often decked out in sailor suits and sailor-clothing motifs were picked up in ladies' fashions. One of the earlier depictions of a child wearing a sailor's uniform is a picture of the Prince of Wales, in 1849, wearing a tailor-made sailor suit, and labelled as 'The Young Sailor'. Later, sheet music, popular magazines, advertising, commercial art, and mass-produced clothing for boys, girls, and young women, would echo the sailor's uniform, well into the twentieth century.

A careful study of uniform books sometimes makes it possible to identify by date a particular picture or sculpture thereby placing the seaman in his time. Similarly, badges of insignia, important for identifying the particular role or specialization of warrant and petty officers, may be traced using such uniform books.

4. 'Punishments', U.S. Navy, 1848, Report to Congress, in WH Collection.

Crew Aboard Marpesia.
Photograph.

This is a group photograph of the crew of the cargo ship *Marpesia* in 1894. The *Marpesia* carried coal from New Castle to San Francisco; lumber from Tacoma, Washington, to Melbourne, Australia; coal from Newcastle to Callao; manganese ore from Carrizol, Chile, to Philadelphia and barrel oil from Philadelphia to Liverpool.

Prince George and others.
Photograph.

A photographer, probably on board HMS *Bacchante* in the 1880s, captured the portraits of Prince George and Prince Edward as naval cadets and British naval officer E.R. LeMarchant. The photograph is part of LeMarchant's souvenir album. A grandson of Queen Victoria, Prince George later reigned as King George V of the United Kingdom, 1910-1936. Then, as now, photographers tended to take pictures of celebrities and the near great rather than capturing for posterity images of everyday life.

Officers and Crew of the USS Dolphin.
Toned photograph.

In this photograph aboard the USS *Dolphin*, the officers and crew marshal on deck for the photographer. As often seen in such group photographs, the African-American members of the crew take up positions at the far rear. The *Dolphin* was one of the first four steel ships of the New Navy of the United States, commissioned in 1885.

Photography and Reality

In the middle of the nineteenth century, with the coming of daguerreotypes, ambrotypes and tintypes, and then the development of paper print photography, further democratization crept in. With heavy equipment at first, photographic work was conducted in studios, with relatively formal portraits taken as keepsakes. Such pictures were set and posed, with the man in uniform or occasionally holding some instrument or tool which provided a clue to his rank. Like earlier portrayals done by snipped-out silhouette and painting, these small pictures would sometimes be framed in little pressed metallic frames or miniature lockets to be kept as valuable reminders of sailors absent at sea.

With more mobile cameras, new categories of pictures became more common in the 1860s and 1870s. Aboard various ships in the 1850s, and then during and after the American Civil war, photographers sometimes moved beyond pictures of single individuals to try to capture some sense of life aboard ship. However, many of these photographs were formally posed, again putting up a barrier to the modern viewer who seeks in them some clues to the ordinary and everyday life. Among some of the simplest such poses, a whole crew or part of a crew would stand on the deck in rows, facing the camera so that every face would be caught on film. Those in back rows would climb up on hatch covers or upper decks so their faces could be caught by the camera.

Much like class pictures from schools with the students arrayed on bleachers or on stairs, such group portraits conveyed very little information about life as it was lived aboard.

Photographers must have understood that such a picture could serve only to memorialize a whole crew and not depict much in the way of reality. A further step in the direction of realism required that small groups of men pose in various departments, such as during gun drill, practicing with swords, swabbing a deck, or playing with pets. Among such pictures we often find classic scenes repeated from literature in which the photographer, attempting to capture what people expected, would arrange several sailors in an appropriate pose. One photographer in the 1880s set up a group, with beards and pipes, all listening to the oldest among them spinning a yarn of the sea, echoing a scene common in the great sea novels.

In group photographs aboard the decks of American naval ships from the 1870s and 1880s, one can still note some interesting, and perhaps unintended, messages about the social setting on ship. The attentive viewer can sometimes discern, usually in the rear of a group, an African-American sailor or two, isolated among, and sometimes, peeking out from behind the white faces. The fact that such men would rarely be found in the front ranks of the photographs itself tells the modern viewer something. Black sailors perhaps knew that they were part of the crew and deserved to be included in any complete photograph; at the same time, their position in the rear suggests something about their standing in the crew. The visual presentation captures the felt discrimination. The pictures echoed the ambiguity of belonging to a crew and being placed on its social edge, the 'two-ness' of identity noted at the turn of the century by W.E.B. Du Bois, the noted African-American scholar and co-founder of the NAACP.

As cameras became cheaper in the 1890s, officers sometimes took them along on voyages. With this stage, pictures went through one more step of democratization and one more step in capturing a more complete reality. Albums of pictures taken by officers from before the turn of the century begin to include visits ashore, pictures of native peoples and foreign architecture, views from the ship of shorelines, and views of the ship from the dock or beach. Much like the men who a century before would keep a personal log or journal, these early camera-buffs tried to capture the exotic, the unusual, and the memories that would stand out, to bring home some frozen moments to share with their families. Whole albums in the Collection give clues of the interests of the amateur photographers. One was captivated by the pets aboard ship; another, with the exotic port visits.

Even after George Eastman introduced the Kodak No. 1 camera in 1889, an ordinary merchant seaman or naval sailor was in no position to spare $5 for a camera and more money for film and developing. Yet as officers took pictures of deck scenes and foreign ports to send home or paste in albums, other sailors found postcards proliferating in ports. Commercial photographers ashore in some ports of call might provide portraits. By 1900, Eastman brought the price of his simple portable camera down to one dollar, and taking snapshots soon became a national and international fad. Commemorative packets issued in the early 1900s would depict life aboard a major ship.

Ship Lovely Matilda *of Philadelphia. Cap.*ᵗⁿ *Benj.*ⁿ *Huggins. Jacob Johnson Master. Signed Ant Roux à Marseille 1808.* Watercolor.

The ship *Lovely Matilda* of 231 tons was built in Philadelphia in 1805 for the Franco-American wine and silk importing firm of Ducoing and Lacombe. The ship was evidently sold foreign or lost soon after the painting was completed. It would appear that this painting was done specifically for the Master Jacob Johnson as the title of the example at the Peabody Essex Museum, Salem, Massachusetts, lists only the captain.

By the early 1900s, therefore, with postcards and snapshots, depictions of men aboard ship and of the ships themselves had become much more democratic and widespread. Photographs of men sewing their clothing at sewing machines, of others mopping the deck or standing watch, or sitting around in a truly candid, unposed moment of relaxation, are valuable finds for a sense of the sailing man's real life, rather than a romanticized version of it.

Images of Ships

Pictures of ships rarely give much sense of what life was like on deck or below deck in the age of sail and early sail-and-steam. Often depicted from a distance, ships have always had a kind of beauty that caught the eye of artists. The ship itself, with its tracery of rigging, its curved lines, its air of mystery and its hints of distant voyages was a fine subject. Looking at a painting or print of an East Indiaman, a frigate, a man-of-war, or a clipper ship, however, it is very difficult to gain much sense of what the men, the boys, and the occasional woman aboard experienced, and what conditions prevailed.

(Above) *Ship Model of the Clipper Ship* Sovereign of the Seas.
(Right) *Print of the Clipper Ship* Sovereign of the Seas.

Ship Model: Clipper Ship. Sovereign of the Seas.

Famous East Boston shipbuilder, Donald McKay built the *Sovereign of the Seas* on his own account and launched her in June 1852. He gave command to his brother, Captain Lauchlan McKay. An extreme clipper, she was considered the largest merchant ship of her day. This model is believed to have been sailor-built about 1880. She may have been the fastest two-deck clipper ever built. Her maiden voyage was to San Francisco. Later she sailed between Liverpool and Melbourne, going out in 78 days and returning in 68 days, outsailing everything in the trade. On one passage to Melbourne, it was stated that she had several runs of 22 knots. Unfortunately, in 1859 she ran on the Pyramid Shoals in the Malacca Straits, becoming a total loss.

George Hodge Diary: watercolor of British vessels.

The Hodge Diary includes a number of well-executed watercolors. This one from 1798 depicts two British vessels in Yarmouth Harbor. One is the brig *Jannet* [*sic*] on which he had sailed from Leith with a load of bottles and coal. While walking on shore, a press gang seized him and took him to a rendezvous. He was transferred to the other vessel in the picture, HMS *Lancaster*, rated 64 guns. He was put to duty first in the maintops and later on the forecastle. Shortly thereafter the *Lancaster* would be taking in troops at Spithead for Ireland.

Large sailing warships might carry many men, perhaps 500 to 800, to both man the ship and fight the enemy during battle. While the highest ranking officers would have cabins of varying sizes as a private space in which to sleep and change their clothes, the crew slept in hammocks, strung between the decks side by side, often so close they would sway against each other with the ship's motion. Normally in daytime, hammocks were stowed in nettings along the sides of the upper deck to act as protection from flying splinters or musket shot.

Merchant ships were manned by far smaller crews. Here again, the privilege of rank included a measure of privacy. Officers would have cabins, sometimes made comfortable with built-in furnishings. The crew's quarters were usually in the most forward part of the ship, in the forecastle, with narrow bunks.

On naval ships in the age of sail, officers had their own mess. Enlisted men gathered in messes usually on the gun-decks. While officers might have their food brought by stewards, each group of seamen messing together would select one man, to bring the meals from the galley

George Hodge Diary. Early 19th century.

Hodge in this watercolor depicted HMS *Lancaster* dressed with signal flags and various national colors during a visit to the Cape of Good Hope. Table Mountain and the settlement can be made out in the background. Hodge tended not to show any crew aboard the ships he painted, but his rendering of the detailed flags and pennants in a stiff breeze made this a lively illustration in his diary.

to where they ate. Normally the task of bringing meals would rotate among the messmates.

Original artwork depictions of quarters below deck from the age of sail are hard to come by. As with the images of men at work, it is often difficult to determine the authenticity and accuracy of such images, but when such a picture is compared to descriptions in journals or diaries, it is possible to get a sense of life below decks.

Ships, like the men who sailed them, would sometimes be presented realistically, sometimes in stereotypes. Some careful artists depicted every line of a ship's rigging, and such fine pictures allow modern model makers and ship historians to capture the exact look of a great many sailing vessels. Indeed, to depict a truly typical ship may be a far easier task than attempting to depict a typical sailor.

Due to the cost of elaborate ship carvings and the need for the British government to economize, the vessels in the latter eighteenth century onwards tended to be less highly decorated. The East Indiamen was an armed merchant cruiser employed by the British-owned East India Company and the Dutch East India Company in trade to India, the spice

English woolie by British sailor. Mid-19th century.

This excellent woolie depicts a British ship of the line flying the royal standard suggesting that Queen Victoria was aboard. With the vessel dressed with flags and the yardarms manned with sailors, the ship is at the peak of a ceremonial moment. The delicate yarn work in this picture conveyed the details of what was probably the Royal Yacht and seamen aloft.

islands and China in the eighteenth and early nineteenth century. American sailing merchantmen and naval vessels, steam vessels, and clipper ships from the nineteenth century were the subject of thousands of ship portraits. Sometimes shown at anchor, tossed in a storm, fighting in battles, or resting quietly at dock, ships were a natural subject for the artist. The full-rigged clipper ship was so beautiful that artists captured them under full sail many times, as they were built to capture the wind with a cloud of canvas.

With the coming of steam, sidewheel-driven ships could always be identified from a distance by the large wheel, while later propeller-driven steam boats could only be recognized as such by the funnel in amongst the masts and rigging. Some early steamships

Schooner Superior *of Baltimore by Antoine Roux, Sr.* Watercolor.

This watercolor, probably before 1806, by Antoine Roux, père (Sr.), of Marseilles, depicts the schooner *Superior* of Baltimore at anchor. She appears to be pierced for cannon.

Shadow box model of the USS Maine.

This shadow box model dated 1898 is of the battleship USS *Maine* of 6,682 tons, a design speed of 17 knots, and commissioned in 1895. She is shown in the Brooklyn Navy Yard. Her destruction in Havana harbor on 15 February, 1898, precipitated the Spanish American War. Although no men are shown, the item is interesting in that it is a model in a case against a painted background of the navy yard facility.

had retractable funnels, as steam might only be employed for entering or leaving harbors or part-time propulsion. Paddle-driven steam vessels, while appropriate for shallow waters in rivers and harbors, tended to be less successful at sea. The transition from sail to steam was not a sudden change, but a gradual shift over many decades as the problems with steam propulsion were solved one by one.

However, in much popular nautical art, ships were stylized and casually presented; copies of copies allowed an engraver or artist to convey the sense of a ship as a symbol in the background, with no need to represent each line of rigging or each mast and spar with accuracy. Ceramics, silverware, medals, tattoo art, sheet music, greeting cards, magazine prints, and engravings showed many simplified versions of sailing vessels. A dark hull, two or three masts, a suggestion of square-rigged sails, and a few lines let the viewer know that the artist intended a ship.

Thus the collector is gratified to find a depiction of a known ship, or two known ships in an engagement or chase, or an accurate portrayal of a famous vessel at anchor. Marine art collectors cherish such pictures. However, as the modern viewer seeks to learn more of the day-to-day life of the sailor, such grand visions of elegant sailing vessels, whether accurate to the last line, or simply stylized symbols in the background of a portrait, do little to let us know how the sailor passed his everyday life, or what he truly thought, felt, and believed. Life below decks, in wardroom and gun deck on warships, in cabin and forecastle aboard merchant ships remains difficult to recapture and every glimpse gained through art can add to the reconstruction of the life of Jack Tar.

The handsome ships of eighteenth and nineteenth century art give little sense of life below decks, and the elegant officer's uniforms and the jaunty rigging of Jack Tar were external to the man. But among the images of ships and men, there are hints about how life was lived.

Deck Scene.
Oil Painting.

In this busy deck scene aboard an armed vessel of the mid-19th century, details suggest the ship is engaged in gun drill. In the foreground, a slow-match is kept burning, while to the right, a gunner sits ready for orders. A sailor kneels with one hand on a box marked 'Telegraph' which would contain signal flags. A boy attends an officer who has a speaking trumpet under his arm, while in a cabin an officer fills out a report using quill pen and ink. An apparent midshipman is being instructed in the use of a telescope by an officer on the upper deck, as a passenger, perhaps a planter, in a broad-brimmed hat, looks on. To the right, another apparent midshipman descends the ladder to the main deck, telescope in hand. Although nothing remarkable takes place in this illustration, the very ordinary business of the deck serves as testimony to the painting's authenticity. Oil paintings of deck scenes from this period are extremely rare.

Equipages de ligne.
Costume de fatigue.

CHAPTER THREE
Day to Day Life Aboard Ship

The daily routine of the seaman aboard a sailing vessel or early steam-and-sail powered ship varied from intense periods of hard work, much of it dangerous, to long periods of enforced idleness. The working day varied a great deal between warships, merchant vessels, and whalers. Of all such groups of seamen in the early and mid-nineteenth century, probably those experiencing the longest periods of simply standing watch were American whalers, whose voyages sometimes lasted as long as three or even five years.

Since so much of the sailor's work and life seemed quite ordinary, and even sometimes very dull, it becomes difficult for later students of the subject to find visual evidence which captures the essence of actual day to day work schedules. Painters, sketchbook-artists, and later, photographers, tended to make images of extraordinary, not ordinary, events. Clearly, a picture of a violent storm, a shipwreck, a burial at sea, a battle, or an exotic port and its colorful inhabitants were all more popular subjects than a cook at work, a seaman holystoning the deck or working aloft on the yardarms or in the rigging, or sailors sitting down to a meal. So, in visual art which survives from the age of sail, the collector discovers the apparently contradictory principle: what was commonplace in life is rare in art and what was rare in life has become commonplace in art.

Even on explorations like those of Captain Cook to the South Pacific, when he engaged several artists to capture and record the high points of the voyages, the vast majority of the art work was of the unusual, not the routine events. Exotic sights, hostile or friendly

(Above) *'Equipages de Ligne'*.
Mid-19th century.
Hand-colored lithograph.

The sailor is depicted at work at an ordinary task. He is part way through the process of worming, parcelling and serving a rope to make it watertight.

Starboard-Watch.		Larboard-Watch.		Starboard-Watch.		Larboard-Watch.	
1	Will᷾ Drisdale, Cap	2	Will᷾ Thompson. c	45	Tho᷾ Backstone. c	46	John Forster. Capt
3		4	Henry Evans	47	James Lee	48	Ja᷾ Dayley
5	Pompey Peeker	6	Thompson	49	John Doyle	50	Phi᷾ Hind
7	Joseph Thompson	8	Dun᷾ Campbell	51	Tho᷾ Weston	52	John Frazier
9	Robert M᷾Neil	10	John Jennings	53	Arch᷾ Rogers	54	Will᷾ Thomas
11	Robert Robinson	12	Hugh Develin	55	Dirk Raaskeys	56	
13	Thomas Davis (2)	14	Tho᷾ Edwards	57	James Latimore	58	John Wright
15	William Norman	16	Tho᷾ Cosgrove	59	Jos᷾ West	60	Will᷾ Davis
17	M᷾Donald	18	Jos᷾ Patterson	61	James Crevey	62	Will᷾ Lansdown
19	Patrick Harding	20	Will᷾ Anderson	63	James Woods (2)	64	Peter Keensden

(Above and opposite) *HMS* Plantagenet.

The HMS *Plantagenet* of 74 guns was built at Woolwich, launched in 1801 and broken up in 1817. Therefore, it is probable that the watch bill, headed by handsome pen and ink patriotic artwork, was for use during the Napoleonic Wars. It contains in great detail the positions of the crew members on various watches. Also bound with the watch bill is a quarter bill listing Robert Lloyd, Esquire, as captain. This also has, in great detail, the positions of the various seamen when reefing, furling and loosing sails; mooring or unmooring; making sail; shortening sail; making sail with studding sails; and shortening sail with studding sails. Each of these sections is headed by a handsome watercolor. Also included is an officer's watch and station bill.

encounters with natives, ports of call, flora and fauna, would all be clearly depicted, but the work and life aboard the ship was mostly too unremarkable for an artist to want to capture.

A collector is faced with a very personal decision: whether or not to collect art work created many years after the scene depicted or to try to obtain work created contemporaneously. Welles Henderson's guide-post has been the latter, with the goal of creating a reference collection based on that criterion. He approaches any 'visual' with a questioning and curious eye. Even some photographs, when carefully posed, could reflect an effort to reproduce what the photographer had come to conclude should be recorded, rather than a candid shot of an actual situation or setting.

It is a great rarity to have a depiction of a calm day aboard ship in the first half of the nineteenth century, with men going about their duties: with the ship being worked, no one being punished, no one falling overboard, the weather pleasant. One such painting in the collection depicts a man peering from an upper deck with a telescope, attended by a young midshipman, while other sailors and officers are distributed casually about the deck, some at work, and others at rest in natural poses. The work presents a straightforward representation, without excessive nostalgic touches, of what an ordinary deck scene probably looked like aboard an armed vessel of the mid-nineteenth century.

The modern observer can piece together such images from a variety of sources, building up, like a quilt made of vari-coloured cloth, a sense of what the fabric of life was probably like aboard British and American ships of the eighteenth and nineteenth century.

Insights into the daily life aboard sailing ships and early sail-and-steam ships can be gleaned from scattered documents, from log and diary entries, and from narratives. Yet even in written or printed sources, some of the ephemera relating to commonplace events or daily routines of that time are difficult to find. For example, one of the most ordinary of documents, the watch-list, although hand-written on many merchant ships, is not easily found today among the paper works handled by dealers. In one of these simple lists, an

'Furling Sail'. Watercolor. Early 19th century.

The difficulty of furling sails in a high wind is captured in this watercolor, as the men struggle to hold on and at the same time catch and bring in the billowing canvas. There are not many watercolors in the early days of sail showing sailors working aloft.

officer would note the division of the officers and men into 'starboard' and 'larboard' (or 'port') watches. Aside from the dog watches of two hours each between 4 and 8 p.m., men from one watch would serve at their duty stations four hours while men from the other watch slept below in bunks or hammocks, or simply rested.

The disadvantages of the watch system were quite clear: no member of the crew aboard got a full night's sleep, and serving a four-hour watch beginning at midnight or 4:00 a.m after four hours' sleep led many a seaman into trouble for dozing off on duty. A print by Cruikshank, *The Progress of a Midshipman* (1821) shows the misery of keeping a midnight watch in a rainstorm. Aboard naval vessels, another commonplace document, is an artistically decorated quarter bill, station bill, or watch bill, drawn up to assign men to their posts and to their different duties. A few fine examples of these bills are in the Henderson Collection, some illustrated with watercolors to indicate the different positions taken by the different members of the crew. Perhaps the finest and most richly illustrated quarter bill is that of HMS *Plantagenet* from the period of the Napoleonic Wars, showing positions of sailors in furling and reefing sails and in other tasks, and giving exact numbered positions

Henry Powlett, R.N, Station Bill 1788.

One of the types of documents that help define the life of the seaman was the 'station bill' which showed exactly where men should work on different maneuvers and sail evolutions of a ship. Here men are loosing sails, standing on footropes below the yardarms and the jib boom. Such carefully executed illustrations give a good sense of some of the day-to-day tasks aboard sailing vessels. The station bill was created in a tabbed book so that an officer could readily turn to the illustration he needed for a particular evolution. This is a particularly handsome manuscript station bill because of the watercolors depicting the positions of the individual sailors for loosing sails, furling sails and manning ship.

for each particular seaman and officer during specific situations and actions. The complexity and difficulty of handling the lines and sails on a daily basis is revealed through several instruction manuals and a variety of quarter or station bills in the Collection.[1]

Other promising sources are accounts of voyages. Aboard naval and merchant ships sailing out of both Britain and America, a designated officer would keep an official ship's log that was a journal of the happenings aboard the ship itself, with entries as to speed through the sea, setting of the sails, force of wind, weather, latitude and longitude, encounters with other ships at sea, ports of call, accidents, and death. As such, official logs tended to record routine information about the ship and the voyage itself, usually not containing very much about the daily life of the men aboard. However, the many log-books in the collection, when taken together, can provide some information about the seaman's life against a background of events such as calling on ports and exchanging mail with other ships. The rhythms and routines, the long quiet periods, and the daily round of shifting watches, are noted in the log-books, giving a sense of how time passed aboard ship – and it often passed extremely slowly, with long, uneventful days following one upon the

1. Capt. C. Chapman, *All About Ships* (London, Edward Colyer, 1869); B.F. Shattuck, USS *John Adams* 1855, watch and quarter bills spell out duties aloft.

Log of Schooner President *from Newport*. 1797.

The log from the schooner *President* sailing from Newport R.I. is most unusual in that it is of an American merchant vessel in the eighteenth century with the entries for each day in rhyming verse; i.e., 'On Feb.ʸ The thirteenth day of Ninety Seven we sailed away...' In addition, watercolors at the bottom of each day's entries depict the vessel at some stage; i.e., 'taking our Departure from Block Island.' On her way to Hispaniola, she was captured by the English. Her eventual fate is unknown.

News From Home. Lithograph, hand-colored. Mid-19th century.

'Decks cleared up for the night and enjoying in the forecastle the first three letters from friends after twelve months' absence.' The four men are all entranced by a single letter, as it is read aloud. The looped-rope handle on the sea chest at the right is a becket, a common piece of handiwork by seamen. All are wearing the characteristic, slipper-like flexible shoes suitable for keeping one's footing on deck and aloft in the rigging. The simple pleasure of hearing news from home comes across in this print.

(Opposite) *Letter From Home*. Painted by T. Whittaker, 1865.

This oil painting shows a scene often mentioned in diaries, journals and letters from sailors. A cherished letter from home, sometimes delivered on the high seas from a passing ship, would be read and re-read to the rapt attention of other sailors, hungry for any reminder of the loved ones they left behind, even in such a second-hand fashion. Beards, intently clenched pipes, and bare feet among the six listeners suggest that this painter repeated motifs and themes that had become common in the attempt to portray the nautical flavor and the heartfelt emotions of the moment.

other. British and American midshipmen, as part of their training, kept journals or logs that were reviewed by a superior officer.

Sometimes officers, doctors, passengers, and a few crew members kept journals or diaries, as distinct from official logs. In such accounts the diarist would often remark on the long periods of inactivity and sometimes make note in passing, of completion of routine duties. Such accounts, often more personal and intended to capture memories of voyages, help flesh out the bare essentials of the log books, watch-bills, quarter-bills, and station bills.

Yet the writing of a diary or a journal imposed its own logic. The diarist wanted to note down, so that it would not escape memory, the interesting and memorable event. Tantalizing, sporadic entries referring to the passage of several 'uneventful days' only

Une Chambre d'Officier à Bord. Engraving. Mid–19th century.

Here an officer is in his cabin, writing a letter, surrounded by everyday furnishings and equipment including: a bookcase, a pitcher and basin for washing, a speaking trumpet and a candle and candlestick for light. Hanging on the side of the desk is his dress equipment, including a sword and his hat. Note the locket, the reason for his thoughts of absent love.

Caulking Tools.
Mid-19th century.

An ambrotype photograph shows a young sailor holding a caulking iron and caulking mallet. The job of pounding rope junk into seams between the deck and hull planking and then treating it with tar was a standard protection against leaks.

Medicine Chest for Shipping and Families., c.1800.
Tooth Extractor.

The ship's captain usually acted as a doctor aboard merchant ships. This wooden chest has a nautical motif label of Wm. Evans Druggist and Apothecary (No. 134 South Front St. 3rd house above the Drawbridge Philada.) Some bottles, a few perhaps from a later date, are labeled 'Epsom salts', 'Spiced Syrup of Rhubarb', 'Castor Oil', 'Sweet Spirits of Nitre', 'Elixir Paregoric' and 'Ipecacuanha'. The wooden-handled instrument with a metal shaft in front of the chest is a tooth extractor. It looks medieval but sailors with rotting teeth had little choice but to be relieved of the pain by extraction. Oil of cloves would only help to a certain degree.

enforced the impression that it was the extraordinary event that most diarists felt worthy to record. Passengers and crew members who kept personal journals, like the keepers of official logs, put in their accounts the unusual events that stood out, including deaths, accidents, episodes of mutinous behavior, punishments, ship encounters, storms, and the like. On balance, the use of diaries to gain access to the ordinary daily life poses a challenge. Horace Elmer, an officer in the US Navy, in keeping his journal aboard USS *Hartford* in 1866, would skip many days, and then when he took up writing again, would even remark upon the fact that he had forgotten the few memorable events he had hoped to record.[2]

Other insights into routine life can be gained from the tools used in daily work. Handling a tool gives a feeling for how difficult a particular job would be. A heavy caulking mallet for use with a caulking iron for pounding oakum, made from unravelled rope or 'rope junk', into the seams of a ship's wooden deck or sides to keep water from leaking in, captures the feel of one day to day chore aboard ships. Pointed 'fids' were used in working rope and splicing it. These were made of wood, metal or whalebone. Sometimes the care taken in making the tools themselves conveys a sense of the regard a man had for his work and for the tools he had to use. And such workmanship in crafting the tool itself suggests the long hours often available.

A carpenter's square made of one piece of whalebone gives just such a sense of the value attached by the worker to the tools of his craft. Similarly, one can feel the care that went into a neatly kept sailmaker's kit, in which some needles would be kept in a tube usually carved from wood and sometimes covered with macramé. Another tool used in rope work, in the collection, is a serving mallet used for worming, parcelling and servicing a rope as protection from wear and weather, that is decorated with an incised heart. In the way of medical instruments and equipment, the Collection includes a medicine chest, with various medicines some of which appear to serve specifically as laxatives or preventatives against diarrhea. A tooth-extractor gives a sense of the crude dental work performed aboard ships.

2. Horace Elmer, 'The Cruise of the Hartford,' ms. copy, entry for 6 May, 1866 (catalog A-68). He often began entries with such a remark.

Jack Hove Down with a Grog Blossom Fever.
Artist: Cruikshank, 1811. Hand-colored engraving.

In this elaborate cartoon, several early 19th century stereotypes of the sailor as well as of the medical profession are presented simultaneously. The sailor obviously has nothing wrong with him except a severe hangover, and his love of alcoholic spirits makes up the central theme. By his bed, a box with rum, grog and brandy is labeled his 'sea stock'. His salty talk is parodied as he says, 'Stop my grog? Belay there Doctor – Shiver my timbers but your lingo bothers me – You may batter my Hull as long as you like, but I'll be d--'nd if ever you board me with your Glyster pipe.' The doctor's Glyster pipe is intended to provide a quick enema, which Jack clearly dreads, although the doctor, with apparent sadistic glee, is eager to put it to work.

An inventory of a sea-doctor's chest from aboard a US naval vessel in the American Revolution shows that 'medicine' consisted of a very few drugs supplemented with a supply of chocolate, raisins, and other treats.

Much of the ordinary is conveyed only by very indirect evidence. We can only imagine the noise of a ship during a heavy storm, and how difficult it would be for an officer to be heard above the crashing waves and howl of the wind. Speaking trumpets and bosuns' whistles would be essential. There is one such trumpet and two bosuns' whistles in the Collection. One of the whistles is engraved with the name of its owner, John Robinson, who served aboard the HMS *Ringdove* in 1870; the other bosun's whistle is decorated with a Chinese dragon (see page 48). Drums were also used aboard ship to give commands, such as summoning men to quarters, and these are depicted in a few prints.

The quality and quantity of the daily diet varied a great deal over the period of sail. Although officers were entitled to the same food as seamen, they usually improved their lot by purchase at their own expense. In Nelson's day, the usual fare for seamen consisted of

Unloading Cattle.
Mid–19th century.

This sketch shows the method of unloading cattle, hoisted from below deck by block and tackle hitched to their horns. Some are corralled on deck, while one is being driven off by ramp to the shore. The text tells us this steamship from Argentina at the port of Dunkirk, is unloading live beef, a common type of cargo in the 19th century.

ship's biscuit, beef (usually salted), pork (usually salted), peas, oatmeal, sugar, butter and cheese, with possible substitution of such items as flour, raisins, and rice. In port, the purser, under certain provisions, was allowed to buy fresh vegetables. Entries in many logs in the Collection show, while vessels were in port, the bringing on board of quantities of fresh beef. Some of the sketchbooks in the Collection demonstrate that some vessels,

Hand-colored engraving.
Early 19th century.

The galley was essential, and cooks often killed chickens and other livestock brought aboard. This print captures several mundane details of daily life: the smoking galley stovepipe, called a Charley Noble in the American Navy, a black cook, the labor of plucking a chicken and the bedraggled clothing that was probably more typical than the fancy dress shown in more formal art.

'Soft Bread and Shore Grub'.
Harper's Weekly, 7 September, 1895.
Magazine Illustration.

This scene by R.F. Zogbaum depicts several aspects of loading provisions aboard a US warship in the mid 1890s. In reviewing the prints and photographs of the Collection it would appear that at the time depicted, Afro-American sailors' duties were primarily as cooks and stewards. Many photographs aboard federal naval vessels during the Civil War, however, show large numbers of black sailors.

Photograph of Berth Deck Cooks.
Aboard USS *Tennessee.*

With mock seriousness, this group of Berth Deck Cooks aboard the steam and sail frigate USS *Tennessee* have fun posing with the tools of their trade from pots and pans to culinary instruments and foodstuffs. Due to her comfortable quarters and handling characteristics she was a favorite duty station, at one time being the flagship of the Asiatic Squadron. By 1879 she was the flagship of the North Atlantic Squadron. She was sold out of the Navy in 1886.

merchantman and naval, depending on the Captain's desires, seemed veritable farmyards, with chickens, sheep, pigs and cattle. Usually the livestock was a supplement to the officers' victuals. Fish, sea-turtles, or porpoises were caught at sea. Sometimes land tortoises, goats, wild birds and game were acquired from visits ashore on remote islands or coasts. Without refrigeration, of course, the meat had to be consumed within a few days of slaughter to ensure its freshness, and occasional journal entries show, for example, pork served two or three times a day after a slaughter, or turtles or tortoises being kept alive for later consumption.[3]

Surviving pictures, in the form of sketches, paintings, prints, and later photographs, of life aboard can lead us to a feel for the routine events as well as the more extraordinary events. On naval vessels, as we see from the *Bellone* illustrations, men often took their meals right at their duty station, with tables set up, for example, between the great guns on a gun deck. One member of the mess would bring food for the others, as a *Bellone* etching demonstrates. The rules and regulations of the USS *Lexington* from the 1820s specify that one man of each mess of nine men is to oversee cleanliness and distribution of food. Some seventy years later, in various vessels, a similar practice of eating next to some of the guns remained common aboard ships of the US Navy, as recorded by R.F. Zogbaum, many of whose illustrations were published in *Harper's Weekly* through the 1890s. Despite the variation in so many details between fleets and over time, it is instructive to find the same practice reported on French, British, and American naval ships.

Aboard merchant ships, the ordinary seamen often ate in the forecastle (fo'c'sle), sitting

3. Journal of Jarias Beal, Master of the Barque *Apthorpe*. 1840: entry for 31 March, notes that pork was eaten for several meals in a row; *Log of the Ship Ida*, 1821 provides details of catching porpoises and turtles for meals.

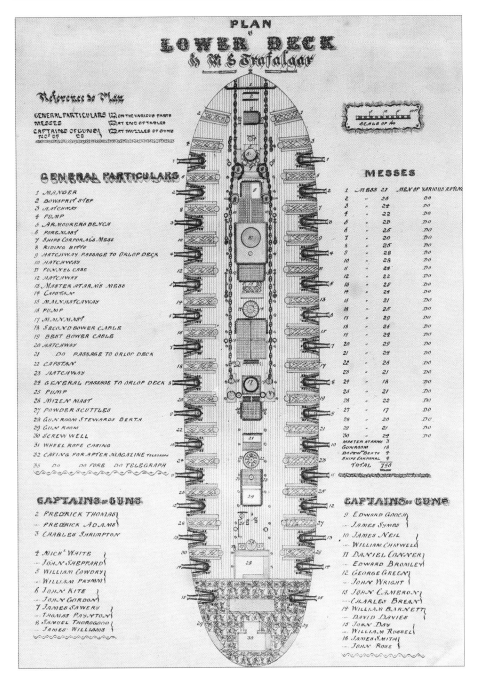

Gun Deck of HMS Trafalgar.
Mid-19th century.
Sepia pen and watercolor.

This plan of the lower gun deck of HMS *Trafalgar*, launched in 1841, clearly details the location and number of guns and the names of the gun captains. In addition, it shows the messes, reflecting the same arrangement for taking meals that prevailed on the French ship *Bellone*. In the plan, the tables for meals can be seen between the guns.

'Le Dîner'. Aboard Bellone.

In the French navy, as in the British and American, gun crews often took their meals between the guns. One of the crew would bring the food to the others from the galley in buckets and pans, to be dished out at the table. Aboard crowded warships such eating arrangements were almost a matter of necessity.

(Above left) *Galley on board the* Union of London.
Watercolor, 1823.

Three men huddle by the light and warmth of the stove in the galley, having a smoke and a coffee or tea break. The galley was often a refuge on cold nights.

(Above right) *Deck of the* Union of London.
Watercolor, 1823.

The deck of the schooner is depicted on a fair but chilly day, with men going about their duties. Several sailors handle a sail. One sailor is fixing the rigging, while three others can be seen in the background. The sails of another ship are visible ahead. The name of the vessel can be made out on the deckhouse. The vessel was purchased by the Royal Navy in 1823. Unfortunately it was wrecked in the West Indies five years later.

on their bunks or sea-chests, while officers more often sat at tables in an officers' mess cabin. A fair number of pictures have survived of officers sitting down to eat at a table which is slanted and pitching under a heavy sea, with food and drink spilling. Some officers, accustomed to such conditions, are frequently shown calmly eating despite the difficulty, while others are queasy with sea-sickness, sometimes running from the table in distress.

Duties tended to be more extensive and varied for the individual aboard merchant ships, usually staffed with fewer men than naval ships. In both the British and American navies through the nineteenth century, a sufficient crew, often numbering in the hundreds, was sought for both fighting and sailing the ship.

Dinner on Board the Union of London *after the Gale.*
Watercolor, 1823.

Five men at the slanted table deal with the ship's roll at dinner. The hanging lamp and the level of wine in the bottle help provide the clues to the number of degrees of roll. The attendant bringing the roast navigates the pitching deck. Such scenes of attempting to eat at a pitching table were commonplace, often replicating the same elements of distressed steward, sliding and spilling food, and a group of diners attempting to maintain their decorum.

Of course, who did what aboard ship depended on their rating. In the Royal Navy, the ratings were landsmen (abolished in 1862), ordinary seamen, able seamen, and various petty officers, such as bosuns' and carpenters' mates. Warrant officers included pursers, bosuns and gunners. Aboard merchant ships, the ranks were usually fewer. The purser was a crucial person aboard a naval ship. Many were accused of issuing short, poor, or inferior supplies, as shown by court-martial or trial records, and as an occasional log, such as that kept aboard HMS *Stag*, 1778-81 (in the Collection) demonstrates.

Aboard both merchant ships and naval ships, the captain had clear power of decision making, as set forth in a remarkable document establishing, in 1821, the regulations for the ship *Ida*. The manuscript preamble began very formally:

> When any number of persons have associated themselves together for
> any particular purpose, it is absolutely necessary that some one should
> command and that others so associated should obey, therefore the
> following instructions are intended not with a wish to exercise any

Gunnery Practice Between Decks on the HMS Donegal.
Artist: Captain James Marshall. Pen and Ink and Watercolor.

Six men have positioned the gun, while the captain of the gun crew is about to pull the lanyard. Only the man holding the lanyard is barefoot. Cannon balls lie in a row, ready for use. The watercolor was done by the ship's captain in the mid-1830s. Aboard warships practice with the weapons relieved long periods of routine and boredom. At the same time, gunnery drill was a serious business, crucial experience which could be called upon when the ship engaged in action.

Gunnery Drill On Board HMS Excellent.
Pen and ink.
Mid-19th century.

In this scene aboard *Excellent* (the Royal Navy's gunnery training school, Portsmouth) sketched from life, the handwritten text makes note of the man with white pants and a cap, looking 'disgusted and done up'. The particular drill exercise here was to train the muzzle to the extreme right.

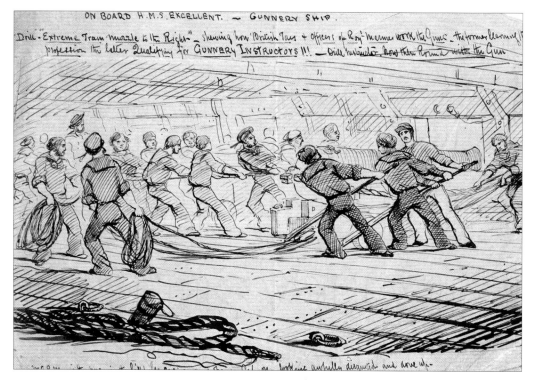

Preparing to Signal.
Watercolor.

Four seamen and probably the captain are engaged in a routine activity. One of the seamen handles the wheel, another is getting out signal flags from the locker, while a third is attaching a flag to the hoist. The fourth sailor is looking through binoculars at the nearby vessel to read her flag hoist. The well-dressed man is no doubt looking at a signal book. All are wearing very similar beards, suggesting a scene from about 1845-1855.

arbitrary power on our part but to point out as far as possible the duty of every officer and seaman now engaged on this our intended voyage as the voyage will be long and many unpleasant circumstances may arise though it is sincerely hoped that no difficultly will take place which may be avoided by every officer and seaman endeavoring to do his duty, with cheerfulness and to feel the ship his home and his shipmates his brothers and that we all form one family, and as I am appointed to command and you by your voluntary shipping under me have chosen me to command you, it is therefore ordered...

This regulation, with its tone of social compact reminiscent of the Constitution of the United States, went on to spell out the specific duties of each of the officers, the bosun, the gunner, the steward, and the carpenter. As to the crew, 'no sleeping in the watch can be allowed', and all crew members were to see that orders from officers were faithfully executed.

Specific tasks when the vessel was sailing would depend on the position to which crewmen were assigned, whether aloft, on deck, or below decks. For example, ship's carpenters and sailmakers would many times work on deck. A pencil drawing, an oil painting, and a sepia watercolor in the Collection capture this aspect of life. A few 'cutaway' ship illustrations attempt to depict life on deck and below decks simultaneously.

Other journals, logs, and sketchbooks give hints of regular duties and daily work. British midshipman Horatio Nelson Head pictured the lowering of topmasts off Bermuda in 1813 during a gale; Lt. L.A. Kimberly, aboard the USS *Germantown,* sketched the exercising of the great guns, and detailed almost humorously, the infestation of the ship with cockroaches. On an 1884 voyage of a French ship, a sailor was shown shearing a sheep. The book of etchings from the *Voyage of the Bellone* offers a range of pictures of daily life, including not only the unusual, but some mundane images showing men at work on deck.

To find original depictions of life aboard vessels before the 1850s is particularly difficult.

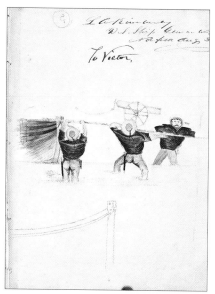

L.A. Kimberly Sketchbook.
Pen and ink and watercolor.

In 1855 Kimberly was promoted to Lieutenant and this was his rank during the period he created this sketchbook. Some of his work ranges from faithful depictions of men at gun drill to stylized and cartoon-like comments on such constant concerns as death by battle and infestation by cockroaches. In 1871, a US naval squadron sailed to Korea with a goal of negotiating a treaty of amity and commerce. The crew of an American merchantman had been massacred there in 1866. The Koreans fired on the American squadron and a naval brigade under Commander L.A. Kimberly went ashore to do battle. He was a rear-admiral commanding the Pacific Station in 1889 when his flagship *Trenton* sank at Samoa in a hurricane (see page 194).

Some prints give clues. In the middle of the century, popular printmakers like Currier distributed illustrations, some of which were clearly copied from earlier works. Later in the century, the popularity of illustrated magazines and newspapers and photography helped flesh out the story of how life aboard looked. A number of photograph albums, sketchbooks, and postcards (beginning in the 1890s) in the Collection, help put together impressions of what the ordinary day was like at sea. Of all the works, perhaps the one that is most immediate is a personal photograph album. An intriguing photograph album of junior officer E.R. Le Marchant shows a view of HMS *Bacchante* in Sydney Harbour in 1881. Two pages later is a photograph of Prince George and his brother Prince Edward, as naval cadets, Lord F.G. Osborne, and Lt. Le Marchant. The two princes spent three years sailing the world aboard HMS *Bacchante*; George would be crowned George V of England in 1910. Almost inadvertently, however, despite the selectivity of the photographer's eye, we sometimes catch accidental glimpses of more mundane features. The album also includes photographs of HMS *Wild Swan* on an around-the-world cruise in 1888 and 1889. Along with the picture of the future king, are scenes such as carpenters planing a piece of wood and a photograph

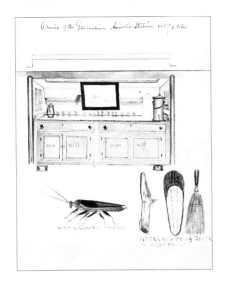  

of a captain's cabin, showing plants, a bird cage, and the other common clutter of late nineteenth century life in a confined space, similar in feel to photographs of Victorian interiors. Close examination of the photograph of the cabin shows that the captain himself kept a photograph of family members next to him as he worked at his desk.

Then, as now, people with cameras could hardly resist taking animal pictures. The *Wild Swan* photograph album, like an album from aboard the USS *Monterey*, includes shots of the ship's pets, including monkeys and dogs. Another photograph from the USS *Miami* similarly depicts officers grouped with their pet dogs.

The mix of exotic and ordinary is quite rich in some of the albums. The officers on the *Wild Swan* visited ashore in the Straits of Magellan and other places in South America, British Columbia, Honolulu and other distant ports of call. All were worth snapshots. Sometimes a photograph would convey a sense of the social distance between officers and petty officers, as in a picture from this album labelled 'Lieutenant Tizard' who is finely dressed, accompanied by a shoeless bosun's mate, identified by his whistle.

Selecting individual pictures from these collections, as well as by choosing individual illustrations from prints, sketches, and paintings, we gain a sense of the nature of meals aboard, the ordinary work on deck and in the rigging, the cramped quarters of seamen, their idle time, and the handling of tools, weapons, sails, livestock, and the equipment necessary for navigation.

Navigation was the responsibility of the officers. The problems of locating latitude and especially longitude at sea required constant attention and work. By using 'lunar tables' published in 1767 in *The Nautical Almanac and Astronomical Ephemeris*, written by the British Astronomer Royal, Neville Maskelyne, an officer could determine longitude by a relatively complicated procedure. The American mariner from Salem, Nathaniel Bowditch, found thousands of errors in the standard English tables, and published in 1802 the first edition of his revised version, the *American Practical Navigator*, when he was only twenty-eight years old.

By the early nineteenth century, the much more common and somewhat easier method of finding longitude was to take an accurate chronometer on the voyage which would maintain Greenwich (London) time, never gaining or losing more than a few seconds per month. The exploration of Captain Cook 1772-75 was among the first to successfully demonstrate the chronometer method. The development of the first such accurate sea-going clock was the life's work in the eighteenth century of John Harrison, who eventually collected a royal prize for his achievement. By comparing Greenwich time as kept on the

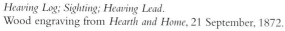

Heaving Log; Sighting; Heaving Lead.
Wood engraving from *Hearth and Home*, 21 September, 1872.

This scene illustrates the common method of determining speed at sea. One sailor holds the log-line spool aloft, while a sailor stands by with a 28-second glass. At the rail, another sailor counts as the knots that payed out in 28 seconds would equal the speed of the ship in nautical miles per hour. The triangular float which arrested the end of the line in the water can be seen dangling from another log-line which hangs from the rail, and can also be seen in the photograph of the whole device opposite. To speak of nautical miles per hour as 'knots' derives from the ship log-line procedure.

chronometer with local time found by a noon sighting of the sun, one could determine longitude, with each hour of difference equal to 15 degrees of longitude.[4]

The Collection has a fine edition of Thomas Truxtun's *Remarks, Instructions, and Examples Relating to the Latitude and Longitude* (Philadelphia, 1794) that relied on the astronomical method, and a review of the text reveals how difficult the task would be. Not only did the observations have to be accurate, but the numerous mathematical calculations allowed error to creep in.[5]

A chronometer in the Collection from aboard HMS *Challenger* on her voyage around the world 1872-76, illustrates that instrument, so essential to nineteenth century and early twentieth century navigation. A commemorative plate in the Collection was presented to a supercargo who apparently forgot to wind the chronometer on a voyage in the early 1800s. One can imagine the 'roast' dinner at which the plate was presented.

Still another, and much more ancient method of charting a course, was to make a rough calculation of the nautical miles travelled by keeping a record of the course and speed through the water. The speed was determined with a 'log'. A log was simply a large spindle, with a knotted string wound around it. A float was attached to the end of the line. A sailor would throw the float and line over the stern of the ship, while another sailor counted the knots, placed forty-seven feet, three inches apart, which slipped through his fingers as the ship moved away from the float. Another sailor or officer timed the process with a sand glass that ran through in twenty-eight seconds. It was clearly a two- or three-man job, as depicted in several illustrations. Recording the speeds as determined by the log method in a log-book led to that form of document.

Officers used sextants and quadrants to measure the angle of the sun above the horizon, for the much simpler calculation of latitudes north and south of the equator. All such navigation equipment, together with compasses, charts, dividers, and parallel rules for

4. Capt. Thomas H. Sumner: *A New Method of Finding a Ship's position at Sea* (Boston, Thomas Groom, 1845) gives details of the chronometer method.
5. The dispute between the lunar method and the chronometer method is ably discussed in Dava Sobel, *Longitude* (New York, 1995).

Log-line and spool with triangular wooden float and 28-second glass.
Mid-19th century.

tracing courses on charts were essential to the sailing voyage. The numerous artifacts and navigation books in the Collection give echoes of the haunting problem of getting lost on the trackless ocean.

The Collection includes a rare eighteenth century Joseph Roux dry-card compass, which allowed the seaman at the wheel to stay on a prescribed directional course.

A mundane and daily task, heaving the lead, showed the depth of the water and the nature of the bottom. A cavity in the lead filled with tallow would capture sand, mud, shells, or weeds, enabling the captain or pilot, especially when near shore, to ascertain the ship's location from charts. The sailor would sing out the number of fathoms to the bottom after each time he cast the line.

Chinese export porcelain plate.
Early 19th century.
Chronometer.
Mid-19th century.

Charles Ross, a supercargo on a Philadelphia ship's voyage to Canton, China, in the early 1800s, obviously forgot to wind the chronometer. One of his shipmates probably arranged for the decoration of a Chinese export porcelain plate with the wording: 'Charles Ross Remember the Chronometer' and gave it to him as a reminder. Beginning in the latter part of the 1700s, mariners could find their longitude at sea by comparing the local time determined by the sun with that given for Greenwich by an accurate chronometer.

'Navire Prenant Un Pilote'. Artist: Eugene Isabey. After 1823. Lithograph mid-19th century.

Bringing a pilot aboard a sailing vessel was sometimes difficult and here the man is being hoisted aboard during heavy seas by two sailors. Meanwhile, aloft, men furl the foresail and others attempt to gather in a jib. Even small merchant ships required the services of a pilot who would know local waters, shoals, shallows, and harbors. This print, full of action and detail, is an unusual depiction of a common event.

'Makeing a Compass at Sea'. Hand-colored engraving Early 19th century.

In this exchange, one sailor has broken the ship's compass but a Scot explains that by releasing a louse, and noting the direction it runs, one can always find south. Scotch lice, it appears, could not stand the cold and headed south, perhaps preferring to dine on Englishmen. The 'bog-trotter', guilty of smashing the compass, is thus gotten out of this scrape. Some of the tensions of the time are reflected in the heavy-handed ethnic jokes among Celts and Englishmen.

'Loading Coal', c.1885.
H. Coish. Watercolor.

A dirty job, despised by many sailors, was loading coal aboard ship. Canvas would protect the hull from accidents like the broken bag in the background, yet the loose chunks of coal and flying dust could still mar the snappy appearance of a naval vessel. The adjustment to the demands of steam power took decades in the US and British navies.

Day to day duties were routine, but many were matters of life and death. Neglect of ship, sails, rigging, hull, or navigation equipment could mean the loss of a ship by foundering or by stranding on a known and charted shore. Repairs, maintenance, daily checking of location by sightings or against deduced reckoning of miles travelled, were not busy work, but essential to survival at sea. The tasks may have been routine and unremarkable, but we can trace them through some of the artifacts, art, and literature left from the age of sail and the early days of sail-and-steam.

'Middy Mastheaded'.
Oil Painting, *c.*1873. Chinese.

The midshipman depicted here has been sent aloft for punishment. This oil painting was apparently a copy of an earlier magazine illustration, entitled 'Mastheaded – A Middy in Disgrace'. From the caption of that *Harper's Weekly* illustration (page 103) we learn that the original print illustrated an episode from the novel *Midshipman Easy* in which the young midshipman took a copy of the 'Articles of War' aloft. The artist conveys a rather wistful scene, with the boy sitting in an almost languid pose. Together with the finger marking a page in the reading material, the posture suggests that this later artist did not understand 'mastheading' as too severe a form of punishment but rather as a quiet perch in which the lad could get in some reading. However, sending midshipmen to sit in the rigging was a common form of punishment for these boys and young men.

CHAPTER FOUR
Law and Order Aboard Ship

The world of the seaman, his day-to-day life, his working conditions, and especially, the system of law and order aboard many ships, imposed by a series of harsh physical punishments, may strike the modern observer as archaic, cruel, and oppressive. During the late eighteenth and through the nineteenth century, we encounter pictorial representations and vivid accounts of flogging, or of disobedient seamen chained in irons. The effort to reform such practices in both the United States and Britain produced volumes of literature and many illustrations intended to provoke sympathy for the plight of the seaman.

The punishments were rooted in both the law governing merchant shipping and in common practice aboard naval vessels. In both the British and American navies, a system of punishments was defined and spelled out in published regulations. William M. Hunter, of the US Navy, who is well-represented in the Collection, with a portrait and with a preserved coat and epaulettes, produced a hand-written copy of the 'Rules and Regulations of the USS *Independence* (1815)'. Among some eighty-two general regulations which he copied, were rules for a great variety of details, ranging from exactly how laundry should be hung on deck, to specific rules regarding the issuance of grog.[1]

Hunter revealed himself as a man of very fixed opinions, when he noted with hand-written entries in a published set of the rules issued by the US Naval commissioners in 1818, that several were unsatisfactory. When he disagreed with certain provisions, he would simply scratch them out and enter his own version. For example, in pencil on his copy of the 1818 regulations, he indicated 1) that sailors when ashore should not be under command of the local naval yard officer; 2) that it was 'nonsense' to declare that all in the naval service should be there voluntarily and that there should be no slaves in the service; 3) and that permission to take a woman to sea could not be granted by a commander, but

(Above) *'The Point of Honor'*.

The Henderson Collection has an oil painting depicting flogging aboard an American warship and a watercolor of a bosun about to flog a British sailor. It appears that the print 'The Point of Honor' by George Cruikshank in Barker's 'Greenwich Hospital' (1826) is the depiction used on numerous occasions to show flogging in the British Navy.

1. 'General Orders for Crew of USS *Independence*, 1815'.

only 'by an Act of Congress'. Since it was common practice to ask naval officers their opinions of existing rules, it seems likely that Hunter's notes were intended to form the basis of changes he might suggest, rather than a set that he unilaterally chose to impose.[2]

Aboard ship, the ancient master-seaman relationship remained one based on the paternal relationship between father and child. In a Treatise on maritime law published in 1810 in Britain, and annotated in an American edition by Joseph Story (Associate Justice of the Supreme Court, 1811-1845), Charles Abbott of Inner Temple commented on the master-seaman relationship:

> By the common law, the master has authority over all the mariners on board the ship, and it is their duty to obey his commands in all lawful matters relating to the navigation of the ship, and the preservation of good order: and such obedience they expressly promise to yield to him by the agreement usually made for their service. In case of disobedience or disorderly conduct, he may lawfully correct them in a reasonable manner; his authority in this respect being analogous to that of a parent over his child or of a master over his apprentice or scholar.[3]

From the 1790s through the first decades of the nineteenth century, sailors like Englishman George Hodge regarded lashes and capital punishment as part of the seaman's life. Hodge had been held ashore as a prisoner of war, with some fifty other seamen, in Norway, housed by a Consul among the local people. After several weeks of forced idleness, arrangements were made to ship Hodge and his fellow-prisoners back to Britain as part of a cartel, a prisoner-exchange arrangement with the French. As preparations were under way, Hodge took a knife from the household where he had been staying, was caught, and in a matter-of-fact way, he reported his punishment '...at the last day I supply myself with a knife from the house that we lived in but was found out and I was punished for that with a dozen lashes for the same.'[4]

Similarly, Hodge reported other punishments of himself and shipmates as a matter of course. While complaining on one occasion of being falsely accused of stealing sugar and receiving an unjust punishment for it, it was the injustice of the decision, not of the flogging itself, that seemed to arouse his indignation. Other minor punishments were noted dryly:

> 1813: January 4th: Mr Dover stopt a pint of grog from me for not bring my mess mate hammock down
> February 17th: ...punishment round the fleet on the seaman belong to the NARCISSUS, received 105 lashes
> August 24th: ...several men under sentence of punishment belong to the fleet one to suffer death belong to the MOHAWK brig and several to go round the fleet
> September 20th: ...Robert Colter got 11 lashes for a woman in the NARCISSUS
> 1814: December 21: My grog was stopd in the first mess

2. 'Rules, Regulations, and Instructions for Service of the US Navy, 1818', signed copy by W.H. Hunter. The changes noted are on pages 3, 16, and 29. The suggestion that rules were circulated for opinions is made by H.R. Skallerup, editor, in the facsimile edition of *Naval Regulations Issued by Command of the President of the United States of America January 25, 1802* (Annapolis, MD: Naval Institute Press, 1970), following page 36.
3. *Treatise of the Law Relative to Merchant Ships and Seamen*, Charles Abbott of Inner Temple, second American (edition) from the Third London Edition with annotations, by Joseph Story, esq. counsellor at law Newburyport: Edward Little & Co., 1810 (signed by Henry Phelps, New York, October 1817), pp. 185-6.
4. Hodge Diary, entry for 2 December, 1794.

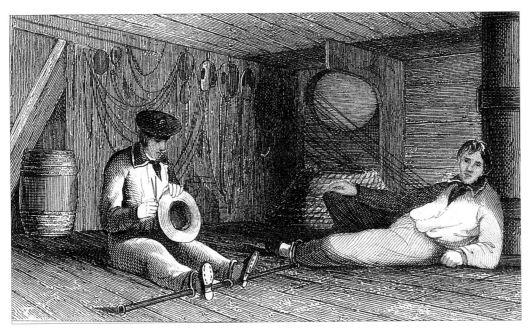

Engraving from Heck's Iconographic Encyclopaedia, *1851.*

Men are confined in irons below deck. Often merchant ships had no formal place of confinement and men would simply be bolted to the deck in a passageway for drunkenness or some other minor offense. Long after the abolition of flogging, merchant officers enforced discipline with similar techniques.

Hodge, perhaps like many seamen of his era, took death, punishment, illness, accidents aboard ship and confinement ashore for drunkenness or getting 'harty', all in his stride as part of the hazards and difficulties of the sailing life.

As was customary in the period, homosexual activity was not only severely punished, but the very act of sodomy would not be explicitly mentioned, even in a private diary. Hodge, in his manuscript diary, noted several cases of harsh punishment for the act. 26 October, 1808: 'a Court martial onboard of HMShip London over David Wilson for the committing the unnatural sin... Sentence'd to suffer death at the yard arm off the ship that the Admiral would a point.' 29 October, 1808: 'a Courtmartial onboard of HMLondon over a marine for going to another man's hammock sentence'd a 150 lashes.' In his entry for 20 January, 1812, he intentionally left the crime unspoken: 'two men executed on board of the KITT brig for_____; a black man and a marien [*sic*] (marine).' Again, however, Hodge recorded such punishments, not with implication that he regarded them as unjust or harsh, but simply as matters of note, along with battles, ship encounters, shore leave, storms and various other mishaps of the sailing life.[5]

Merchant seamen who signed on board a ship for the duration of a voyage would be exposed to day-to-day methods of discipline and punishment following the traditional formula employed aboard both naval and merchant ships through the first decades of the nineteenth century. One mode of punishment, depending on the offense, was placing the offender in irons. In the Navy it remained the norm to subject men to flogging, who had been drunk, disobedient, who wilfully challenged the authority of an officer, or who had neglected their duties. Aboard merchant ships, a knotted rope was at times the instrument of punishment, while a cat-o'-nine-tails was employed on both British and American naval ships.[6]

However, by the 1840s, sailors and visitors aboard both naval and merchant ships who

5. Excerpts from Hodge Diary, WH Collection.
6. Hodge Diary. The difficulty of research into a subject which could not even be mentioned, is detailed in, Eugene L. Rasor, *Reform in the Royal Navy, A Social History of the Lower Deck, 1850-1880.* Hamden, CT: Archon Books, 1976.

witnessed flogging and other punishments began to consider them inappropriate, similar to the conditions of slavery, and subjects for legislative and judicial reform. Visitors, articulate seamen, and passengers contributed to a genre of literature which combined the sea narrative with a critique of its social conditions.

Particularly when an abusive ship master would apply punishment either for his own sadistic enjoyment, or because of some trivial episode of disobedient behavior or attitude, the injustice of flogging appeared even greater. Such episodes would be noted in emerging literature of protest, precisely because the injustice would draw more sympathy to the plight of seamen than would attention to more routine or deserved discipline. As in anti-slavery literature, details of the most sensational and cruel abuses could help draw sympathy to the oppressed group, with the hope of mounting reform.

Part of Richard Henry Dana, Jun.'s motivation in writing *Two Years Before the Mast* in 1840 was to make a contribution to reform literature, much in the tradition of one genre of anti-slavery literature, the narrative of a victim of the system, being published at the same time. Just as the slave narratives presented the case for abolition in a true-to-life setting, later fictionalized by Harriet Beecher Stowe in *Uncle Tom's Cabin*, so did a group of published narratives of voyages present the case for reform of seamen's conditions. Dana's work was the best known and best remembered of several such sailor narratives, some fictionalized, written as part of the reform effort of the period.

Other writers drew attention to seamen's conditions, both aboard ship and ashore, using other genres besides the narrative. Early in the nineteenth century, the Seaman's Home Societies in Britain and the United States attempted to bring to public attention both the conditions of discipline and many other forms of social exploitation of seamen. The Societies also sought to provide decent living conditions to sailors while ashore, setting up dormitories or 'homes' ashore. Its founders claimed that the first 'sailor's home' was started by the Reverend George Charles Smith in London, in 1829. Within a few years, the American Seamen's Friends Society established similar refuges in the United States.

The reforms in both countries directed at sailors were part of a much wider and rapidly-growing, religiously-inspired concern with conditions of various groups of unfortunate people: prisoners, slaves, the insane, orphans and the poor. Many reformers and writers in both Britain and the United States hoped to build consciousness of abuses to which sailors were exposed among a middle-class reading public. As in the movements to abolish slavery or to improve the conditions of prisoners, a first step was to bring awareness of abuses to the attention of a public who could then agitate for legislation. Reform writers knew that to arouse the public would require vivid descriptions and a sense of horror at the cruelties practiced.[7]

Dana's narration of a flogging incident aboard the *Puritan* captured the direct connection between the treatment of slaves in the period and the treatment of seamen. The captain asks:

7. The WH Collection includes a scrapbook of cuttings from the *Seaman's Home Journal* published in the 1840s. The journal collected news and reports from many independent Seamen's Homes. The scrapbook contains a rare episode of a serialized novel by Charles Dickens, published in the journal. A detailed history of the seamen's home movement and the role of Rev. Smith can be found in Roald Kverndal, *Seamen's Missions: Their Origin and Early Growth* (Pasadena, CA: William Carey Library, 1986).

'A Picture for Philanthropists',
J.Ross Browne, *Etchings of a Whaling Cruise,* Harper & Brothers, NY, 1846.

The flogging episode is described by J. Ross Browne. The episode may have served as the basis for Melville's description of a similar incident in *Moby Dick*. The sailor, lashed to a ratline, is flogged by the captain while officers and men witness the punishment. By the 1840s, mounting criticism of the practice of corporal punishment was bringing pressure for reform in the US Navy and in the merchant and whaling vessels. Twelve lashes were often meted out aboard naval, merchant and whaling ships for offenses ranging from drunkenness and fighting to insubordinate remarks. The episode depicted here arose on a whaler from a fight between two seamen. In the Navy the lash was usually handled by a bosun's mate, not the ship's captain, as in this case. The severity of punishment in many instances depended upon the particular officer in command of the vessel. In 1850 Congress abolished flogging aboard US naval vessels. Flogging and all other forms of corporal punishment were prohibited on any merchant vessel by Act of Congress, 21 December 1898.

> '...Will you ever be impudent to me again?' 'I have never been, sir,' said Sam. 'Answer my question, or I'll make a spread eagle of you! I'll flog you, by G-d.' 'I'm no negro slave,' said Sam. 'Then I'll make you one,' said the captain; and he came to the hatchway, and sprang on deck, and rolling up his sleeves, called out to the mate – 'Seize that man up, Mr. A – ... I'll teach you all who is master aboard!'[8]

An 1839 work by an American William McNally, *Evils and Abuses in the Naval and Merchant Services Exposed with Proposals for their Remedy and Redress* also drew the connection between the treatment of seaman and slaves very clearly.

> Those who exclaim loudest against slavery had better turn their attention to objects of suffering and benevolence at home, before they look for them abroad, hundreds of whom will be found to stand as much in need of assistance and emancipation from the yoke of tyranny and oppression as the swarthy sons and daughters of Africa.[9]

8. Richard H. Dana, Jun., *Two Years Before the Mast,* pp. 123-124.
9. William McNally, *Evils and Abuses in the Naval and Merchant Services Exposed with Proposals for their Remedy and Redress* (Boston: Cassady and March, 1839), p. 129.

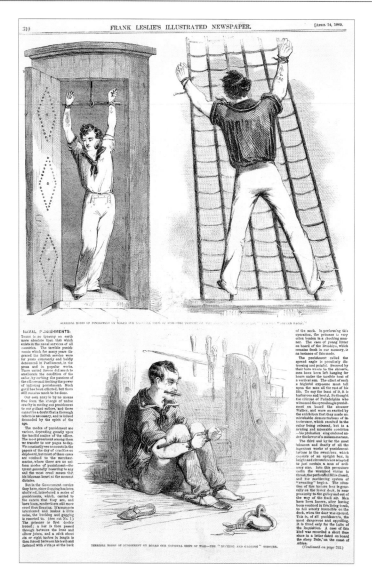

Frank Leslie's Illustrated Newspaper, *14 April, 1860.*
Wood engraving.

Even after flogging was abolished aboard US naval ships in 1850, various tortures were still practiced aboard US naval vessels. First, was being spread-eagled in the rigging and being trussed in the 'bucking and gagging torture'; second, being locked in irons; third, and described by the journalist as 'by far, the most inhuman and deadly of all the ingenious works of punishment – torture in the sweatbox.' Reform of such abuses continued to be an issue into the 1860s and 1870s and even afterwards. (Note tattoos on two of the sailors' arms, both sporting an anchor as well as initials. One tattoo on the sailor's right forearm might be the goddess of liberty.)

McNally's slim book was entirely dedicated to abuses and reforms needed both in the Navy and the merchant service, and may have affected legislation more directly than Dana's better-remembered and oft re-published narrative.

J. Ross Browne published a narrative of a voyage, a few years after Dana.[10] Browne detailed a flogging incident, much as had Dana, in which the flogging was ill-deserved, and seemed motivated more by the sadism of the master. After two men had fought over spilled coffee, the captain flogged them both. The episode was illustrated with a print in the book.

> 'Now,' said the captain, 'You've been fighting, and I'll flog you both. Mr. D—, seize those men up!' Jack's wrists were lashed to a ratline on the starboard side, and Bully's to a ratline on the larboard. The captain then provided himself with a piece of tarred ratline, and striding up to Bully bared the man's back. 'Remember now, this is for fighting.' 'Oh for God's sake, don't flog me, captain!' said Bully, sensible of the degradation of the punishment about to be inflicted on him. 'Not a word!' said the captain, whose blood was boiling with passion. Take that! and that! and that! Do you feel it? Will you fight again?'

10. Dana's work was not unique, but only the most famous of a group of works along the same lines published in the period, including those cited here.

Court martial.
Engraving, 1851.

This print of a court martial on the deck of a ship from the *Heck's Encyclopaedia* depicts the accused under guard while his shipmates look on from the bulwarks in which their hammocks are stored. Very few illustrations of court martials from British and American sailing navies can be found but, from accounts, this depiction seems fairly accurate.

Poor Bully groaned and writhed with agony. Each stripe of the ratline raised a blood-red mark on his back.

> '.. I'll skin your back worse than that! Cut him down now! See if he'll behave himself!' Jack's turn came next. At the first stroke he yelled with all his might. 'Oh Lord, captain! Oh for God's sake. Oh don't flog me! I'll never fight again.' 'I'll take care you won't. If you do, I'll lay you up for a month. Your back's been itching for a flogging. Now take it! Take that ! Take that! Yes you feel it, don't you? Cut him down, Mr. D—.'[11]

Browne depicted flogging, not as a regular part of the ship's discipline, but as a case of 'blood boiling with passion', and a concerted attempt to degrade the seaman, while the author of *Evils and Abuses* saw the practice as very widespread and requiring fundamental reform.

Long after reforms of the 1850s had improved conditions in the US Navy, J. Grey Jewell, who served as US Consul in Singapore, wrote of the conditions of merchant seamen in 1874. Jewell found such practices continued, and he wrote with motives very similar to those of the reformers some thirty years earlier. Jewell directly stated that his motive was to seek further reform aboard the merchant vessels. In his preface, he noted:

> I have vainly examined many libraries in the hope of discovering some work deprecating the unjust expectations which ship-owners, underwriters, and consignees have of the officers commanding their ships; some work that would denounce the unmerited, unmerciful, and cruel punishments inflicted upon American sailors, when at sea, in the merchant and naval services; some work that would expose the defective and unjust laws which enslave the sailor and screen his oppressors. I have long waited, hoping that some one more capable would come forward and defend the defenseless sailor, and awaken an interest in his behalf.[12]

11. J. Ross Browne: *Browne's Whaling Cruise*, full title: *Etchings of a Whaling Cruise, with notes of a Sojourn on the Island of Zanzibar, to which is appended a brief history of the whale fishery, its past and present condition.* (New York, Harper and Brothers, 1846), JWH Collection. This now rare book served as a source for Melville in *Moby Dick.*
12. J. Grey Jewell, *Among our Sailors*, (New York, Harper and Brothers, 1874), Preface, in the JWH Collection.

Jewell went on, like his predecessors, to describe excessive punishments, emphasizing the sadistic nature of the masters' and mates' behavior towards seamen, despite the intent of Congress to limit in recent legislation (1871) the right of masters to inflict corporal punishment.

> Congress never intended to permit or authorize a ship-master or his officers to starve seamen, to beat them on the head with a belaying-pin or marlin-spike, to shoot or stab them, to trice them up to the yards or rigging, or to chain their feet to the deck, and chain their wrists together, and then by the aid of block and tackle stretch the poor helpless creatures upward until they are pulled almost limb from limb! Congress never intended to give any such permission; and yet, as the reader proceeds in this work, he will find that all these cruel and brutal punishments are inflicted on board American vessels. He will find cases reported where seamen are nailed up in coffins called 'sweat-boxes', for days, on board a vessel of the United States Navy, and where they are suffocated by the commanding officers forcing a deck mop into their mouths.[13]

Jewell provided details of the incidents he described, basing his information on court records in these excessive cases.[14]

However, Jewell believed that some punishment, which did not need to be cruel, had to be allowed. Writing in 1874, he echoed the Abbott Treatise of 1810:

> A ship captain has a well-understood authority to inflict punishment, or order it to be inflicted, on seamen who disregard or disobey legitimate orders, when the carrying out of such orders is necessary to the navigation or safety of the ship or cargo. Proper punishment for these offenses, such as placing in irons, solitary confinement between decks, or a diet of bread and water for a reasonable time, will generally bring the offending party to speedy and humble terms, and can not be said to be either cruel or unusual...[15]

In both the British and American navies, flogging continued to be employed as a form of punishment up to 1850. However, both navies attempted to regulate its administration, suggesting a limit to the number of strokes which could be applied in the course of ordinary punishment. Greater or more severe punishments could be administered only on the order of a court-martial.

A listing of offenses for which the punishment was flogging was reported to Congress in 1848. A survey of the document suggests that the most common offense in the US Navy for which twelve lashes were meted out was drunkenness. Offenses meriting flogging included some which were rather unique, and others much more common. Many of the offenses listed in the facing table were reported as occurring many times; others showed up only once or twice.

13. Ibid., pp. 53–54.
14. The two cases are detailed from court records in Jewell, pp. 257–258.
15. Ibid., p. 55.

TABLE

Punishments US NAVY, 1848

TYPE OF OFFENSE	NO. LASHES
Sentence by court martial	48
Sleeping on watch	12
Drunkenness and insolence	12
Stealing	12
Fighting	12
Striking a petty officer	12
Acts of violence on shore	12
Seditious conduct and disobedience of orders	12
Mutinous and seditious conduct	12
Having a naked light in fore passsage	12
Overstaying his liberty	12
Dropping fire in the hold	12
Neglecting the sick	12
Smuggling liquor	12
Selling his clothes	9
Neglect of duty	9
Disrespect of the Commodore	9
Gambling	9
Being naked on the spar deck	9
Improper language to his comrades	8
Making water on gun deck	8
Skulking in his watch	8
Insolence to the gunner	8
Absent from ship without leave	8
Lousy	6
Damning the sentry on post	6
Neglect of duty and filthiness	6
Disobedience of orders	6
Not turning out when the watch was called	6

Source for Table: Report from the Secretary of the Navy, to US Congress, February 8, 1849, Punishments in the Navy, 1848. Original copy of report, WH Collection.

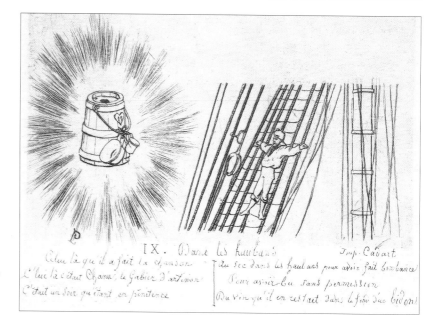

'Souvenir de la Bellone 1870-71-72'.
Etching, 1884.

A sailor is lashed to the rigging and dreams of a water keg and ladle. The artist captures the psychology and the logic of the punishment both in the picture and in the accompanying text. The doggerel verse in French alludes to the concept that having a drink without permission leads to going without drink altogether. Such forms of punishment by deprivation continued in most navies well into the late 19th century.

A review of the list of offenses makes us realize that flogging was not simply administered for reasons of sadism; rather, it was a structured system of punishment for a very wide range of infractions of order, cleanliness, duty, deportment and military order and authority. While punishments for being drunk far outnumber those for other offenses, the inclusion of such offenses as 'lousy' or 'making water on the gun deck' clearly had to do with sanitation, while offenses such as 'insolence to the gunner', 'disrespect to the Commodore', and 'seditious behaviour' were all punished to maintain military authority. Partly due to the congressional investigation, flogging in the US Navy was abolished in 1850. However, despite the protests of humanitarians like Consul Jewell, flogging and other cruel punishments continued in the merchant fleet. It was not until 1898 that the US Congress passed legislation against flogging of merchant seamen.[16]

16. *Report from the Secretary of the Navy to US Congress, 8 February, 1849, Punishments in the Navy, 1848.* Original copy of report, WH Collection. For a detailed treatment of the relationship of the reform movement to the legislation, see James E. Valle, *Rocks and Shoals* (Annapolis, Naval Institute Press, 1980).

The literature of the late eighteenth and early nineteenth century is full of references to the exercise of discipline aboard ship. Flogging attracted the attention of a few painters and print-makers, partly because of its sensational nature, partly because it so resembled the primary punishment of slaves and also because it was the most commonly practiced system of discipline aboard ships. Books describing the punishment in the Royal Navy often used the same Cruikshank print over and over to illustrate the point, suggesting the rarity or perhaps the absence of such images in Britain. The Collection contains an original oil painting depicting a flogging aboard an American naval vessel and a watercolor of a British bosun flogging a sailor. These rare items, together with original editions of some of the more commonly reproduced prints, provide graphic views of this regularly employed form of punishment.

'The Boatswain on duty'.
Watercolor, *c.*1800.

Cartoon-style watercolor in the style of Rowlandson. A British bosun flogs a bound seaman with a cat o' nine tails. The bosun, who appears sadistic, is putting his whole body and spirit into the punishment. He has secured his pipe in his headband so as to have both hands free for the task.

Flogging Scene Aboard a US Naval Warship, c.1840.

This painting depicts flogging aboard a US naval vessel. The offender is bound to the rail and flogged in the presence of the officers and crew. A sense of the social distance between officers and men comes across in the separate grouping of witnesses on deck. Prints alluding to flogging provided a visual side to the reform movement in the late 1830s and early 1840s. This extremely rare painting is perhaps the only oil painting depicting flogging aboard a US naval ship in the first half of the nineteenth century; no nineteenth century oil painting of a British flogging scene is presently known. George Cruikshank's print, 'Point of Honor' from Barker's work *Greenwich Hospital,* (1826) appears to be the only representation of flogging aboard a British naval vessel in the days of sail (page 89) except for the watercolor 'The Boatswain on duty' (page 98), which is in the Collection.

'The Merry Ship's Crew or Nautical Philosophers'.
Hand-colored engraving, *c.*1800.

The ironic humor often employed in the period served as a form of protest against conditions aboard ships. The captain, accompanied by a female companion, greets his bosun's mate, just alighting from a boat to the shore. Their ship is in the background. The bosun's mate, with an allusion to a passage from Dryden, reports the crew are all happy: those who have not been whipped are happy to have escaped, and those whipped are happy it is over. The whole tongue-in-cheek presentation of this period is in sharp contrast to the more serious, reform-minded material generated by the 1840s, which depicted flogging as a social evil in need of remedy.

Beyond flogging, a few images show other types of punishment. The book of etchings from the *Bellone* depicted a sailor spread-eagled in the rigging, dreaming of a keg of water and a ladle (page 98). The French verse which accompanies the illustration, makes it clear that the sailor is suffering a drying-out period, for drinking without permission.

In the early nineteenth century, before the reform movement was fully underway, print-makers would draw attention to flogging and punishment, sometimes with clumsy attempts at humor which, nevertheless, had a biting edge.

This piece of dialogue is to be found in a British print, *c.*1800, entitled 'The Merry Ship's Crew, or Nautical Philosophers'. The captain greets his bosun's mate, just alighting from a boat to the shore:

> Well Mate! Just come on shore? How did you leave the ship's crew?
> Why captain, I have left all to a man the merriest fellows in the world.
> I flogged seventeen of them as your Honor commanded, and they are
> happy it is over; and the rest are happy because they have escaped.

A note at the bottom of the illustration, in fine print, reads: 'For all the happiness mankind can gain, Is not in pleasure, but in rest from pain. — Dryden'. It was almost as if the cartoonist sought to provide his literary readers with a reference which would provide an intellectual basis for his awkward humor and explain the reference to 'the merry ship's crew or nautical philosophers' in the picture's title.

In another print, entitled 'Skins', a sailor with a bear skin on his back is confronting a laughing captain, mate, and other seamen. The text reads:

> A sailor who had got himself well grog'd
> Staggered and trod upon his captain's Toe;
> "You drunken Swab, you shall be flog'd
> Here, you Boatswain's Mate, I say,
> 1 dozen on this fellow's Bare Skin lay!"
>
> "Well," says the Man, "then if it must be so,
> Suffer me first to go below."
> Now you'll be kind enough to know,
> He kill'd a Bear some time ago,
> And now into the Skin secure he crept
> Which for remembrance he had kept
> Then going to the Captain with a grin —
> "Here, please your Honour, flog my poor BEAR SKIN!"

Such pun-based jokes and allusions to poetic philosophers simply do not appear very funny to the late twentieth century sense of humor. But coupled with later, more serious paintings, sketch-book entries, and the reform-oriented material in the works of writers like McNally, Dana, Melville, Browne, and Jewell, we can gain a picture of the continuation of corporal punishment and the paternal relationship between master and seaman, well into the nineteenth century. What one generation took in its stride and regarded as part of the childish status of the simple seaman, or the seaman himself simply took as a matter of course, the next generation took as a serious matter for the literature of exposé, for reform, and for legislation.

The cartoon-like presentations seen in the 1790s and early 1800s, gave way to more serious depictions which would echo the concerns of reformers in the middle of the nineteenth century. But by the 1870s, Romantic painters gave much more sentimental, even wistful presentations of punishments. A young midshipman, sent aloft as punishment, sits on the cross-trees high on a mast, his legs hanging languidly, his finger inserted to mark his page in a book he has been reading, while he stares longingly out to sea. His isolation hardly seems a punishment, but rather, a moment of almost poetic reflection. Based on an

The Sailor's Defense.
Hand-colored engraving.

This print from about 1800 published by T. Tegg gives a whole story of a seaman encountering shore-side justice. The magistrate rebukes him in front of the victim. The sailor's nautical language and his 'defense' appear to carry little weight. Sailors' fights and carousing ashore were legendary, and such encounters with the law ashore were common, although probably not so amusing.

Mastheaded – A Middy in Disgrace.
Wood engraving.

Drawn from the popular novel, *Midshipman Easy*, the extensive text with this illustration from *Harper's Weekly* July 19, 1873, describes the incident in which the young boy, whose position had been secured through the fact that his father was friends with the Captain, was sent aloft for insubordination. He takes a copy of the 'Articles of War' with him, hoping to find some argument he might use to bolster his side of the dispute. He is no sooner aloft, than all hands are called on deck from aloft, and he is reprieved. The magazine print apparently served as the basis for the Chinese copy (page 88). The novel by Frederick Marryat (1792-1949) originally published in German, was reissued as a dime novel by Beadle and Ames of New York in the 1870s.

episode from a popular novel by Captain Marryat, *Midshipman Easy*, the illustration converted the punishment into a reflective moment. As in other Romantic period art, we are drawn into the emotional state of the depicted character, speculating on what the young boy must feel. Yet confining midshipmen to a position aloft for some minor neglect of duty was indeed a form of punishment.[17]

The change in attitude towards flogging from simple acceptance in 1800 to concern in the 1830s, to a more concerted reform movement directed at the Navy in the 1840s, to legislation,

17. Other illustrations of midshipmen punished show them with a book. G. Cruikshank, *The Progress of a Midshipman* (London 1821), gives such an illustration, while a reproduction of a picture from the novel *Midshipman Easy* from *Harper's Weekly*, 19 July, 1873, made explicit that "middy" took 'Articles of War' aloft.

TRIAL OF CAPTAIN BRAGG,

AND HIS MATE,

FOR THE MURDER OF THE SHIP'S STEWARD

THE Trial of these men took place this morning at the Admiralty Sessions, which were held at the Old Bailey. Bragg was indicted for the Wilful Murder of Lewis Sinclair, on the High Seas, on the 13th of June, 1829, & the Mate was charged as an accomplice. Captain Sampson Bragg was commander of the Francis Watson free trader to India, and from the evidence of Hugh Murray, George Corney, and others, seamen of the said vessel, it was proved that the deceased entered on board the vessel at Liverpool, as steward, & was then a fine healthy young man. At Batavia he got tipsy, and for which offence he was sent before the mast, losing his birth as steward; incapable of doing the duties of a seaman, the Captain inflicted the most cruel punishment upon him, flogging him and afterwards washing the wounds with salt water; ordering him to be slung over the lee-side and the bow, to scrape the ship's side, when going from seven to eight knots an hour; and had no allowance except what he got from the crew. The poor fellow gradually grew worse, & looked like a starved man, and a few days before his death he became quite mad, and roared out for the doctor—he was again cruelly beaten with a capstan-bar, and on endeavouring to get to the ship's bow, he fell, and never rose again. The next morning his body was sewn up in canvass, and hove overboard.—This was the substance of the evidence, but the prisoner's defence stated that in consequence of the obstinacy and neglect of the deceased, he deserved the punishment he received. The learned Judge summed up the evidence, and the Jury returned a Verdict of Not Guilty.

Printed by T. BIRT, No. 10, Great St. Andrew-Street, Seven Dials.

July 1829

Trial of Captain Bragg.

In the days of sail, the captain of a merchant ship, in essence, was, at times, close to an absolute monarch. Some were sadistic and treated members of the crew cruelly. Such was the case as set forth in this broadside. In those days, c.1829, sailors' rights were limited and many times disregarded. The jury returned a verdict of not guilty.

paralleled many other social movements of the century. The British enacted a series of reforms limiting punishments by flogging except in time of war, through the 1860s. Unlike the American legislation, the British reform came through quietly-issued regulations, in stages.[18]

Officers were not immune from court-martial, as a number of items in the Collection demonstrate. The trial and execution of British Admiral John Byng in 1757 is detailed in a rare book in the Collection. Byng had failed in an engagement with the French at Minorca to assist other ships and had hung back. His dereliction of duty was a capital offense. The case in Britain drew international attention. Many viewed the hanging as a face-saving act by the British government to pass blame to officers for larger strategic errors. 'In this country,' noted Voltaire in his novel *Candide*, apparently in reference to the Byng episode, 'it is thought well to kill an admiral from time to time, to encourage the others.'

In another case, a Captain James, is depicted being hanged for starving some members of his crew. The midshipman and two sailors involved in the mutiny aboard the USS *Somers* in 1842 were hanged from the yardarms, depicted in a Currier print. The print shows only the two

18. Eugene L. Rasor, *Reform in the Royal Navy, A Social History of the Lower Deck, 1850-1880*, (Hamden, CT: Archon Books, 1976). Rasor details the step-by-step reforms which were buried in regulatory changes, not in Parliamentary action. A groundbreaking study of the reforms in the US Navy is Harold D. Langley, *Social Reform in the United States Navy, 1798-1862* (Urbana: University of Illinois, 1967).

'The Shooting of Admiral Byng, on board the Monarque'.
Engraving, 1757.

The British Admiral John Byng was executed by a firing squad aboard HMS *Monarch.* He knelt on a cushion and was blindfolded. After a moment's prayer, he dropped a handkerchief as a signal to the firing squad to fire. The engraving captures the falling handkerchief in mid-air as the shots from six redcoats ring out, at 12 noon, 14 March, 1757. Behind Byng, a thick backboard protects the ship's woodwork from bullets and gore. Execution of naval officers for dereliction of duty was extremely rare.

sailors, hanged from the starboard side; the young midshipman, as an officer, was hanged from the port side. The decision to hang the *Somers'* mutineers stirred a great public debate, as many believed the young men deserved a far lesser punishment. (Mutinies are discussed in some greater length in Chapter Nine.)[19]

Ranging from deprivation of grog or being isolated in irons or aloft in the rigging, through flogging and torture, through hanging, the punishments meted out aboard ship generated a rich and colorful literature and pictorial heritage.

In the period from the 1750s through the early 1820s, punishments aboard both British and American ships, even the most severe, were treated by all concerned as simply part of the conditions of life at sea. Under law, in practice, in diaries, and in other accounts, corporal and capital punishment simply fitted into the system. As reformers drew attention to the plight of various oppressed groups in the following decades, depictions and commentaries began to change. The movement to eliminate flogging in both Britain and the United States generated visual artifacts, broadsides, literature, and legislative materials through mid-century, that increasingly viewed corporal punishment and excessive capital punishment as cruel and unusual, worthy of control and elimination. By the last decades of the nineteenth century, some Romantic artists and writers began to treat earlier cruelties as part of the nostalgic heritage of the sea.

19. Officers were traditionally executed by hanging from the port yardarms, and members of the crew, from the starboard yardarms.

CHAPTER FIVE
Sailors' Crafts

When one is trying to fathom Jack Tar, it makes a lot of sense to search far and wide to build up a meaningful collection of the craft work of sailors themselves. Through the items the sailor made in his leisure time, we can see results of skills that seamen regularly used in maintaining and repairing their ships and equipment, and we can sometimes get a glimpse of what the sailor thought about in his long hours aboard ship.

Looking at the crude or intricate work made by sailors' hands, we are struck by the unexpected fact that, even though the labor aboard ship could be strenuous and exhausting, and the sailor had short hours of sleep in rough bunks or swaying hammocks, many sailors still found time to work on personal items, gifts, and memorial items. Handling some of the finest of the objects, we can see that many of the most delicate craft products took countless patient hours to complete. The labor that went into such crafts gives evidence of the tempo of work aboard ship, with its alternation between intense, crucial exertion to keep life and ship safe, and periods when a sailor could turn to some personal project. Sometimes officers, like the seamen, would spend hours creating a hand-crafted item.

(Above) *Sailor doing needlework.* Lithograph.

This mid-19th century print demonstrates the fact that sailors themselves produced woolwork embroidery. This print explicitly states that the sailor is making 'A Present for Home'. The long hours spent on a gift for a wife, mother or girl-friend would show how much she was on his mind and would be part of the implied message of the gift itself.

(Opposite) *Harpooner; Wheeler scrimshaw tooth; small pie crimper; large pie crimper; busk; 'Tudor Lady' tooth and part of unfinished pie crimper.*

This group includes the sculpture of a harpooner together with scrimshaw items: a busk with several motifs common in the craft, including a dove and a weeping willow representing mourning, two pie crimpers decorated with hearts together with an unfinished pie crimper which demonstrates how the work would be carved from a block of whale ivory or bone. The engraver of the 'Tudor Lady' tooth is believed to have been the anonymous *L.C. Richmond* artist. The Wheeler tooth was used as a clothing stamp by a sailor of that name.

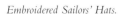
Embroidered Sailors' Hats.

As a way of relieving monotony and adding individual distinguishing decoration, some sailors embroidered their hats. Hat ribbons on these seven include (clockwise): USS *Philadelphia*, commissioned 1890; no ship designation; USS *Texas*, commissioned 1895; USS *Brooklyn*, commissioned 1859 and decommissioned in 1889 or the second *Brooklyn*, commissioned 1896; USS *Minnesota*, commissioned 1855, in 1895 lent to Massachusetts Naval Militia and sold in 1901, or second *Minnesota*, commissioned 1907; (center) USS *Alabama*, commissioned 1900. The seventh hat ribbon reads 'US Training Squadron'.

Handicraft work also suggests how starved sailors were for entertainment. Many were illiterate, and those who enjoyed reading soon ran through every available book, magazine, or newspaper aboard ship; letters would be read and re-read. Music and dancing could occupy time, but on a watch when crew mates were sleeping, it would be natural to turn to quieter pursuits. Individual carving, carpentry, drawing, whittling, knot-tying, macramé, scrimshanding, or sewing and embroidering on a long-term project that could be put away and taken up again fit into the tempo of ship life in a comfortable way.

The craft items often incorporated motifs and symbols that seemed to capture a sailor's innermost thoughts, reflecting what the sailor dreamed about, thought about, and pined for: his women, a safe port, faith in the afterlife, patriotism, fear and courage. Other products were quite utilitarian, yet even so, the careful embellishment of certain ordinary tools of everyday life hints at both their special place in the life and daily ritual of the seaman and at the importance of the very symbol engraved, carved, or etched.

Available material and tools dictated what the sailor could make aboard ship. With skill and imagination, sailors could change scraps of wood, lengths of twine, scraps of canvas, pieces of cloth and daubs of paint into amazing creations. Sailors on board whalers, might have a rich bounty of whale ivory (sperm whale teeth) whalebone, baleen, walrus ivory, abalone shell, mother of pearl and exotic woods. The materials themselves suggested the different pathways each type of sailor encountered around the world. Inventive uses of wood or ivory or bone would sometimes define the look or shape of the final product.

Embroidered blouse and poke bag.
Owned by George W. W. Dove.

George W. W. Dove was the 3rd Assistant Engineer aboard the US steamer *Richmond* (1861-63) during the American Civil War. His richly embroidered uniform blouse and poke bag might be rare examples of a now nearly-forgotten folk-art tradition: sailor-made embroidery. Using silk thread and elaborating on the necessary skill of needlework, sailors produced excellent examples of decorated uniforms and sea bags for holding clothing and other possessions. Both the embroidery and construction stitching of this blouse are of good quality but the difference in techniques suggest that two different hands could have taken part in its making, one of whom might well have been a sailor. Although this was 'non regulation', uniform regulations for enlisted men were so loose and varied at the time that it was common for sailors to embellish their dress uniforms for going ashore wear. The small poke bag (on right), for holding money or other valuables, would be hung around the neck and worn inside the blouse. Symbols of an eagle on an anchor flanked by American flags on the right upper sleeve of the blouse are repeated on the poke bag.

Needlework and Sea-bags

Some sailors became adept at handling needle and thread through their work as sail-makers, and many grew proficient in the art of making and mending their own clothing. Embroidery by sailors is nearly a forgotten art form, and no major book has been located which captures or details this form for collectors, curators and craft *aficionados*. Sailors worked on going-ashore uniforms, sometimes taking a naval uniform and embroidering it with names, silk decorations, mottoes, stars, or anchors.

Some items of uniform can be traced back to individual owners. A highlight of the collection is a richly embroidered and decorated blouse with stitching spelling out 'USS Richmond' across the chest, together with a small poke bag, for hanging around one's neck under the blouse to hold money and other valuables. Embroidery on one side of the poke bag spells 'USN' and on the other, 'DOVE'. George W.W. Dove was Third Assistant Engineer on board the *Richmond* during the Civil War. The stitching in these two items is mostly a typical chain stitch. The wrong side of the blouse is less precise than one would expect from a professional embroiderer, and therefore the work may well have been done

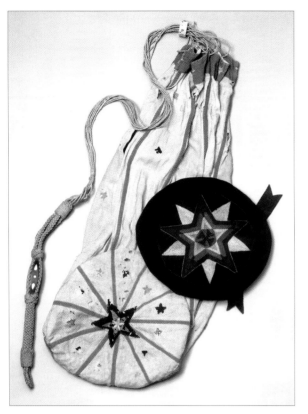

Embroidered seabag.
19th century.

A much-used embroidered seabag with a fine macramé drawstring and an embroidered hat reflect the star pattern frequently found in sailors' handicrafts. The seabag, with its multi-star motif on its bottom, echoes the star pattern on the top of the round hat. Such repeated patterns suggest how sailors may have emulated each other in their work, getting ideas, themes and patterns with which to decorate everyday items.

Embroidered textile.
Late 19th century.

This richly decorated piece was perhaps made aboard the USS *Kansas*. Some sailor, apparently for a 'souvenir' of his naval life, has made a nautical collage of American enlisted rating badges, of embroidered stars, of ribbons of named vessels, and other maritime-related symbols.

Money belt.
Mid-19th century.

A finely embroidered money belt has the owner's initials, 'FG', and a collection of flags of nations, political entities, naval and merchant marine bodies: Great Britain, the United States, Jerusalem, Tunis, the British Admiralty flag and that of the Russian Merchant Marine. The identification of all the flags is a challenge to the collector. The belt had a practical side. Sewn inconspicuously inside the belt is a secret place for hiding money – a forerunner of today's money belt. It appears that the nautical embroiderer wanted to make a visible statement of where he had been on his voyages in many parts of the world. The hours expended on such work speak to the sailor's interests, his needs, his craftsmanship, and a schedule which permitted attention to a project that might take months to complete.

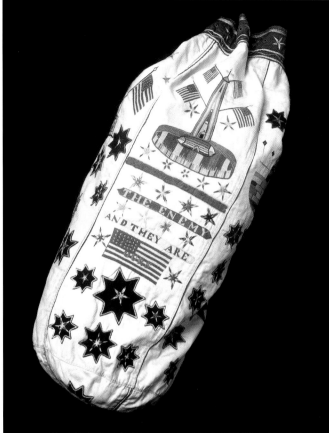

(Above left) *J. Lord seabag.*

Privacy aboard naval vessels was hard to come by and highly valued. A sea-bag hand decorated with a cannon, cannon balls, an anchor, and marked with the sailor's name, 'J. Lord', shows one means of identifying a small private space. Lord was a gunner aboard the USS *Constitution* and died in 1829. The Collection also includes his trunk, some clothing, another sea bag and a ditty box.

(Above right) *Richly decorated seabag – 'we have met the enemy...'* Late 19th century.

This richly decorated seabag is a very fine example of the craft with embroidered stars, flags, the Washington Memorial at Baltimore, Maryland and a famous naval motto done in bright colors. The Battle of Lake Erie on 10 September, 1813, was the most important naval action of the war to that date. Twenty-eight year old Commodore Oliver Hazard Perry, leading a squadron of nine ships mounting 54 guns, defeated the British squadron of six ships mounting 64 guns. After the battle he sent a message to General Harrison: 'We have met the enemy and they are ours: two ships, two brigs, one schooner and one sloop.' Found reversed on the inside bottom of the bag is 'T. Williams' indicating the possibility that part of the bag was an old seabag. This bag may have been the result of a joint effort of a fine embroiderer and a sailor. The entire bag is lined with cotton hiding the stitching. The five point stars along the top of the bag are the same embroidery method as the Dove blouse. A much worn seabag in the Collection appears to be by the same hand with a schooner, topsail schooner and the Washington Memorials at Baltimore, Maryland and Washington, DC.

by a sailor. Some sea-bags, mail-bags, a belt and a memorial fabric hanging recording ships, ratings and symbols, appear very likely to have been made by sailors themselves. Other nautical embroidery may have been made ashore.

In order to store and carry their clothes, sailors had sea bags, usually made of tough sail canvas. Some of these were richly decorated, capturing motifs including patriotic naval mottoes, cannons, shot, stars, anchors, or testimony to George Washington. The combination of patriotic themes and the focus on a useful item which would contain the sailor's possessions gives insight into two issues close to the heart of the average sailing man: his love of country, and his concern about maintaining some private place for his own

Woolie: sailor/woman/doves/bridge.
Late 19th century.

By its use of photographs, this woolie shows the presumed sailor-creator husband and the object of his affections and recipient of the woolie, his wife. The symbolism is shown by turtle doves embroidered above each photograph representing love, affection and constancy of husband and wife. Various types of shipping are depicted with Tower Bridge on the River Thames and London in the background.

Woolie: 'What is a Home without a mother'.
Late 19th century.

Here an interesting story is represented. One actually sees by a photograph what the sailor looked like who undoubtedly made the woolie together with a photograph of his mother, a reproduction of his ship and a legend that explains the son's devotion in making the woolie for his mother. The workmanship is rather crude compared to many of the other woolies made at the time.

Sea Chest.
19th century.

Sailor's sea chest with three rigs painted inside the lid.

possessions while in the crowded and very un-private quarters of the ship. Whether a sailor embroidered the bag or whether he received it as a gift, it was clear that it was a personal item, and that the motifs were close to his heart.

Another form of sail or needle craft was the 'woolie', a picture done in embroidery, believed to be practically all British, from the second half of the nineteenth century. Most are of British naval vessels, while a few show American flags, hinting that possibly some American seamen worked in the craft form. It is rare to find people portrayed in them. Supporting the idea that sailors made woolies, are two English nineteenth century prints. Other evidence that sailors made the woolies is provided on close examination of the work itself.

Chests and Boxes

Keeping a private place with private possessions was extremely difficult on both merchant ships and naval vessels. In journal after journal we see references to sailors 'overhauling' their sea-chest. In a moment of leisure, a sailor would carefully rearrange his private possessions in his own wooden sea-chest, dwelling on each memento and link to life ashore, as well as asserting his own individuality and personal humanity against the constant pressure to be one of the crew and to wrestle for his life with the elements. On a more physical plane, a sea-chest could serve as a seat, a table, a container, a writing desk, as well as a place to keep private possessions.

Some of the finer chests reflected diligent and careful craftsmanship, some perhaps put together by a ship's carpenter. Many were sturdily constructed of wood, painted with names or initials, with internal compartments and sometimes a papered or painted inner lid, showing a ship or other scene. One element of the sea-chest on which sailors would spend dozens of hours, was the pair of rope handles or 'beckets', one on each end of the chest for carrying purposes. These simple loops, held by wooden cleats attached to the chest with screws or nails,

Ditty Boxes and a Bible Box. 19th century.

These two ditty boxes and a bible box reflect a number of notable themes. Many sailors were expert craftsmen, collecting exotic woods and making fine inlay work. They often employed the symbols seen here: diamond shapes, stars and initials or names to personalize an item. The box in the front, with the rosary on it, is inlaid with a compass and belonged to J. Lord, a gunner aboard the US frigate *Constitution*. The top inlay depicts an armed brig flying an American flag. In addition, the inlay on the front of two urns of the Federal period probably dates the box to about 1800. Other inlay spells out 'Daniel Colladay'. The bible box on the right bears the initials 'Z. L. A' standing for 'Zelotes L. Almy' who appears to have been a New England whaling captain.

could become elaborate. Intricate macramé, tightly knotted and waxed or painted, provided strength, flexibility, and an unobtrusive, but handsome decoration. Even the wooden cleats through which the beckets were attached were sometimes carved with symbols and designs or sculpted into the shape of a clenched feminine hand to grasp the looped becket. A rare double-looped becket is another fine example of folk art. If a chest became damaged, the finely crafted beckets and cleats could be transferred to a new one.

To some extent, the degree of elegance of a sea-chest might denote the rank of the owner; one of the finest which has survived clearly belonged to an officer. A few that have names carved in them can be traced to a particular individual, such as a fine one owned by E(llison) Ames, first mate aboard the American merchant sailing vessel *Molo*.

That sailors would expend so many hours on containers for their own private possessions, that is, sea-bags, ditty-boxes, and sea-chests, reminds the modern viewer of the importance of privacy aboard ships in the age

Double Beckets. 19th century.

Woman's hands beckets (handles).

'E. Ames' officer's sea chest.
Mid-19th century.

This chest has the carved gold lettering of 'E. AMES' standing for Ellison Ames who was first mate aboard the *Molo*. The sea chest has exceptional carving, especially the laurel design on the cleats. The *Molo* was built by Thatcher Magoun & Son in 1835.

of sail. Even captains, who had the luxury of a separate cabin, might use the cabin to hold conversations and give orders to their officers.

Sketches

Some sailors and officers kept sketchbooks or made drawings or watercolors in their journals. Such work ranges from very primitive or off-hand work and doodles, through excellent, very high quality work of trained sailor-artists. Nineteenth century British midshipmen and some US Naval Academy graduates were trained in sketching, and exploring ships of both navies usually took along an expedition artist. The log of the American schooner *President*, the journals of British midshipman Horatio Nelson Head, the sketches by Lt. Kimberly aboard USS *Germantown*, of MacArthur, aboard HMS *Chesapeake*, and the Hodge Diary, depicted ships, perhaps coasts and ports, a few pictures of men at work or play on the ships, and sometimes a rare aspect of daily life. Such presentation of life as the artist saw it, is in its way, much richer in communicating what the sailor saw and consciously wanted to put down on paper than the more humble craft work.

Straw Box. Early 19th century.

This elegant straw box was made by a talented prisoner of war in a British land prison or hulk during the Napoleonic Wars. A second view of the same box shows the interior lined with satin and a clear mirror. The craftsman might have been an imprisoned French sailor, formerly an artisan in straw, or an American prisoner who had been taught by a fellow prisoner. Note some of the sailing vessels depicted and also that the interior colors, shielded from oxidization and light, are much fresher.

Not all sailor-produced art was folk-art or 'primitive'. For example, the watercolors of Lt. John B. Dale on the Wilkes Expedition, 1838-42, and on the cruise of the USS *Constitution* around the world in 1844-46, appear to reflect artistic training and a practiced, observant eye, documenting foreign sights as well as some activity of sailors.

By contrast, the message of craft work can be far more subtle and much less explicit. Here we may ask what the symbols conveyed and why they were so loaded with meaning for the seaman. Further, we may ask for whom the work was intended, and what the sailor may have thought as he made the piece. Although less direct in communication than the work of sketch or watercolor artists, the meanings embedded in artifacts may be more profound, offering a better window, because of the very unselfconscious nature of the work, into the souls of the men who created the items.

Ship Models

Just as some sailors created images of their vessel by drawing or painting, and others by woolwork, still others made ship models. Various maritime museums tell us of ships' carpenters making models of varying degrees of finish and exactitude. Some sailors made them aboard ship against amazing odds. Still others made them ashore and at sailors' retirement homes or 'snug harbors'. Professional models go back centuries; British Admiralty models are much sought after nowadays. A special class of models are those made by prisoners of the Napoleonic Wars in British prisons. Some highly skilled Dieppe workers created amazing models and passed on their expertise to some American prisoners of war. This is an area where *caveat emptor* is especially in order. One model in the Collection is believed to be a large sailor's model of the famous American clipper ship *Sovereign of the Seas*.

Bone and glass casket; miniature playing cards; hunting scene box; watch holder.

All of the items in this group were made by prisoners of war of the Napoleonic Wars in British hulks or prisons. All of them were made from bones. The motif of the lady and gentleman hunting appears on other pieces that were probably made by the same hand. The casket contains dominoes and playing cards. The beautifully carved hutch was made to hold a watch.

Mementos

A wide variety of items would capture the names of ships, ports of call, storms, and wrecks that a sailor had survived. Others remembered some well-known historical event such as a sea-battle or a naval hero. If a sailor did not maintain a journal or sketchbook, he might cherish a carved or painted object, in wood, which could serve to remind him of his own personal adventures. A number of decorated items, varying in workmanship, such as boxes, paper cut-outs, and scrimshaw work would give scattered details of a particular sailor's life of voyages. Some of these may have been made in retirement, as a sailor looked back over his adventures.

Sailors made many objects intended as gifts for wives, sweethearts, or mothers. The fact that the gifts and mementos were made primarily for women, rather than for fathers,

Photograph cyanotype of a sailor scrimshanding, c.1890.

This photograph of a young sailor, believed to be at the wharf side New Bedford, carving a sperm whale tooth (scrimshanding) is extremely rare and is believed to be the only one in existence showing an American scrimshander at work in the 19th century. Over his left shoulder is a lower jaw of a sperm whale and scattered on the ground in front of him are sperm whale teeth.

uncles, or brothers, suggests how powerfully the separation from women weighed on the minds of sailors.

Men aboard whaling ships were often at sea for years at a time, on voyages as long as three to five years. A boy would grow into a man aboard such ships, while older men who survived might return visibly greyer. All of them had not only time on their hands, but some excellent materials to work with, including beautiful sperm whale teeth, which could be carved and etched, as well as whalebone and baleen. These particular materials could be worked into a variety of shapes, and the gifts for women that flowed from the hands of 'scrimshanders' were numerous and varied, and have been the subject of a whole separate field of collecting and literature. The Collection includes what many believe is the only known nineteenth century American photograph of a sailor scrimshanding.

Experts have attempted to identify particular workers in scrimshaw, with some success. In quite a few cases, detailed work on whale teeth was inspired by or copied from a well-known print, such as the 'Pilot on the Deep', showing a young man aloft in the rigging, and on the other side, 'Sailor's Return'. This piece in the Collection has been tentatively attributed to 'The Banknote Engraver', so named because of the fine, detailed workmanship he brought to whale teeth.

Gifts made from whale ivory would include pie-crimpers, often quite elaborate, suggesting that the sailor was dreaming of one of those delicious apple pies his mother or wife had made in bygone days. Using tortoise shell, whalebone, and whale ivory, carvers would sometimes inlay one material into another, using familiar themes of hearts, crosses, clasped hands, anchors or other oft-repeated simple symbols. Inlaid boxes to hold multi-coloured thread for sewing, and swifts or yarn-winders, complex and delicate, could also be fashioned from whale bone, whale ivory, and hard woods. Some items may have been made for trading purposes or even to raise some cash.

A bored captain, Jairus Beal, master of the barque *Apthorp*, noted in his 1840 journal that he spent every off-duty hour working on a bird-cage. Captains, like ordinary seamen, suffered from long periods of idleness, perhaps made slightly worse by the loneliness of command.[1]

1. Jairus Beale, Journal aboard the *Apthorp*, 31 March – 26 August, 1840, in the JWH Collection.

Oil painting; scrimshaw knitting needles; coconut dipper; engraved busk and scrimshaw tools.
19th century.

The oil painting depicts 'Ship Spermo Trying with Boats among Whales On California 1821' and is signed
J. Fisher. The try-works of the ship were going full blast to render or melt out whale oil from the blubber.
In the distance dead whales have been marked for future cutting in and other quarry are on the surface. In
1820 the *Spermo* was owned by A. Mitchell. Displayed in front of the painting are several examples of sailors'
crafts, including a ladle with a cup made out of a coconut shell, a busk with heartfelt verses, knitting needles,
a carpenter's square, a seam rubber, two fids, a thimble eye (of whale ivory) and a small block. Both practical
and decorative items could be made from the plentiful whale ivory, baleen and whale bone.

Macramé lady's purse, basket, cup and saucer.
19th century.

Sometimes macramé took the form of objects that could serve as gifts. This lady's purse, basket and cup and saucer are excellent examples.

Busks, flexible strips of whale bone or baleen used to improve a woman's posture by insertion in the front of a corset, were lovingly carved, and often engraved with fond, sweet messages. A sailor concentrating on a busk for days at a time and considering its final use may have found a special satisfaction in his work. One busk in the Collection bears this verse:

> *This trifle, love, from me accept*
> *And wear it for my sake*
> *Oh! May the bosom that it guards*
> *Have never cause to ache.*

The thought continues on another panel on the busk:

> *My dearest girl, pray think on me*
> *When you look at this bone*
> *Oft times my dear, I've thought of you*
> *When far from my sweet home.*

That artist added an eagle with a patriotic reminder: 'E Pluribus Unum'.

In the nineteenth century, images of fully-clad women abounded in scrimshaw work. Many were based on prints from *Godey's Lady's Book* or similar magazines.[2] Idealized wives and sweethearts were never far from the thoughts of sailors.

Sailors aboard merchant or naval ships had far less time and far less interesting material to work with than did whalers, but they too, generated gifts for the women they left behind, using available materials. Such gifts included purses and baskets made of macramé. Small boxes, made from

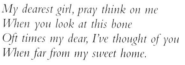

Cutout by Captain Frederick Williams 1828, Portsmouth, Virginia, of storms he experienced and vessels he served on.

This amazing cutout is somewhat in the tradition of European 'ex-voto' pictures which offer praise to the Lord for the rescue of ships. Depicted here are eight separate storm episodes involving either the ship *Protection* or the ship *Indianchief* together with religious sayings. This is one of the most elaborate cutouts known and demonstrates the degree of religious faith sailors sometimes revealed in their craftwork.

Ship Paul Jones *cutout.*

A handicraft by some sailors, as well as shore-side artisans such as the Pennsylvania Dutch, was the fashioning of amazing paper cutouts. This is a remarkable example of the art made by Charles Frances from one piece of paper. This cutout shows the ship *Paul Jones* of Boston arriving at Sandy Hook, New Jersey, 1 January, 1845 from Canton in China. The *Paul Jones* was a well-known vessel in the China trade.

wood, or covered with macramé, could also serve as gifts. Bodkins, inlaid with hearts, would go into a lady's sewing kit.

Paper cut-outs could take literally hundreds of hours. Carved from a single sheet of paper and carefully laid against a dark background, these intricate works must have been done with a razor-edge cutting instrument, rather than snipped with scissors. A few seem to have been cut from a folded piece of paper, much as today, children snip out delicate patterns for valentines. Intricate designs included named ships, biblical sayings, and sometimes prayers of thanks for safe escape from storm or shipwreck. One cut-out by ship captain Frederick Williams of Portsmouth, Virginia and dated 1828, bears quotations from various books of the Bible: Mark 4, v. 37; Luke 2, v. 14; Acts 27, v. 44; and the 91st Psalm. All were appropriate to the sailor who thanked God for his safety at sea.

2. E. Norman Flayderman, *Scrimshaw and Scrimshanders,* (New Milford: N. Flayderman & Co., Inc. 1972) p.39.

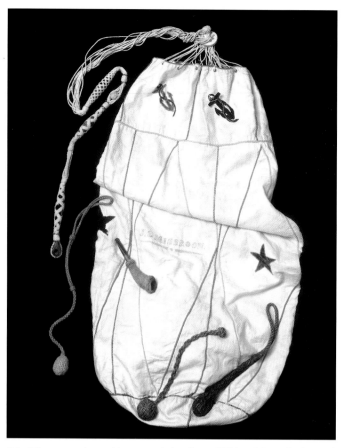

Razor case and razor.
Mid-19th century.

This finely crafted straight-edge razor case was designed to hang on a bulkhead. The inlay of mother of pearl, the fouled anchor in brass and the care taken in making this personal object, all attest to the time sailors would devote to personal items. The razor blade is held in a handmade scrimshaw whale-bone handle.

J.S. Missroon seabag with macramé handle, c.1824. Macramé pipe and slungshots, 19th century.

This seabag, decorated with stars and anchors, once belonged to John S. Missroon who became an American midshipman in 1824 and a commander in 1862. The macramé work of the rope handle is exceedingly well done. Shown here are other pieces which also demonstrate the art of macramé as practiced by sailors. The macramé covering a pipe would provide a cooler and better grip. A man making the slungshots, which might serve as protection in a port of call, could have spent hours day-dreaming about a wild evening ashore. Macramé as a sailor's craft was a natural outgrowth of work with rope, thread and marline in the course of day-to-day work.

Private and Personal Use

Sailors also made items for their own use, either as tools or as part of their own recreation. Wooden boxes that could be hung on the bulkhead to contain a straight-edge razor, 'going-ashore' canes inlaid with whale bone or ivory, baleen or metal, seam rubbers for use in connection with sewing sails, and unique items such as wooden book covers or macramé covers for tobacco pipes, all convey messages to us. Carved wooden sticks, perhaps used by bosun's mates as 'starters' to poke recalcitrant sailors, were crafted of sturdy hardwood. Some wooden items were carved to resemble macramé, showing how these folk arts influenced each other in form.

One elegant piece of scrimshaw in the Collection is a whale tooth, carved with a verse. Verses on teeth are somewhat rare. On the base of the tooth, the sailor had carved his name, W. Wheeler, in reverse, so that, with ink, he could stamp his name on his bag, clothing, and whatever else he desired. The tooth itself was decorated with raised carving, with the name of his ship, HMS *Dublin*, and in an unusual touch, the year, 1837. The verse read:

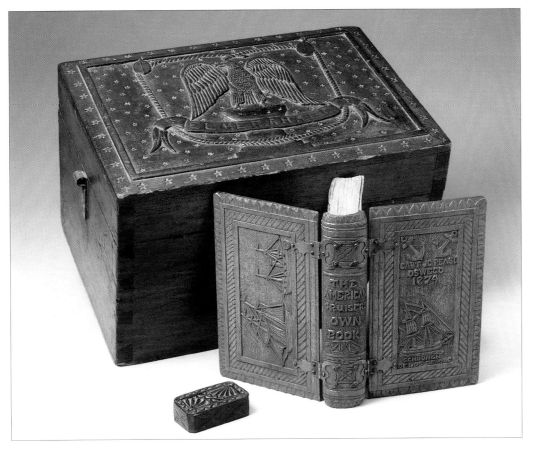

Once the tooth of a Whale
That oft stood the Gale
In the wide Southern Ocean afar
Now would you suppose
I am used to mark clothes
That are stow'd in the bag of a tar.

Patriotic themes, including two crossed British flags, a stylized head of a marine, and an Irish harp also embellished this particular tooth, which the carver had engraved with the words, 'a keepsake'. Here again, we see hints of the need for privacy and assertion of private possessions in the close quarters aboard ship, and can almost feel the satisfaction that Wheeler, aboard the *Dublin*, must have felt as he returned to crowd in more fine work on his carving.

Sailors would cover other common and useful items with macramé, such as telescopes or tinderboxes. Macramé was not only decorative, but by offering friction to the hand, it would allow a better grip on a pitching deck. Sailors covered a lump of lead with macramé or leather, making a 'slungshot' that could serve as a black jack or small personal protective weapon when visiting a rough port of call. Here, the sailor making the device for self-protection might readily have been dreaming about a chance to let off steam or a night of pub and brothel crawling that could be months away. Or the slungshot might be used by a bosun to break up a fight between brawling sailors aboard.

The sailor had spare hours varying from the long idle watches of the whalers, to snatched moments of sailors in the US or British navies, and few personal possessions that could be elaborated or perfected: his own kit, his pipe, his clothing, his walking stick or weapon. The act

'John Chinaman trading with Jack Tar'.
Pen and ink sketch by Lt. John B. Dale,
USN, Canton, China, 1845.

Very few contemporary sketches of
American sailors in the 1840s actually
purchasing the gifts they brought home have
survived. This rare sketch captures the
moment that Jack Tar, a crew member of the
venerable US Frigate *Constitution* on her
round the world cruise, is haggling with
John Chinaman over a possible purchase of
souvenirs. Note carved chessman in a box
in the background.

of smoking a pipe could involve a set of accoutrements that the able craftsman might produce
for his own use: pipe cover of macramé or tobacco tamper made from some type of ivory. One
such tamper in the Collection is in the shape of a very nicely turned lady's leg, also carved with
two tobacco leaves and an anchor. Some clever sailor could smoke and day-dream at the same
time. For those who enjoyed 'smokeless tobacco', a snuff box was another such personal item.
In many of the crafts by sailors, a number of motifs and symbols are repeated again and
again, giving hints of what was on the sailor's mind. A fuller treatment of symbols and the
meanings they appeared to convey is found in Chapter Eleven of this work.

Souvenirs

Through the centuries, it was natural for officers and seamen to want to bring gifts home. The
captain might desire a portrait of his ship either for himself or for the owner. Several ports of
call became well known for port artists, including Le Havre, Marseilles, Malta, Leghorn,
Palermo and Smyrna. An outstanding watercolor artist was Antoine Roux, Sen., of Marseilles
(1765-1835), and several of his ship portraits are in the Collection. Liverpool was home to
several proficient artists, including Samuel Walters, one of the better-known practitioners.

Trying to find ship portraits in watercolors or oils of American flag vessels painted prior

(Opposite: top)
Oil painting of 'Spermo Cutting in Whales on Japan', 1820, signed 'J. Fisher'; scrimshaw checkerboard and two-drawer swift
stand. 19th century.

In 1820 the whale ship, *Spermo* (Captain James Bunker), and two other whalers, the *General Jackson* (Captain John
Fisher) and the *Pacific* (Captain Franklin Chase), left Nantucket to hunt whales in the Pacific Ocean. The *Spermo*
returned in 1823 with 1,920 barrels of sperm oil. A blanket of whale blubber has been cut from the whale and
is about to be hoisted aboard and cut up into much smaller pieces to be converted into oil by trying out. In the
foreground is a rare checkerboard of whale bone and the men are of whale ivory. The two-drawer sewing stand
is topped with a swift and is unusual in that only whale ivory is used throughout rather than the more abundant
whale bone.

Oil painting, Canton c.1835 and export ware.

Captains and fellow officers of British and American ships trading with China would work with the Hong merchants at Canton to sell and buy cargoes. The foreign Hongs or trading houses are depicted in the oil painting by Lamqua *c.*1835. For personal family use, as gifts, or as commercial cargo, huge quantities of Chinese export porcelain were brought home to England and America. The tea set is of the FitzHugh pattern (*c.* 1810–20).

'Life in a Training Ship – sketches on board HMS Boscawen'. Lithograph. Late 19th century.

Several revealing insights into daily life appear in this collection of sketches. On Thursday afternoon apparently sailors could take up their hobbies. In the upper right inset, one man is working on a woolie, one of very few known illustrations of such work aboard a ship. Other shipmates are making and mending their uniforms.

HMS Queen *'A Present from My Son'*. Woolie, *c.* 1855.

Many woolies crafted by British sailors in the last half of the nineteenth century depicted British naval vessels. HMS *Queen,* first rate and of 110 guns, was formerly the *Royal Frederick* renamed in 1839. By her rig, the woolie was probably made prior to 1859. The fact that the work was done by a sailor rather than a shore craftsman seems to be supported by the legend in which the letter 's' is reversed three times: 'HMS Queen - A Present from My Son'. The fine work showing the detail of the rigging and sails demonstrates that the sailor was observant of his surroundings.

Brown Nelson stoneware jug.

This is a Doulton and Watts brown stoneware jug, *c.*1840, representing Admiral Nelson. Innumerable commemorative items were made honoring Horatio Nelson during his lifetime and especially after his death. Probably no other English naval figure has received the amount of adulation and hero worship as that accorded Nelson.

to 1800 is not easy, although there are many more such portraits for British ships. Some captains had their ships memorialized on Liverpool jugs and plates in the period 1790 to about 1820. The Collection has two fine pieces depicting American ships in this category.

For the popular ceramic market, one finds a variety of plaques, mugs, and figurines of sailors with scenes of sailors' farewells and returns, and other nautical motifs and poetry. One apparent favourite had a frog inside the mug. Another medium for souvenir items was glass. A rolling pin shape of dark blue Bristol glass is decorated primarily in gold color, depicting a sailor's farewell and a brig.

From examining prints and sketches, it is apparent that favourite souvenir items included a piece of exotic cloth, parrots in cages and strange and fascinating sea-shells. Many items brought home as gifts for wives, mothers, and sweethearts were ephemeral in nature, and would rarely survive the passage of time. But from the surviving souvenirs and images of sailors buying or bringing home gifts, we have hints of the life of Jack Tar.

Blue glass rolling pin.
19th century.

This glass tube somewhat in the form of a rolling pin captures the recurrent theme of a sailor's departure. A depiction of a ship is on the left and on the right is a sailor bidding goodbye to his wife and home, the oft-repeated sailor's farewell scene. The two scenes are separated with a verse which reads:
Sweet oh sweet is that sensation
When two hearts in union meet
But the pang of separation
Mingles bitter with the sweet
Probably made in the Bristol area, this could be hung up as a sentimental reminder of a loved one at sea.

'Aurora of Newport, John Cahoone' and 'The Mary of Newburyport, Moses Pearson'.
English creamware plates.

Exceptional English creamware plates, *c.* 1795-1801, with American ship transfer-prints painted in enamel colors, each inscribed with the name of a vessel, home port and her master. The 'Aurora' plate is part of a service. The 'Mary of Newbury Port' plate is the only known example. Both were probably custom ordered by the respective captains as a keepsake of their named vessel.
(Left) 'AURORA of NEWPORT, JOHN CAHOONE', a soup plate, impressed 'WILSON' (Staffordshire). From 1790 to 1799 the *Aurora*, carried cargoes of Newport furniture, engaging in trade along the Atlantic coast from New York to the Carolinas. (Right) 'THE MARY OF NEWBURY PORT/MOSES PEARSON', 1803. Probably WILSON (Staffordshire). Moses Pearson was lost at sea in 1803.

Jack Tar: Clues in the Crafts

All of the seamen's crafts, and the souvenirs that seamen purchased or for which they traded, may yield scattered insights into the inner sailor. The sailor was concerned with making a fine appearance once he returned to shore, and hence he would embellish his shore-going finery. He cherished his privacy, and worked on his boxes and bags. He never stopped thinking about women and the love-life he was missing, either representing his fantasy

Sailor's valentine 'A Present from Barbados'.
19th century.

As a collector, one is delighted to find an object that is self-explanatory as to its origin. Over the years many people have thought that 'sailors' valentines' were made by sailors. This example helps prove that a large number of 'sailors' valentines' were purchased as souvenirs by sailors who stopped at the island of Barbados.

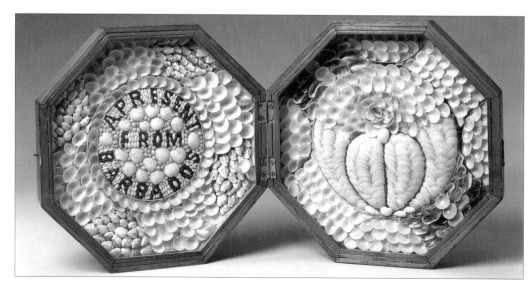

(Far left)
Pottery figure of Nelson.
!9th century.

(Left) *Toby jug.*

This 'Sailor' Toby jug, pearlware with enamel painted decoration, Staffordshire, *c.*1800-10, captures a sense of sailors as hearty drinkers. The sailor is sitting on a sea chest.

directly in art, or preparing or buying a gift he would later lavish on a particular woman. He worried about the afterlife, and memorialized departed ones and pictured crosses and moments of deliverance from disaster and death. The anchor and a safe port were on his mind, as was friendship and love shown by clasped hands and hearts. To memorialize his own experience, he would identify the particular ships on which he had served, and often take note on ivory, wood, cut-out paper, or embroidery, of his ports of call.

The few private possessions the sailor kept — clothing, pipe, tinderbox, snuff-box and razor — with the chests, ditty boxes and bags that held them, might be decorated, asserting an element of individuality in a harsh world whose forces could stifle the human spirit of self. The sailor converted the long hours into cherished artifacts and bought still others. Those that survive bear quiet messages into the present.

'Joseph Rob Seaman Aboard the Abercrombie of 74 Guns'.
English creamware mug.

This is an exceptional English creamware mug, *c.*1810 (possibly Staffordshire). The ship, the sailor, the lettering and the fouled anchor were hand painted in enamel colors. The *Abercrombie* was formerly a French warship captured in 1809 during the Napoleonic Wars and her name was changed. That an ordinary seaman would have this souvenir made for himself is remarkable.

(Above) *Portsmouth Point*.
Hand-colored engraving. Late 18th century.

Rowlandson visited Portsmouth in 1784 and may have combined what he saw there with several stock elements of
cavorting and carousing – sailors taking leave of their girlfriends or wives at the door of a ship's tavern, orgiastic love-
making upstairs and in the plaza, a one-legged fiddler, alcoholic stupor, a money-lender and plentiful street girls.

(Opposite) *'An Engagement with a Storm'*.
P.S. Duval Lith. Phil<u>a</u>, *c.*1845. Hand-colored lithograph.

This bar-room brawl print is one of a series of eight entitled 'Sailors on Shore'. The series depicts the same group,
each with a nautical caption, as they walk in the country, approach a tavern, have a few drinks, start cavorting outside,
then in 'an engagement, with a storm' stir up a great fight inside the tavern with the owner, other customers and the
owner's wife. One of the bystanders, 'Timberto', with a wooden leg, has more regard for his ale than his own safety.
In the final panel of the series, the miscreants are confined to the local jail.

CHAPTER SIX

Cavorting & Carousing

Throughout the eighteenth and much of the nineteenth century, recurrent themes in literature, song, and art depicting the life of the sailor were scenes of drinking, whoring, and fighting. Cavorting and carousing went hand in hand with being a sailor. The reputation for rough good times drinking ashore, and with ladies of easy virtue in port cities, and often in great numbers aboard ship, was well earned. The reality of sailors finding available prostitutes, getting in fights, and drinking themselves into oblivion derived from the very nature of the sailing life.

For the ordinary seaman, a long voyage meant deprivation from sexual contact for months at a time. Throughout the period from the 1750s to the early twentieth century, homosexual sex among sailors at sea was treated as such an unspeakable crime that it was rarely mentioned. When discovered in the early period, it was punished by death, or at least, severe flogging. It was not surprising that when the average sailor arrived in port, one of his first objectives was to find a woman.

The same harsh economic conditions that provided a supply of men for navies and merchant fleets also drove many young women into lives of prostitution. Girls born into poverty in the late eighteenth and the nineteenth century in both the United States and Britain had very few choices for earning a living as they reached adulthood. For those who were widowed or never married, there was simply no social 'safety net' in the modern sense.

'Launching a Frigate'.
Hand-colored engraving.
*c.*1800.

This print published by Thomas Tegg depicts a noticeably ugly woman, apparently a madam, sending forth an attractive young woman on to the streets of Portsmouth. In the background, a sailor calls up to another welcoming lass.

If a woman had no support from family or husband, very few legitimate jobs beyond domestic servitude were open. Such women, especially in port cities, were easy victims of the tavern keepers and brothel operators who needed a constant supply of young women. Venereal disease, miscarriage and abortion, malnutrition, alcohol, and urban epidemics all contributed to a short career and a shortened life expectancy for these young women. Although often depicted in the prints of the late eighteenth and early nineteenth century as

(Right) *Sailors Drinking the Tunbridge Waters.*
Hand-colored engraving.

The sailor's preference for liquor over water was notorious, as the expressions of these three attest. The sailor in the midddle finds it a 'D- - d Queer Tipple to be sure!' Aboard ship, beer, grog and wine were preferable to water for health reasons in the 18th and part of the 19th century as water would soon go bad in wooden barrels while alcoholic beverages could remain drinkable for months.

Presentation spirit cask 'HMS Warrior'.

This small spirit cask was presented to the Captain's Mess of HMS *Warrior* by the Thames Ironworks and Shipbuilding Company (builder of the warship) in August 1861. The brass lettering, 'God Save the Queen', replicates the wording on the full scale grog barrel on deck from which the mix of rum and water was issued daily. HMS *Warrior* was the first ironclad ship built for the British Navy.

enthusiastic and lecherous temptresses, with modern eyes we look past such stereotypes to understand that 'women of easy virtue' was a polite way of referring to a class of sex laborers, who were as much victims of the times as were their customers. Furthermore, such terms implied the practice could be attributed to a moral choice on the part of the women, when in fact it was the social structure and economic conditions which had created flourishing seaport prostitution.

The nature of the work for seamen aboard ship, often boring, usually perilous, strenuous and difficult, and frequently extremely tense and nerve-wracking, demanded some form of relief. Perhaps the most common relief in the navy came from the rum ration aboard and the bottle ashore. From the earliest days of ocean sailing, wine and spirits were taken aboard ship to alleviate thirst, as alcoholic drinks did not spoil as did water in wooden casks. By the eighteenth century, rum and brandy were common aboard ship.

Admiral Edward Vernon (1684-1757) introduced watered rum as a regular ration in the Royal Navy, to reduce the drunkeness that impaired efficiency when sailors drank straight rum. Vernon, a hot-tempered but effective British naval officer who had served in Parliament before being given a last command to attack the Spanish Main, was known to his crew as 'Old Grog' for the 'grogram' foul-weather cloak he wore. Having led a small naval squadron of six ships against the Spanish in the Caribbean, in 1739, the next year he gave an order that his men be issued rum in the amount of a half-pint per day, in two rations per day. Mixing one part of rum with four parts of water, the ration became known thereafter in the English language as 'grog'. Later the standard ratio of water to rum became three parts of water to one part of rum. Vernon required the grog to be consumed at the barrel where it was doled out, but other captains were less strict, allowing all the

Ceramic mug 'Women make men love…'.

The mug was probably made in Sunderland, *c*.1870-80. There is a frog inside and two compelling verses on the outside that reflect the linkage between loneliness and finding solace in drink:

> *Women make men love*
> *Love makes them sad*
> *Sadness makes them drink*
> *And Drinking makes them mad.*

On the reverse side, a more serious and spiritual message is found:

> *The sailor tost in stormy seas,*
> *Though far his bark may roam*
> *Still hears a voice in every breeze*
> *That wakens thoughts of home*
> *He thinks upon his distant friends*
> *His wife, his humble cot*
> *And from his inmost heart ascends*
> *The prayer – Forget me not.*

1. James Pack, *Nelson's Blood* (Annapolis, MD: United States Naval Institute Press, 1983), pp. 10-11.
2. William M. Hunter, 'General Orders for Crew of USS Independence, 1815.' Ms. in WH Collection, page 15.
3. Order by Secretary Gideon Welles, 1862, in WH Collection.
4. Pack, *Nelson's Blood*.

seamen to take their grog ration to their quarters and to store it up for several days.

The rationing of grog in the American Navy became the subject of special rules for its distribution. The Rules and Regulations for the men aboard the USS *Independence* in 1815 carefully prescribed exactly how the liquor should be given out:

> The Grog must be served from the tub and no person is to be permitted to carry their allowance from the tub except petty officers and Then [it] may be served to them in messes. The warrant officers to receive their allowance raw. The place for serving out must be on the main deck, abreast the Mainmast, abaft a line stretched across the deck before the Grog tubs. A masters mate must always attend to this...[2]

An order issued by the US Secretary of the Navy in 1862 brought the issuance of grog to an end in the American service,[3] although it continued for decades longer on British ships. Several reforms allowed sailors in the Royal Navy to take a cash allowance rather than grog. In 1970 the issuance of rum was totally discontinued aboard British naval ships.

As the custom spread throughout the British navy, the twice-daily ration of grog allowed sailors to ameliorate tension slightly. The rule issued aboard the USS *Independence*, that sailors not be allowed to carry the ration away from the tub from which it was served, requiring it to be consumed on the spot, guarded against hoarding the ration to accumulate enough for a true drinking bout. Nevertheless, aboard both American and British ships, it was common for sailors to trade their allowance, so that the heavy drinkers could generally find more than the minimum if they wanted. Often, officers in both navies had their own personal supply.[4]

This original Chinese watercolor, by Sunqua from about 1860, depicts a severely contorted British sailor with the ubiquitous bottle. Chinese and Japanese artists, like many of those in the West, disapproved of the public spectacle of drunk sailors. It was, however, a universal phenomenon – sailors ashore got drunk.

Pseudo-Armorial Tankard.

The pseudo-coat of arms on this drinking tankard, from about 1790, is a humorous commentary on the habits of sailors, with a British lion and flag, and on the quarters of the shield an anchor and cannon to represent the naval ancestry, three tankards and a drinking bowl and glass. The traditional Latin motto underneath is here replaced with a spoof version in English and the words – 'Grog is the liquor of life'. This rare ceramic was made in China for export.

'No More Whiskey Shall I Ship'.
Pen and ink sketch by Charles Dwight Sigsbee. Early 1860s.

With the outlawing of alcohol, except for medicinal purposes, in 1862 aboard US naval ships, Sigsbee captured the depressed state of the affected sailors. Advancing moral reforms may have improved conditions but from the point of view of sailors, this one form of refreshment would be sorely missed.

'Jack in a White Squall amongst Breakers on the Lee Shore of St Catherines'.
Hand-colored engraving, *c.*1800.

The irony of the title and the several nautical puns in both title and text would be readily understood. St Catherines was a sailors' neighborhood of taverns and houses of ill repute. The sailor cannot pay for drinks, indicated on the chalk-board (upper right), as his empty pockets show. One of the enraged entertainers is about to smash him with a fiddle, as he laments, 'I am hard up, not a Quid left or Shot in the Locker to pay the Fiddler. Mieyes what a Squall. How it Whistles through the Ratlines. I must Braill up and Scudd under Bare Poles.' Tavern keepers and bawds took advantage of Jack on shore.

A custom aboard some ships led to somewhat more celebration, weather and sea state permitting, on Saturday evenings during the last dog watch between six p.m. to eight p.m. A ritual toast to 'Wives and Sweethearts – May they never meet!' would be followed by named toasts to particular women.[5]

When a sailor had shore leave in a strange port, he would head immediately to the taverns and brothels, with his pay burning a hole in his pocket. When the seaman was paid off at the end of the voyage, he would have the equivalent of several months' or possibly several years' back pay due to him. In those circumstances, he was an easy target for tavern-keepers, pimps, owners of 'flag houses' or brothels, and street girls. When he was broke, he could then be victimized by crimps.

So cavorting and carousing whether in home port after a voyage or during a visited foreign port were a real part of the sailor's life as well as being a much-depicted motif in art, poetry, song, and literature. The sprees contributed to the public impression of the sailor, at home and abroad.

Aboard ship, cavorting took several forms repeatedly shown in literature and art. George Little, in his account of the voyage of an American cruiser during the War of 1812, recorded an episode, rarely described, but which occurred from time to time. The captain would order the men to cavort, with the command, 'all hands to mischief.'

Little carefully explained that the order turned over the main deck and foredeck to the complete control of the men especially for the purpose of relaxing them from nerve-

5. George Little, *The American Cruiser's Own Book*, New York: Richard Marsh, 1846, p. 100).

Sailors Carousing.
Hand-colored mezzotint, 1807.

This print of a painting by Julius Caesar Ibbetson portrays all the elements of carousing: dancing, fiddlers, love-making, sellers of cheap watches and the sailors who would be swindled into buying them, and of course, lots of drinking.

wracking strict discipline.

> All hands were piped to mischief, and a scene ensued which baffles description. There was singing, dancing, swearing, and fighting. The old salts were running with bowlines, in which they caught the green horns, and would trice them up to the lower mast-head, and to the no small annoyance of the sufferer; while others by the same purchase, drew water aloft, which was soused upon those on deck. Some had a bucket of tar thrown over them; others were well-greased from the slush barrel.[6]

A print of the scene in the book captures this moment. Yet some of the sailors became so enraged at the pranks that a serious fight soon broke out.

> These last tricks were borne with a very ill grace, and yet it was of little use, for in every instance it brought down a double portion of suffering to any who offered resistance. This buffoonery lasted until some of the heroes ... lost all their patience, and some half dozen clubbing together, assumed an attitude of defiance, and sided out for a regular knockdown.[7]

6. Little, p. 101.
7. Little, p. 102.

'All Hands to Skylark'.
Magazine illustration.

In this print by R.F. Zogbaum, reproduced in *Harper's Weekly*, 1891 and in Zogbaum's 1896 volume of prints on the American Navy, *All Hands*, an entertainment on deck reveals a limited degree of 'skylarking'. Here two sailors dance a hornpipe, while a white fiddler and black banjo player, apparently a cook, from his clothing, provide the music. At the back of the print another black man, probably a steward, looks on. The expressions of the audience range from participation to outright boredom.

Apparently the officers found the fight dangerous, for a similar 'piping all hands to mischief' was never tried again for the remainder of the cruise. Yet the experience was not unique, for a repetition of a more sedate scene, some sixty-eight years later, is captured in an 1891 print, 'All Hands to Skylark', with music and dancing.

Playing of jokes and pranks could get out of hand, and journals and accounts are full of stories of midshipmen playing one trick or another on each other and on officers. Midshipman Basil Hall, aboard HMS *Leander*, noted that he and his friends made fun of the captain by dressing the pigs in mourning after the captain's dog died. The captain, 'Old Daddy', took it in good grace, but punished the whole group by mastheading them all:

> Some were sent to sit on the top-mast cross-trees, some on the top gallant yard-arms, and one small gentleman being perched at the jibboom end, was very properly balanced abaft by another little culprit at the extremity of the gaff. In this predicament we were hung out to dry for six or eight hours, as old Daddy remarked to us with a grin, when we were called down as the night fell.[8]

8. Dean King, *Every Man Will Do His Duty: An Anthology of Firsthand Accounts from the Age of Nelson*, New York, Holt, 1997. p. 153.

'The Interior of a Midshipman's Birth'.
Hand-colored aquatint, *c.*1840.

Drinking appears to be one of the main occupations of midshipmen in this British print. Obviously, one middy has fallen asleep and is on the receiving end of a practical joke by having his face colored. Cards are being played – on some ships gambling was forbidden. The jollity of the occasion is increased by a flute player and a fiddler. Some midshipmen were very young and their frivolous antics could get out of hand.

Telling of yarns was a much milder form of recreation than organized mischief, and both in fictional works and seamen's journals, a sailor's yarn often provided a framework for a story within a story, as the main narrator would reproduce an account by a sailor of his adventures. In Tobias Smollett's *Roderick Random* several such encapsulated stories give accounts of the sailor's life, a pattern later echoed by novelists like Dana and Melville. Depictions of sailors sitting enraptured and smoking their pipes as one of their number regaled them with his own exploits or handed-down legends of the sea, abound in print and art.

Bringing prostitutes aboard ship while in port was a common practice in the British Navy, indulged by many British naval captains and often depicted in raucous cartoons and engravings of the 1790s and early 1800s. Hodge, in his diary, reported as many as 300 women aboard ship in 1807. Those officers who urged the prohibition or reform of the practice found it deeply ingrained and very common.

In a report addressed to the 'Right Honourable The Lords Commissioners of the Admiralty' published in limited circulation of 150 copies in 1821, a naval officer addressed in detail the practice of bringing prostitutes aboard ship, providing detailed testimony and anecdotes drawn from episodes over the prior twenty years. British naval captains allowed prostitutes to visit ships while in harbor, with the women often numbering several hundred at a time. The report condemned the practice: 'The tendency of this practice is to render a ship of war, while in port, a continual scene of riot and disorder, of obscenity and blasphemy, of drunkenness, lewdness, and debauchery.'[9] The prostitutes and their customers would all inhabit the same deck, 'huddled promiscuously together.' The report noted with distaste that in these conditions, 'in the sight and hearing of all around them, they live in the unrestrained indulgence of every licentious propensity which may be supposed to actuate inmates of this description.'

9. *Statement Respecting the Prevalence of Certain Immoral Practices in His Majesty's Navy: Addressed to the Right Honourable The Lords Commissioners of the Admiralty.* London: Elerton and Henderson, in WH Collection, pp. 5-6. Hereafter, 'Report'.

A Scene on the Main Deck.
Hand-colored aquatint.

This 1830 print reflects the practice, then undergoing reform, of bringing prostitutes aboard British naval ships while in port. In this fairly sedate depiction the girls are being welcomed aboard with kisses, gentlemanly assistance, cards and dancing. Such scenes tend to include a fiddler, frequently one-legged, ample supplies of grog and two women fighting.

The report described how, immediately after arrival in port, crowds of boats would swarm off from the docks with cargoes of prostitutes. The women had no ready cash to pay for being rowed to the ship, and each waterman would take out as many as his boat would carry, 'on speculation.' Many of the boats would hover around the naval ship, and then each man aboard the ship would select from the boats one or two women, paying a shilling or two for their passage. The women would be examined at the gangway for smuggled liquor, sometimes inspected by officers as to their health, and then would accompany their temporary 'husbands' below deck. A number of bawdy prints capture the process of bringing the women aboard.

The 1821 report pointed out many disastrous results of prostitutes aboard ship. One was the rapid spread of venereal disease among nearly all of a ship's company. Another ill-effect was the conversion of young boys and midshipmen to an early familiarity with sexual promiscuity. The anecdotal presentation with a tone of strict disapproval, like much such reform writing, itself became a form of near-pornographic literature through the vividness of the scenes described.

> A woman, who supplied the ship with vegetables, &c., had come on board with her two daughters, and they along with the midshipmen, and the prostitutes who were in their birth, all got drunk together; in which state they never thought of going to bed, but lay all night like brutes on the deck, while every kind of abomination was going forward – mother, daughters, prostitutes, old midshipmen, and young boys, all mixed together.[10]

In another account in the same report, based on an episode in 1809, the officer noted that the number of women brought on board happened to exceed the total number of seamen

10. Report, pp. 5-6.

'Exporting Cattle, Not Insurable'.
Hand-colored engraving, *c.*1800.

These buxom women, being brought to entertain sailors aboard ship, are the subject of a cruel pun in the title of the print. They try to smuggle supplies of alcohol for consumption on the ship and one of them is already being hauled aboard. Despite the efforts of reformers, the practice of bringing hundreds of prostitutes aboard ships of the Royal Navy while in port continued well into the 1820s. A companion print shows a group of bullocks being rowed out to a ship and is labeled 'Exporting Cattle, Insurable'.

and officers. As a consequence, even though some officers were in bed with two women at a time, the surplus provided an inducement to the younger midshipmen.

> The effect of this licentiousness was of the most pernicious tendency, particularly on the minds of the young midshipmen and boys of the ship, and the writer can well bring to mind that it was the practice of some two or three of the younger midshipmen and boys to 'row guard' between the decks, as it is termed, after dark, seeking a connection with the supernumerary women.[11]

In another case from 1808, the captain allowed nine women to go out to sea with the ship. Two or three behaved so outrageously that they were shipped back to England in a brig, but the remainder 'were common to the ship's company,' one of whom 'admitted nineteen men to her embraces in one night.'[12]

Not only were the diseases these women brought contagious, but their attitudes and values spread like a plague, which some officers found even more disturbing. One remarked that a particular group of prostitutes sang 'openly the most grossly indecent parodies on the Lord's Prayer and the Creed: they were of too coarse a nature to bear repetition.' The officer noted that the 'tendency of such compositions to promote disloyalty is well known.' He believed that verses of that kind had contributed to the mutiny of the British fleet at the Nore in 1797.[13]

The British Naval Regulations of 1790 prohibited women aboard ships, except those who were married to the men aboard, and allowed those legitimate wives aboard only

11. Report
12. Report, p. 9.
13. Report, p. 11.

141

Milling Match.
Thomas Tegg, Hand-colored engraving, *c.*1800.

Two sailors are tied to a chest and engage in a sit-down fist fight as messmates and several visiting women make wagers and encourage them. In the confined space below decks, the chest could substitute for a roped boxing ring.

while the ship was in port. A revision of the regulations in 1808 had charged the officers to set examples of morality, and to prevent 'drunkenness, gaming, rioting, and quarreling' or anything which might tend to the promotion of vice and immorality. Nevertheless, it was clear from the gathered testimony that the law was widely violated, and the practice of violating one regulation, the report pointed out, could easily lead to a general lack of order and a tendency to break other laws and regulations. 'One excess draws on another', the report noted, quoting from a text on moral philosophy.[14]

In a classic essay style, the report introduced arguments in favor of the prostitution practice and then dismissed those arguments with counterpoints. The report, in very circumspect language, examined the question of whether or not admitting prostitutes to warships had the effect of reducing 'unnatural crimes', that is to say, homosexual encounters.[15]

Along with other supposed justifications of prostitution aboard ship, this argument was dismissed as based on faulty reasoning: only a very small proportion of seamen would fall into the 'vice' of homosexuality, but at the same time thousands more were introduced to licentiousness and disease by the presence of prostitutes aboard.

Several common expressions found their way into the language from women being aboard ship. A child born aboard ship on the gun deck of the British Navy was known as a 'son of a gun'. When the watch was being turned out of their hammocks in the mornings, a bosun would ask each hammock to 'show a leg'. The smooth-legged girls would be left to sleep in, the hairy-legged men turned out to their watch.[16]

The degree to which the practice of bringing prostitutes on board ship occurred in the British merchant fleet is difficult to determine. Apparently it was not common in the United States Navy. On an early voyage of the USS *North Carolina*, 1824-27, August Beers, the Surgeon's Mate, kept a careful and detailed journal. While calling in Spanish ports, he found the women rather diffident, and certainly a far cry from the loose women reported by the British reformers in the same period.

14. Report, p. 20.
15. Ms. Diary of Voyages Aboard several British ships, 1790-1833, by George Hodge. 26 October, 1808 entry.
16. *Oxford Companion to Ships & the Sea*, Oxford, 1976, pp. 799-800.

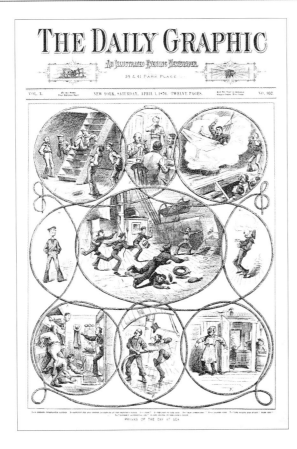

'Pranks of the Day at Sea'.
The Daily Graphic, 1 April, 1876.
Wood engraving.

The April Fool's Day pranks at sea echo those of 'The Midshipman's Birth'. In nine separate episodes, the young practical jokers take over the ship for a day. There is a greased forecastle ladder, sawdust pie and cotton doughnuts, a fire set under a hammock, the 'pest' of the ship, a false cry of man overboard, a loaded pipe, a false cry of a burst boiler, a fire hose aimed at an officer's stomach and red pepper spread on the cook's stove.

The dress of the men as well as of the women is full of finery. Some of the latter may be called handsome but most of them are the reverse. What strikes a stranger most is their confidence and indifference. They view the ship with curiosity but the officers do not attract their attention.[17]

Dr Beers did discover, however, that in some of the Spanish ports, sailors could find other entertainments. He noted with some disdain:

> The taverns in this place are miserable... At one of them called the Three Anchors – where a trade is carried on too disgusting to be mentioned – there is a theater in the place. Their favorite amusement is bull baiting. The Andalusian bulls being the most furious in Spain makes this sport in perfection here...

He may have found the trade at the Three Anchors Tavern too disgusting to mention explicitly, but he apparently spent some time enjoying himself there, for he went on to comment in a later entry: 'While in the tavern in the evening I was surprised to see two ruffian Spaniards ride into the barroom on horseback – but I learnt it was the custom in Spain.'[18]

Of course, sailors found many other forms of entertainment aboard ship and ashore besides liaisons with women of ill repute, bull-baiting, and noisy taverns, as various depictions of card games, yarning, chess sets, checkers, drinking parties, and even organized fist fights attest. In one print, two sailors, one black and one white, are tied by their waists to a chest and engage in a sit-down fist fight as their messmates and several visiting women make wagers and urge them on. In another illustration from *The Daily Graphic*, a popular magazine, young pranksters aboard a US naval ship commit a whole series of practical jokes

17. Ms. 'Journal of a Voyage to the Mediterranean in the US Ship *North Carolina*, 1824-1827', by Dr Aug. P. Beers, Surgeon's Mate. pp. 34-35. WH Collection.
18. Beers, journal, p. 37

'The Wapping Landlady'.
Hand-colored copper plate engraving.

In this fairly proper 1743 print of sailors cavorting, the landlady chalks up the tally of drinks served while a sailor dances to a fiddler and his companion looks on. Violin players, bar girls and dancing tended to go together in these scenes and this is a very early example of all three elements.

on April Fool's Day, 1876.

In the late eighteenth and early nineteenth century prints and cartoons proliferated showing sailors in taverns, grog shops, outside flag houses or brothels, and dancing and drinking with women or in all male groups. Early nineteenth century art of this type by Rowlandson and others appeared to mix a bawdy tone with implied disapproval of such robust entertainments of sailors. Close examination of the detailed illustrations sometimes shows bits of social commentary in the exaggerated ugliness of the women, debauched sailors deprived of their money, or various exploitative merchants, tavern keepers, pimps, pickpockets, and brothel madams. Yet to an extent, some artists before the 1850s seemed to suggest, wild cavorting and carousing by seamen was not so much a social evil, but rather an amusing, and to the observer, perhaps a titillating, form of entertainment.

One common theme among the humorous depictions of sailors cavorting ashore was the incongruous attempt of a sailor to ride horseback. Almost as a standing joke, sailors were shown mounting horses in the wrong direction, out of confusion or inebriation, or out of their habit of rowing a boat while facing aft. Sailors tied to the saddle or hanging on for their life abounded, suggesting that in this one respect, a landsman might have a skill that was absent among sailors.[19]

With the growth of reform sentiments through the nineteenth century, pictures of sailors' entertainments changed in several ways. On the one hand, the mission or Bethel movement began to emphasize that sailors' hard-earned money was being taken from them by tough prostitutes, boarding house keepers, crimps, thieves, tavern owners and barkeeps. An 1853 report in the *Sailor's Home Journal* by an early-day muckraking journalist described in detail

19. One scholar traces the motif of sailors on horseback as a 'dependable comic type' to Chaucer: Nathan Comfort Starr, 'Smollett's Sailors,' *American Neptune*, vol. 32, April 1972, p. 81.

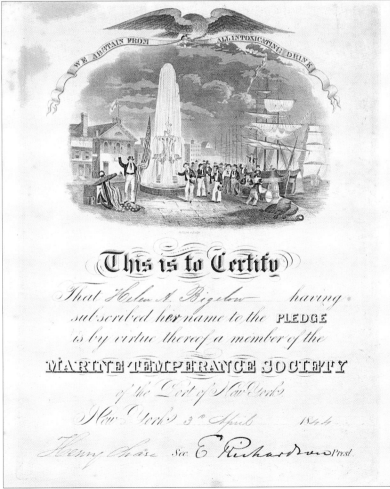

Snuff Box.
19th century.

The illustration on this musical snuff box plays on the tradition since Smollett of sailors being humorously ill-adapted to horseback riding.

'Coning and Steering
Starboard Tom Starboard
Aye Aye Starboard it is'

The sailor facing forward issuing commands is waving a speaking trumpet pretending it is a telescope to see where he is going and the sailor facing aft is holding the reins as if he is steering a ship to starboard.

Marine Temperance Society Pledge.
Engraving.

In 1833 the Marine Temperance Society was founded at a time when a general temperance movement was making great strides in America. Most of this was due to growing public interest in humanitarian reforms and the spread of revivalistic religion. In 1842, Congress passed a law cutting the spirit ration in half and forbade it entirely to those under 21 years of age.

On this 1844 pledge form from New York, a group of sailors are around a water fountain at the dockside, supposedly demonstrating their preference for water over alcohol. Reformers worked to overcome the vices of alcohol, prostitution and blasphemy.

Theatrical entertainment aboard HMS Chesapeake, *at Aden, 1859.* Pen and ink by Alex[r] D.M. McArthur.

McArthur was the editor of 'The Young Idea', the *Chesapeake's* 'Chronicle' and 'Weekly Journal'. The play of 'King Charles the Second' was a comedy and performed as a Christmas play, 29 December, 1859.

how prostitutes and their associates continued to fleece sailors.

> I proceeded down Ratcliffe Highway towards Shadwell. On my way I met with half-intoxicated seamen, accompanied by drunken women, sallying forth from those low licensed public-houses, which are kept by the most unprincipled persons, who retain in their pay agents of both sexes whose duty it is to watch the arrival of vessels and to pounce upon the seamen the moment they put their foot on shore. These miscreants, on hearing of a man of war being paid off, at any of the naval ports, look out for the sailors as they reach London, many a good man of war's man being thus decoyed into their dens of infamy, and there drugged, robbed, and irretrievably ruined.[20]

The reform-minded writer was protected by the presence of a policeman he took with him. He was stunned by what he encountered in one of the establishments.

> To describe the fearful scene I there witnessed, among the principal actors in which were wretched women, half dressed, blaspheming and fighting, under the maddening influence of intoxication, would be a task as difficult as it would be painful... I discovered three human beings, two of them sailors, in a state of stupefaction, the other a woman, who was plying them with drink, giving them no doubt just sufficient to keep them in her power, till all their money was gone. One of these poor fellows was just sober enough to tell me — the woman having left the room in a rage at my appearance — that he had given the last of his money two days ago and that the previous day he

20. *Sailors' Home Journal,* scrapbook, WH Collection.

146

(Left and right) '*British Plenty*' and '*Scarcity in India*'.
Hand-colored stipple engravings. Late 18th century.

Two paintings by H. Singleton, reproduced here as prints, convey some charming contrasts and a lesson in Adam Smith's Law of Supply and Demand. In Britain a single sailor, who apparently has recently been paid and by his clothing shows it, sails between two charming young ladies simultaneously, while in India the reverse is true. There, a poorly dressed sailor and soldier offer gifts to a single native lady.

had been prevailed upon to send the best of his clothes to be pawned...
On returning down stairs I found my visit had raised a hurricane of abuse against me; thanks however to the policeman, my companion, I passed through a crowd of angry women without being attacked by them, which they seemed inclined to attempt...[21]

Another aspect of the changing values of the mid-nineteenth century was to show alternate sailors' entertainments in a more respectable fashion, with dancing scenes, weddings, or gatherings ashore that suggested not so much an orgy of debauchery but simply some decent, morally acceptable, entertainment. Prints of the period following the 1850s took a far less tolerant view of carousing, beginning to reflect the consciousness that sailors in the company of loose women were not so much the beneficiaries of a relaxed morality, but victims of an exploitative system which used prostitutes to strip the sailors of their meager earnings.

Sometimes the flirtation of sailors with local women was depicted in quite an ambiguously innocent or at least semi-respectable fashion, with a form of tongue-in cheek humour. One

21. *Sailors' Home Journal* scrapbook. Reports in this publication could serve as an excellent source for a fuller treatment of the reform movement directed against prostitution.

'Holiday Sports'.
Hand-colored wood engraving.

This print from *Harper's Weekly*, 23 October, 1875 reflects the fact that bored sailors on ships of the US Navy resorted to some quite innocent entertainments on their time off. Skipping rope was a vigorous workout, as the perspiration and serious faces demonstrate.

famous pair of illustrations, entitled 'British Plenty' and 'Scarcity in India', made a point about supply and demand. In the Indian scene, a British sailor and a soldier with ragged uniforms simultaneously offer gifts to a single pretty young Indian woman; in the British scene, a prosperous looking sailor is walking arm in arm with two young women. The viewer was left to draw conclusions as to the sexual and economic implications.

In the mid- and late nineteenth century, some sailors' manuscript journals reflected the growing sense of propriety found at the same time in published work. Some of the entertainments aboard ship described by sailors, artists, and journalists became much more refined, with theatrical performances, quiet sessions of reading aloud, singing, spinning yarns, contemplative tobacco smoking, or even sailors standing in line to skip rope.

The manuscript journal of letters sent by Boatswain William Hill on the USS *Galena* told of girls visiting aboard as tourists on the naval ship when in New Orleans over Christmas, 1884. While a few practical jokes and flirtations took place, the sailors did not expect anything other than a social call, nor did the girls get more out of their visit than some innocuous souvenirs.

Dancing the Hornpipe.

Painted in 1878 by English painter George Green, this watercolor captures a sailor dancing the hornpipe, to the amusement of six of his fellow sailors and their lady friends. A civilian plays the fiddle while several soldiers in the background look on. Green's realistic portrayal of this moment of carousing suggests a fairly sedate group, standing in some contrast to more riotous and sexually explicit scenes from earlier in the century. By the height of the Victorian era, depictions of sailors cavorting and carousing had been transformed from drunken orgies to the sort of staid and proper social event shown here.

Richard Van Lennep Sketchbook.

This watercolor scene of men dancing aboard ship was painted in 1807 by Richard Van Lennep on his voyage in the topsail schooner *Tryal* from Smyrna, Turkey, to her home port, Boston. The black musician appears to be playing a homemade fiddle.

> The midshipmen are in clover, 'catching on' as they call it, to the pretty girls. There were five young ladies hailing from Wisconsin off here the other day. ...While they were on board I had occasion to go forward in the berth deck, when I was stopped by quite a rumpus. One girl was holding Fahs while another was cutting a lock of hair from the top of his head, with a dull pen knife. It was quite amusing for lookers on. They left the ship with several trophies. One had some of Fahs' hair pinned to her dress, another some buttons, while the rest had pieces of lace and portions of coats, etc. One of the fellows opened a bottle of wine, but they all refused.[22]

Bosun Hill took a very proper tone in his letters home, even complaining of nude statuary displayed at an exposition hall in New Orleans, and alluding to various uplifting experiences. Even allowing for the fact that Hill appeared to be an exceptionally proper gentlemen, the 'rumpus' he depicted was a far cry from the orgiastic scenes depicted as typical aboard British naval ships sixty-five years earlier.

Yet Hill could not avoid noticing, in various ports of call in Central and South America, that the usual entertainments provided for sailors of less discriminating taste than himself appeared to still flourish. In Panama, he reported several such aspects of the trip:

> Field had an adventure in the shape of a dusky Belle wanting him to kiss her. I did not learn whether he complied with the damsel's request or not...We walked into the town through the main street through the usual rabble of street gamblers, lazy negroes, naked children and half naked women and were glad to get down to the landing in time to take the four o'clock boat.[23]

Other late nineteenth century journals, authored by writers less prudish than Hill, conveyed the fact that sailors still sought out feminine companionship and 'sensual gratification' while ashore. Even when not couched in disapproving tones, their descriptions of such excursions reflected a changed set of values and a less ribald and rowdy sort of adventure common a few decades before. George Cochrane, the paymaster on a US naval supply mission along the coast of Greenland in 1871, coyly described how sailors sought out several good-looking girls of mixed Eskimo and European ancestry in the port of Disko. Cochrane expressed himself in very proper language, noting that one such young woman of mixed ancestry might have been the result of a whaling captain following 'the deviation of his magnetic needle' towards an attractive native woman some years earlier. In another passage, he noted that one young woman, Mary, was reputed to have 'a lamb whose fleece was white as snow', and that all the sailors sought to get a peek at her 'lamb', without success. Cochrane delighted in such Victorian allusions to salacious aspects of his trip which were encoded in *double entendres* and innocent language.

22. Cruise of the USS *Galena*; Extracts from letters written by Boatswain William L. Hill, in WH Collection.
23. Hill, letters of 11 and 14 March, 1885.

Automaton showing British Sailors dancing, c. 1880.

This working wind-up British automaton from about 1880 presents two sailors who dance to the music-box rendition of the hornpipe. The pagoda, the moored sampan, palm-trees and witnesses in oriental garb show western sailors taking their traditional form of frolicking to exotic locations.

The propriety of tone found in the journals of American naval officers may have reflected not only the gradually growing moral uplift in the period, but the increasing professionalising of the naval service. For example, the Rules and Regulations at the US Naval Academy as published in 1855 made it clear that the Navy set a rather stiff-necked definition of proper behavior, when compared to the debauchery of the 1820s reported and apparently somewhat tolerated up until that decade in the British fleet.

Frank Leslie's Illustrated Newspaper. 27 November, 1880.
Wood engraving.

Despite years of the temperance movement, alcohol remained a universal problem for sailors of all nations. Here four very strict United States Marines bring three inebriated American sailors through the streets of Norfolk, Virginia after a naval review. The black on-lookers include some spirited children and their more reserved elders. The sobriety of the black gentleman and his wife contrasts rather sharply and may offer a comment on the behavior of the sailors.

3. Any student who shall be intoxicated, or shall use, or bring into the academy, or the grounds belonging thereto, or have in his quarters, or elsewhere within the limits of the academy walls, any spiritous, vinous, fermented, or other intoxicating drinks, may be dismissed from the academy, or from the navy...

6. Any student who shall play at cards, chess, back gammon, or any game of chance; bring, or cause to be brought, within the limits of the academy, any cards, dice, or other implements used in such games may be dismissed from the naval service.

7. Profane, obscene, or vulgar language is strictly prohibited.[24]

As photography began to supplement and supplant painting and sketching among sailors at the end of the nineteenth century and as moral reform took much firmer hold, the pictures sent home showed a more proper sort of visit ashore. Victorian morality seemed to be taking hold, as pictures reflected social calls on local expatriates, visits to various architectural landmarks and local natural wonders, and tourist excursions into the interior or to the local market to buy curios.

No doubt part of the reason for the survival of pictures of such innocent enjoyments is

24. *Revised Regulations of the Naval Academy,* Washington: A.O.P. Nicholson, Printer, 1855, Chapter XI, p. 28ff. Copy in WH Collection.

1. J.H. BLOOMER (THE ONLY SAVED)
2. C. SHILLINGTON
3. W. HOWE
4. W. LAMBERT
5. W. TINSMAN
6. P. NEWTON

7. CAPT. C.W. EIERMAN.
8. J. MERTZ
9. B. MASDEN
10. W. GORMAN
11. L. BOUNER

COPYRIGHT 1898 GEO. C. MAGES CHICAGO.

Photograph of baseball team of the Maine.

This rare photograph depicts the baseball team, with goat mascot, of the Battleship *Maine*, early in 1898. The legend notes that only J.J. Bloomer, upper left, survived the explosion in Havana Harbor on 15 February, 1898. Sailors took up team sports eagerly, a method of recreation encouraged by the Navy. The black sailor in the upper right with the baseball appears to be the pitcher.

that the pictures themselves were intended as souvenirs to be shown to relatives, wives, and sweethearts at home. Sailor artists who sketched scenes of their trips into their illustrated journals which they kept for themselves had always captured the exotic and unusual on their visits ashore. Such art included pictures of ports, natives, landscapes, and local architecture. The tradition of sending home little memento pictures of innocent tourist attractions expanded into an international cultural phenomenon when sketches and snapshots became replaced by purchased postcards.

However, cultural memories and candid depictions of the sailor's entertainments such as storytelling and singing, grog and girls, fist fights and philandering, cavorting and carousing, all survived through the era of reform and Victorian propriety, well into the twentieth century.

Tho' distant climes may us divide
To think on you shall be my pride
Tho' Winds and Waves may prove unkind
In me no change you'll ever find.

F. Bartolozzi R.A. Inv. Delt. et Sculp.

A Magic Spell will bind me fast
And make me love you to the last
Let Cupid then your Heart incline
To take me for your Valentine.

Sailor's valentine.
Hand-colored engraving. Mid-19th century.

This touching sailor's valentine uses the oft-replicated 'Sailor's Return' motif, with cottage, ship in distance, and sailor and girlfriend or wife greeting each other.

(Opposite) *Woolie, c.1860.*

This woolie depicts two sailors lifting their glasses in an apparent toast to the lady between them, with a floating depiction of two ladies, above in an oval, suggesting a locket. We can only guess as to the story behind this, but the two in the oval would seem to be the subject of the toast with raised glasses of wine. Depiction of people, such as sailors and their women-folk, in woolies, is very unusual. Most known woolies are of British warships.

CHAPTER SEVEN
Sweethearts and Wives

I n the world of the sailor in the eighteenth and nineteenth century as depicted in contemporary art, writing, and artifact, we see repeated over and over the theme of the women left behind. Every Saturday night aboard many US and British ships, during the dogwatch, men would lift their cups to toast wives and sweethearts, each sailor calling out the name of his own in a separate toast.[1] The special place in the lore of sailors reserved for women left a rich legacy in the maritime art collections of our times, and the ways in which sailors fantasized about the women at home colored their songs, shaped their letters and showed up again and again in their handicrafts.

Sailing was entry into a man's world. Thus, seamen about to depart were almost always

1 Little, as cited in chapter 6; also
Creighton, p. 132

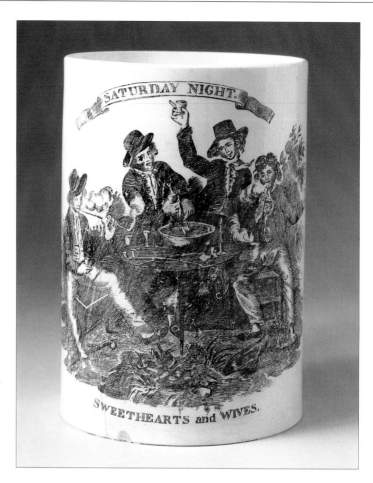

Saturday Night 'Sweethearts and Wives' Mug.
19th century.

This drinking mug captures the moment customarily reserved on Saturday evenings for toasts, with the issue of grog, to 'Sweethearts and Wives', often with each sailor naming his own particular wife or sweetheart at home. The jocular version is 'To our Sweethearts and Wives – May they Never Meet!' For many sailors, however, the toast was heartfelt.

depicted in engravings and paintings as breaking away and leaving women and children, most commonly daughters, not sons. In this fashion, the art symbolically presented the act of sailing away on a ship as putting things feminine behind them. Comparatively few pictures show young seamen saying farewell to their fathers or show the father attempting to restrain or to hold back the son. In fact, various pictures can be interpreted as showing the father encouraging the son to take up the sea. The convention is so implicit and the implications are so standardized that, like the sentimental departure from women-folk, the conventions of father and son discussing the sea need not be made explicit to the audience. No label explains the serious demeanor of father with a sailing vessel on the horizon, nor the attentive look on the son's face. But the body postures reflect, not agony of departure, but instruction, advice and serious passing on of sage wisdom. Again, the signals had become understood; the masculine quality of the life of the sea was so universally comprehended that no viewer in the era of sail would misunderstand the depicted moment.

This tendency to think of the sea as drawing men away from women, recurred again and again in art, and reflected a real psychological and cultural tradition in sailing itself. Marcus Rediker, in his definitive study of Anglo-American merchant sailors and pirates in the early eighteenth century demonstrated that the culture of the sea was a masculine one, not only because sailing crews in the early period were all male, but because the sailing life represented and incorporated a whole series of male values in contrast with feminine values. He shows how masculine entertainments, direct and forthright expression, and coarse language of the seamen that he defines as 'plain dealing', were conventionally contrasted with the etiquette, polite mannerisms, and the feminine styles of shore-bound life in the early eighteenth century. In the early eighteenth century Anglo-American maritime world, women were regarded as bad omens

'Father and son', c.1810.
Watercolor.

Here a gentleman discusses a sea career with his thoughtful son. The small telescope indicates that the son is about to go to sea, as the father gestures. The stance of the two men is ambiguous. Is the father encouraging or warning the son? Is the son resolute in his decision to go to sea? Does the older man expect his son to live up to his own exploits? The mood, unlike so many in which a sailor about to depart must take agonizing leave of his womenfolk, gives an entirely different feeling, in which men can somberly discuss life at sea, its perils and rewards.

aboard ships, and among pirates in the period 1714-1726, it was a capital offense to bring a woman aboard, one among very few violations of pirate custom and rules which would result in execution by pirates of members of their own group.[2] In the eighteenth and early nineteenth century, the sense that a ship was a man's world prevailed, even as British and American merchant ships began to carry women passengers and wives of officers, and as an occasional woman who passed herself off as a man would be discovered among the ranks of naval sailors.

2. Marcus Rediker, *Between the Devil and the Deep Blue Sea: Merchant Seamen, Pirates, and the Anglo American Maritime World, 1700-1750* (Cambridge University Press, 1987), p. 266.

George Hodge's Diary.

In a rare watercolor of people in his diary, George Hodge suggests a blissful scene of what appears to be a sailor husband and his wife blessed by cherubs. This is evidence that Hodge was married at one time and had a daughter. Hodge's long voyages left him little time to enjoy the pleasures of domesticity.

3. Margaret S. Creighton and Lisa Norling, *Iron Men, Wooden Women: Gender and Seafaring in the Atlantic World, 1700-1920* (Baltimore: Johns Hopkins University Press, 1996), p. ix.

4. Lilian Nader suggests that in the works of Joseph Conrad, the wooden sailing vessel resembled the angelic, domestic woman, while the steam ship was replete with images of a sexually promiscuous woman. See Nader, 'Sailing Ships and Steamers, Angels and Whores: History and Gender in Conrad's Maritime Fiction', in Margaret Creighton, ed., *Iron Men, Wooden Women*.

In a recent collection of essays on the topic, Margaret Creighton and Lisa Norling, the editors, offered this analytic comment on the relationship of gender and seafaring: 'The view of the ocean as a single-sex masculine space, in contrast to a feminized and domesticated society on land, reflected the nineteenth-century projection of bourgeois social mores onto a time-honored division of seafaring labor.'[3] Paintings, prints, sea shanty songs and ballads, poetry, as well as memoirs and journals from the period all reflect these overtones in ways that come alive for us today.

It was no accident that ships themselves were named for women (often a wife or daughter of the owner or captain) and always referred to by the feminine pronoun. For the sailor had abandoned human feminine companionship for a masculine world in which the ship herself was the bride. Like a woman, a ship appeared to have moods, and had to be treated with respect if her cooperation in a crisis was to be expected.[4] In a rather overblown passage, echoing literary conventions, Dr Samuel Beers, an officer aboard the *Augusta Mayhew*, noted in his journal:

Eighteenth century Chinese export plate.

The sailor's departure scenes spread world-wide. This eighteenth century Chinese export plate depicts a Dutch sailor taking leave of his wife, with a porcelain castle-like home in the rear. The poignancy of the scene was understood across cultures.

So, once more I am afloat on the fearce rolling tide, the ocean is my home and the Bark is my bride and as highlands fade fast from our view I cannot feel but sad, sad to think that years must pass ere I again behold these well known scenes or revisit the haunts of my childhood, yet such is my fate, ever to be roving in some foreign clime.[5]

Despite his self-conscious style, Beers captured the notion of the ship as substitute for love life, and how it replaced all the familiar scenes of home with a far more difficult marriage. For many such men, the 'bark' would indeed become the 'bride'.

In sailing humor, the sailor often made analogies between women and sailing vessels. Sailors would 'rig out' their lady friends, or when flirting with girls, would be 'on a cruise' hailing a woman with nautical terms. Over and over, a woman's bustle would be a 'stern', her bosom, her 'bow' in such humor. In the rollicking sea-song, 'Bangidero', Chilean girls were described as 'trim and neat'. The older women were 'frigate molded from truck to keel, with their quarter-galleries and breadth of beam'.[6]

Many artists would produce pairs of pictures entitled 'The Sailor's Departure' or 'Farewell' and 'The Sailor's Return'. Even tattoo art, ceramic ware, and Valentine cards emulated the motifs common in these scenes. On one side of the departure scene we would see a cottage

5. Log book of the *Augusta Mayhew*, 1858. Original manuscript copy in the WH Collection, catalogue number A-94.
6. Joanna Colcord, *Roll and Go: Songs of American Sailormen* (Boston: Lauriat, 1924), 41-42, as cited in Mary Malloy, 'The Sailor's Fantasy: Images of Women in the Songs of American Whalemen', *The Log of Mystic Seaport*, Autumn, 1997, 38.

Tradesman's locket sampler and individual locket, c.1800.

In this saleman's sample of nine oil on ivory ovals, *c.*1795, three represent the sailor's farewell, two, in memoriam and four others in various poses. When purchased, the painting would be mounted in an attractive locket as shown below. In the back of it was a compartment to hold a lock of hair. That sailors and their wives and sweethearts used such lockets as remembrances while they were apart is indicated in several prints.

Patch box.

This fine patch box bears the sailor's verse:

> *Take this, Dear Girl*
> *May you prove true*
> *Till I return*
> *From Sea to you.*

Metal boxes were made in Birmingham. The enamelers in various places; i.e., Bilston, personalized the boxes as they wished. This poem is indicative of the British public's awareness of the importance of sailors and the sea in their lives. Patch and snuff boxes represented still another type of gift for the girls and wives at home. Inside the lid, a girl could check the application of the cosmetic patch to her cheek in a miniature mirror.

'Sailor's Return' ceramic figure.

This Staffordshire pearlware figure with enamel decoration, c.1815-25, inscribed 'Return' shows a sailor about to embrace his sweetheart or wife while clutching a bag full of money earned the hard way. His right foot rests on a chest marked 'Dollars' suggesting that he may have received a share of prize money.

wall pierced by window and door. This opening in the wall gives a view into the domestic life which the sailor left behind. Ivy or climbing roses softened the building's hard edges, echoing the feminine tresses of the woman in the foreground. In the center, the separating couple stood between domesticity on one side and the life of the sea on the other, with the woman near the house, the man nearer the seascape. Often a ship's boat would be pulled ashore, representing for the viewer the future moment, when the sailor would step into the boat and be rowed out to his waiting ship.

(Above) *Ambrotype of sailor with lock of hair, c.1855.*

This photograph in a case contains a lock of the sailor's hair, and a short verse, which was originally pasted on the back of the photograph:

> *Say when I plough the watr'y deep*
> *Wilt then this slight memento keep*

Photographs of sailors were frequently mounted in such cases to leave with wives, sweethearts and mothers ashore.

(Right) *Design for a tattoo book.*

This colored design from a tattoo book, *c.*1890, shows a young US Navy sailor leaving his loved one, and hearth and home behind him for the unknown on board a sailing ship on the high seas. Like prints and ceramics, tattoos often showed one or another aspect of the sailor's longing for women and often, for a particular sweetheart. The price for this tattoo was $2.00.

'Wialliam of the Ship Philadelphia *Taking Leave of Nancy'.*
Print, *c.*1795. Philadelphia.

In this primitive and very unusual print, a sailor departs from his sweetheart, echoing some of the themes of departure for reasons of patriotism and leaving things feminine behind. Nancy's chaperon stands behind her while the sailor and Nancy touch but do not embrace. His ship awaits, with two men in the rowboat ashore. In an appeal to early patriotism echoing the ideas of the young republic, the legend reads, 'The rights of America we'll maintain, And then return to you sweet girls again.' The artist misspelled 'William'. The use of the name 'Nancy' may derive from the fact that Dibden, the popular English song writer, often used the name to represent the sailor's sweetheart left behind.

Sailor-Far-Far At Sea.
Lithograph.

In this 1845 Currier print, a sailor dwells on the locket Sally has given him.

A token then my Sally gave
Tis this which now I view
And in my heart shall ever be

A US warship rocks at anchor in the background. The sailor's beard and costume are typical of the US Navy, mid-1840s.

In 'The Sailor's Return', the elements would all be there again, but now conveying a different message and a different past and future beyond the frame of the picture. From the posture, the smiles, the embrace, we would know the sailor had returned to his wife or sweetheart. The cottage, with its glimpsed interior, offered a waiting refuge.

'Departure' and 'Return' prints caught many elements of the gender values echoed in many other forms of art and popular literature. For example, some prints, including song sheet music illustrations, depict a sailor day-dreaming on the deck of a ship, thinking of the sweetheart he left behind. Again, the two worlds were in contrast, the immediate and real world of the sailor at sea, and the remembered girl depicted in the miniature locket.

In a more subtle fashion, the fact that sailors thought of their women while at sea could be caught in a depiction of a sailor purchasing gifts to give to wife, sweetheart, or mother

'Sailor's Adieu' and *'Sailor's Return'*.
Hand-colored lithographs, *c*.1850.

These American 'Sailor's Adieu' and 'Sailor's Return' prints by N. Currier contain all the stock elements, including a ship and a vine-draped cottage. The girl is wearing a locket which probably contains the sailor's picture. The prints capture the sailor's imminent departure and his anxiously awaited return.

upon his return. Some 'Sailor's Return' pictures would repeat, almost as stock elements, certain specific gifts: a parrot, a cage, a silken shawl. The sailor had been thinking of his women while in far-away lands; his return with gifts in hand reflected a story which would be easy to imagine: his visit to an exotic port, and the thoughts that went through his mind as he purchased the objects.

One unique form of craft work, usually made and purchased in Barbados, was the 'Sailor's Valentine', a mosaic made of colored sea-shells. Because of their intricate craft work and beauty, and their fragility, Sailor's Valentines made of sea shells are much sought after as modern collectibles.

Another theme recurrent in the literature is the flirtation of sailors with girls at home and abroad. The boundary line between innocent flirtation and negotiation with a prostitute is

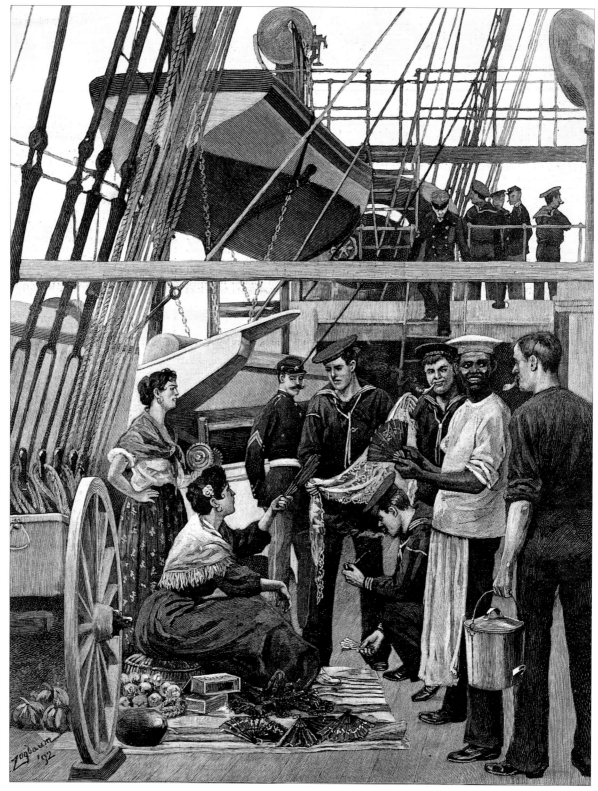

Harper's Weekly: *Souvenirs.*
Magazine illustration.

This 1892 print by Zogbaum shows US sailors purchasing souvenirs from women bringing them aboard ship while in a foreign port. Gifts for wives and sweethearts, especially the delicate fans, appear to be popular with several members of the crew. R.F. Zogbaum tried to be extremely realistic in his work, much of it printed in *Harper's Weekly.*

(Above) *Woolie of sailor's return, 1850-1880.*

This woolie depicting a sailor's return to his wife from a sail-and-steam warship features a large lavender house, probably accenting the sailor's devotion to his home. As in many woolies, the art as well as the artistry suggest the work was done by sailors themselves, rather than by professionals ashore.

'Sailor's Return'.
Liverpool painted ceramic tile.
Mid-18th century.

This Liverpool painted tile by John Sadler, *c.*1760, depicts two sailors returning home – one with a possible sweetheart or wife and the other embracing what appears to be his mother. The smiling faces are in obvious contrast to the tearful goodbye depicted in the companion tile, *'Sailor's Farewell'* illustrated in Chapter One (page 34).

difficult to determine in some art, but many items of this type survive.

Literature made much of the relationship between sailors and their wives. Melville, in *White Jacket* put a rough-and-ready image of the value of a good wife into the mouth of his narrator: '...Of all chamber furniture in the world, best calculated to cure a bad temper and breed a pleasant one, is the sight of a lovely wife.'[7] The narrator's voice becomes even more characteristic of the plain dealing and coarse values of sailors, as noted by Marcus Rediker. In one passage, Melville makes the following comparison: 'The band...messed by themselves, forming a dinner party not to be exceeded in mirthfulness by a club of young bridegrooms, three months after marriage, completely satisfied with their bargains, after testing them.'[8]

Later in the nineteenth century, some writers adopted a much more sentimental view of the plight of wives left behind. A laudatory family biography of Admiral John Markham, describing his life in the 1790s and early 1800s, but written and published in 1883, presented this romantic picture:

7. Romances of Herman Melville, *White Jacket*, (NY: Tudor Publishing Co., 1931)
8. *White Jacket*, p.49.

Decorated picture frames / photographs.

These plaster frames, which look home-made, are decorated with sea shells and hold photographs of a sea captain and his wife. They were another type of sentimental souvenir for a sailing officer to give to his wife.

Sailor's Shell Valentine, c.1870.

This sailor's shell valentine, a hinged pair of boxes with the motto, 'Home Again' and a heart, opens like a book. Usually purchased in Barbados for wives, sweethearts, and mothers at home, elaborate and well-preserved examples are becoming harder to find and are much sought after. The gifts made by, and purchased by, sailors for the women they left behind tell us something about Jack Tar's emotional life.

> There is such sorrow and anxiety to be born by the wife of a naval officer who is actively employed, but there are compensations. It is her lot to lead a lonely life, sometimes for years together, while she sees other married couples living on without any separation. Yet these know nothing of the intense pleasure of anticipation as the time for reunion approaches, nor of the great joy of home-coming. The sailor's wife also sees the bickerings of many of her acquaintances. 'I am married [she says] to an honest tar, who although absent in the service of his country, is good and true.'[9]

In sailor art, narrative, and song, there seem to be two views of women held by sailors. On the one side there is the sentimental, romantic, Victorian image, embodying the domestic ideal or ideology which emerged in the nineteenth century. In this view, women were virtuous, faithful, religious, frail, and they bore children and raised them. The other view held women to be objects of lust, promiscuous, flirtatious, and who consciously tempted men and enjoyed the results. The songs of sailors appeared to divide between the work chanteys which often had an overtly sexual and bawdy tone, and the leisure-time ballads, often sung at home, which spoke of fidelity and the romantic vision of women. The key to the division in song may have been that the chanteys were sung by the sailors as they worked aboard, and were rarely heard in parlors, while the ballads were intended for mixed company.[10]

9. *A Naval Career During the Old War: Being a Narrative of the Life of Admiral John Markham (Lord of the Admiralty, 1801-04 and 1806-7)* (London, Sampson-Low, 1883), p.154.
10. Mary Malloy, 'The Sailor's Fantasy', p. 36.

'Jack on a Cruise'.
Hand-colored engraving, *c.*1785.

Jack calls out 'Avast there, back your Main top-sail' and the young lady, not at all distressed, gives him an impish smile. The flirtations of a sailor ashore, depicted in this print also, became the subject of ceramic reproduction on the drinking mug (opposite).

JACK on a CRUISE.
Avast there, back your Main-top-sail.
Printed for Robert Sayer, No 53 Fleet Street

Another aspect of the division between the two views of women held by sailors was the difference in attitude between the young bachelor sailors and the older officers and petty officers who were older. The ordinary seaman was often a young man who had left home before he had attained an age to develop attachments to a wife or sweetheart, and he usually had his first sexual experiences in foreign ports. The older officer or sailor was more likely to be married and to have a woman to return to. The dichotomy in the image of women, on the one hand, as wives and sweethearts, and on the other, as part of the bawdy entertainment of brothels and port-girls to some extent may have been a product of the divide between two cultures, that of the older and younger sailing men aboard ship. The social division between cabin and forecastle was profound, and no doubt shaped the ideas, images, and values of the two groups.[11]

Sea chanteys, the work songs sung by sailors, captured many of the themes popular in the sailor's own self-image through the nineteenth century. Among the many recorded chanteys that echoed the themes of girls awaiting in ports was 'Rolling Home', which captured the concept of girls in every port, and at the same time, mentioned the wife or sweetheart waiting at home:

Heave away ye sons-of-thunder
For the nor'ard we will steer
Where the gals and wives are waiting
Standin' there upon the pier.

Cheer up, Jack, bright smiles await you
From the fairest of the fair,
There are lovin' hearts to greet you,
An' kind welcomes everywhere.

An' the gal you love most dearly
She's been constant, firm and tru.
She will clasp ye to her bosom,
Saying, 'Jack, I still love you.'

Jack on a Cruise.

This mug with enameled decoration and printed inscription, 'Jack on a Cruise Avast there – Back your Maintopsail' was probably Staffordshire, *c.*1780–1800 and perhaps based on a popular print of the same title. Comparison of girls with ships, often complimentary to both, became part of the lore of sailors ashore.

Yet another had a slightly more cynical line:

> *A John he is true to his Sal an' his Sue,*
> *So long as he's able to keep 'em in view.*[12]

Valentine cards from the era of course reflected only the most sentimental of such responses, the overly romantic side, often utilizing the stylized departure or return pictures with cottage, couple, waiting rowboat and distant ship, and all the themes of separation echoed in the verse:

Stay on shore oh stay with me
Trust no more the boistrous sea
Oh attempt the main no more
Stay with me, oh stay on shore!

Shall I say my heart is thine
Will you be my Valentine?
Stay thee on your native land
And accept your lover's hand.

Another, similarly illustrated, captured much the same thought:

The distant climes may us divide
To think on you shall be my pride
The Winds and Waves may prove unkind
In me no change you'll ever find.

A magic spell will bind us fast
And make me love you to the last
Let Cupid then your heart incline
To take me for your Valentine.[13]

11. (Opposite page) Mary Malloy, 'The Sailor's Fantasy', p. 35, and note 2.
12. Stan Hugill, *Shanties from the Seven Seas* (Mystic, CN: Mystic Seaport Museum, 1994) pp.147, 233.
13. Text from Valentines in WH Collection.

'The Honest Waterman'.

This is an English creamware baluster-shaped jug with transfer print in sepia (probably Staffordshire, *c.*1795-1805). Based on a spirited song by Charles Dibden, 'Poll and My Partner Joe', this scene illustrates the final verse in which the returning Honest Waterman catches his Poll in the arms of his Partner, Joe. The reproduction at the top of the jug of a stag's horns is symbolic of ages-old cuckoldry – the unfaithfulness of a man's wife. Sailors, as well as their wives, had reason to question the fidelity of their spouses after long separations.

As the eighteenth century popular song writer Charles Dibden captured in his rollicking song, 'Poll and My Partner Joe', sailors remained very insecure about whether their girlfriends, fiancées, or wives would remain loyal to them while the men went off to sea. The theme of the jealous sailor speculating that his sweetheart might find another man recurs throughout the art and literature. The protestations of loyalty on both the seaman's part and reflected in the Valentine verses no doubt covered a real anxiety, captured in this verse by Lyttleton, which was used as a caption for a poignant print of a sailor observing his sweetheart with another man, entitled 'Love and Jealousy'.

> *O pain to think another shall possess*
> *Those balmy lips that I was wont to press*
> *Another! on that panting bosom lie*
> *And catch sweet madness from her shining eye.*[14]

Sailing men were known for their powerful sex appeal to women, and the subject made for political scandal and some very ribald humor. One depiction of Lady Emma Hamilton, made clear by several cartoon-style allusions in the picture to her lover, Admiral Nelson, was hardly complimentary to her, her husband, nor to Nelson. Behind the politics and the

14. Print E138 in the WH Collection.

'Love and Jealousy'.
Hand-colored stipple engraving.

This romantic depiction of 1786 captures in verse the sailor's distress that his girlfriend will find another while he is away at sea. The separation of a sailor and his sweetheart became a subject of verse and song, as well as visual art, reproduced on canvas, paper, in scrimshaw and in ceramics during the romantic era. The legend that a sailor might have a girl in every port did not detract from his expectation that the girl at home should remain faithful.

humorous bedroom scene was a whole cultural background which suggested that sailors would often cuckold the landsmen, as much as they were cuckolded by them. Lady Hamilton laments:

> *Ah where & Ah where is my gallant sailor gone*
> *He's gone to fight the Frenchman, for George upon the throne,*
> *He's gone to fight the Frenchman, t'loose t'other arm & eye*
> *And left me with the old Antiques to lay me down & cry.*[15]

The illustration is rife with *double entendres*, but at the time most of them would have been obvious to the informed British public. Nelson, renowned for his love affair with Lady Hamilton, was off to fight the French in Egypt and had only one arm and one eye; Sir William Hamilton was a collector of antiquities, was his wife's senior by many years, and could be regarded as an antique. Lady Hamilton, however, was a good looking woman, and hardly as gross as the cartoon suggested.

Dr Beers, an astute observer, who tried to give his journal elements of literary style, remarked on a 'departure' scene as an eyewitness. His response to the scene suggested that his emotions may have been colored by his conventional expectations of what he should feel: 'Preparations are making for sailing...Some of our men whose wives have been aboard ship for some time took their leave of them to day making quite an affecting scene.'[16] In the romantic era, 'affecting scenes' were those which had an emotional effect, bringing forth inner feelings from the soul. Yet in the same entry, Beers showed that he had the ability to look beneath the surface of events in a rational and analytic fashion, to the less romantic side of relationships between sailors and their women. He noted that, while provisions were made to provide pay for sailors' wives, other young women (presumably prostitutes) took advantage of the situation.

> It is usual for those who are married to leave a part of their wages for the maintenance of their wives — for which purposes the Purser gives out a Half Pay Ticket entitling those who hold it to Half Pay, — This custom is often taken advantage of by the cunning ones of the tender sex who getting themselves in favor with the seamen enable themselves to pass [for] their wives and deprive the poor sailor of half his wages.[17]

15. Print E-692, 'Dido in Despair', in the WH Collection.
16. *Ms. Journal of a Voyage to the Mediterranean in the US Ship North Carolina, 1824-1827,* by Dr Aug. P. Beers, Surgeon's Mate, entry for 4 Jan. 1825.
17. Ms. Journal of a Voyage to the Mediterranean in the US Ship North Carolina, 1824-1827, by Dr. Aug. P. Beers, Surgeon's Mate, entry for 4 Jan. 1825.

Finding the social reality behind the romantic images conveyed in song, art, and literature is made difficult by the repetition of sentimental and maudlin ideas. Even Samuel Beers, a professional, and sometimes quite a prudish observer, tried to see the romantic, 'affecting' side of events. So such primary sources as journals provide no absolute guarantee that we are looking past the romantic vision to the social reality. Sailors' own self-image, and their images of their women, were often shaped by the expectations of culture.

The economic reality of being a sailor's wife was difficult throughout the eighteenth and

'Dido in Despair'.
Hand–colored engraving.

This 1801 print makes allusions that would be well-understood at the time. Lady Emma Hamilton, whose affair with Admiral Nelson was notorious, despairs over her lover's departure to fight the Frenchmen in Egypt. Lady Hamilton, despite this scurrilous depiction, was a beautiful woman. Her husband, Sir William Hamilton, was somewhat older than her and a collector of antiquities, which helps to explain her lament that her lover left her with 'the old Antiques to lay me down and cry'.

nineteenth century. In Britain in the eighteenth century, sailors' wives received so little pay that poverty drove many to prostitution. The subject was so painful that many allusions to infidelity on the part of sailors wives may have been a delicate way of suggesting a much darker reality, in which women had no choice but to find a source of income. Even though a sailor's wife sometimes received an allotment of a portion of a sailor's pay before he set sail, on long voyages, such resources would soon be depleted. Direct documentary evidence of how such women survived is rare; many depended on their parents or other relatives. If opportunities to enter domestic service were rare, some were left destitute. One letter in the Henderson Collection tells a poignant tale as a sailor's wife in Nantucket appealed for assistance in August 1857.

> I appeal to you (wrote Mrs George Cleveland), once more for assistance. I am entirely destitute. I have delayed writing as long as I could in hopes to have some successful news from the Virginia. I have been living on my father — he says he is not able to do any more for me untill (*sic*) I can remit him part of what is due him. I have done all I can to keep my child and myself decently clad, and that is all. ...I know my husband has tried all he could to get a voyage if they do not see the whales, they can not get them... I am needy and appeal to you for assistance. Please let me have one hundred dollars and place the same to my husbands acct....[18]

18. Letter from Mrs. George S. Cleveland to Hathaway, August 23, 1857, original in the WH Collection.

'A Seaman's Wife's Reckoning', c. 1800. Hand-colored engraving.

The sailor's 'wife' has a certain logic to her explanation of how she got pregnant and had a child during the long absence of her 'husband'. The husband is gullible, but his father is a bit more worldly-wise and doubtful of her mathematics. There is very little surviving explicit material about the sexual mores of sailors, their wives and their girlfriends. This cartoon, with its rather coy presentation of the wife's reckoning of the time of her pregnancy, was about as explicit in its message as the period would allow.

The whaler *Virginia*, which had left 15 August, 1855, did not return until 19 June, 1860, and then with a fairly poor showing of whale and sperm oil. There is no record of how Mrs Cleveland survived over the remainder of the nearly five year absence of her husband.[19]

How did the ordinary sailor think of his wife or sweetheart? Was he consumed by jealousy, as suggested repeatedly in prints and song? Or did he remain devoted to her and she to him, which other pictures and verses depict? Or was the truth somehow distributed on a range between the extremes of infidelity and jealousy on the one hand, and loyalty and sentiment on the other, both of which so attracted the writers and artists of the romantic era?

Some of the letters and journals of sailors from the era suggest that the sailor's preoccupation with the woman he left behind was much more than a literary conceit or the work of an artist's imagination. The letters of bosun William L. Hill from aboard USS *Galena* are frank and direct. While he made no effort to conceal his contempt for US Naval Academy graduates, for African-Americans, for natives of Latin America in general, for Catholics, or for what he saw as the foolish antics of the young bachelor enlisted men, his honest respect for his wife continually came through in the collected letters. He called her his 'sharer of joys and sorrows', and regretted leaving New Orleans, because it would interfere with their exchange of mail. On New Year's Day, 1884, he looked forward to the next year being happier, because they would spend it together, rather than apart. Even expressed so stiffly, it was clear that bosun Hill thought of his wife often, corresponded with her regularly, and often noted anecdotes and events that he would later recount to her in a way he thought she would enjoy.[20]

Hill's many prejudices suggest that he was from the middle-class of sailors: a warrant officer, not an ordinary seaman, nor an officer; not full of pretense nor highly educated; even though a Congressional Medal of Honor winner, he may have been typical, in several ways, of many warrant officers in the American Navy in the 1880s, especially those who were

19. Alexander Starbuck, *History of the American Whale Fishery*, (Secaucus, NJ: Castle Books, 1989 [reprint]), pp. 526–527.
20. Hill letters, WH Collection, pp. 62, 163.

Painted cigar case, mid-19th century.

This cigar case is painted with an erotic picture of a woman floating above the sailor's hammock, as he day-dreams about her. The painting may be over an applied print. While it is only logical to assume that sailors day-dreamed about the girl they left behind, or about women more generally, it is unusual to find an explicit representation of the act of such day-dreams in the art of the 18th and 19th century.

married and had outgrown the 'youth culture' of the forecastle. He was literate, but made no allusions to literature in his writing, which was straightforward, lively, and full of anecdotes. His letters to his wife reflected several elements: a constant and faithful correspondent, a man who respected her feelings, and someone quite affected by the long separation. Bosun Hill was unusual in that he earned a high medal for valor and took on many duties above his rank, but like the sailors of the songs and pictures who pined for their women, he told his wife that he was lonely for her, and the words have the ring of truth.

Life for the men who shipped out on long voyages was sharply different from the life they left behind in many ways. Many agricultural workers, miners, and laborers in the emerging mills and shops of the period commonly had a style of life which entailed returning at night to a family. Even watermen with their wherries and local river and harbour craft, and most coastal fishermen, were able to return home nightly or after a predictable short voyage. But for the Anglo-American mariner who crossed the oceans of the world in the eighteenth and nineteenth century, perhaps the aspect of their life which set them apart most clearly from those who worked on land was the long separation from women, extending for periods of years in some cases. So it is no wonder that thoughts of wives, sweethearts, mothers, and women more generally informed their art, their poetry, their songs, and their handicrafts that survive from the era of sail and early sail-and-steam into our times.

Diorama.

This diorama presents a wedding scene inside a church. There are miniature figures in appropriate dress and uniform of the bride, her attendant, the sailor groom and his best man, together with a minister and his assistant. Also evidenced are tablets of the Ten Commandments and a bible on the altar. By the costumes, the scene represented was created about 1820.

Playing up the Ensign— God save the Queen   H. Coish

CHAPTER EIGHT
Ceremonies, Protocol, Diplomacy

A rich subject of illustration and a repeated theme in logs and journals kept at sea are the ceremonial moments, often conducted according to ancient traditions. The special place of traditional ceremonies in the life of the seaman was partly due to the fact that, without such events to mark the passage of time, the days at sea could easily blur together, undistinguished from one another on the long voyages of weeks, months, and often, years. The tedious round of watches, the long uneventful stretches between ports, marked only by changes in the weather, almost demanded that some form of human ceremony provide an event to give the calendar significance, and to establish and note the passage of time.

(Above) *Playing up the Ensign – God Save the Queen.* Watercolor.

This original watercolor by H. Coish, *c.*1885, depicts the band playing while the ensign is hoisted and the men stand at attention (compare with the illustration opposite).

(Opposite) *Lowering the Stars and Stripes.*
R. Lufkin. Oil painting.

It is interesting to note that aboard an American warship in 1892 the salute to the flag at sunset was rendered by the officer removing his head-dress. Standing at attention and saluting became, in time, a naval regulation. The raising and lowering of the flag helped mark the time of day aboard ship.

Officers and crew could create a mutual awareness of passage through time by celebrating holidays, by saluting with cannon fire their arrival at, or departure from, a port of call, or by the ritual reception of visitors from another ship or visiting dignitaries from a port city. The initiation-like 'crossing the line' ceremony held in mid-ocean at the Equator, or at the Arctic or Antarctic Circle varied from ship to ship, but was often a very festive occasion. One Captain Basil Hall, writing in 1846, captured the importance of the crossing of the line ceremony, when he remarked that it 'certainly affords Jack a topic for a month beforehand and a fortnight afterwards.'[1]   Officers and men alike participated in these events, treating some very seriously and other customs and ceremonies with a mock seriousness. Artists captured and recorded many of the events, for unlike the mundane daily routine activities, the ceremonial moments, whether serious ritual or humorous relief from toil, stood out as worthy of remark.

Even as a ship was being built, the various stages were often marked by several ancient ceremonies: the laying of the keel would attract merchants and investors for commercial ships, and naval and government authorities for naval ships. The stepping of the mast was accompanied by an ancient custom of inserting coins below the mast, which according to legend, provided the fare for Charon to row the deceased across the River Styx after death. The coins under the mast would serve as passage money for all the sailors aboard who might die suddenly and unattended.[2]

The launching of a ship, again attended by dignitaries or investors, for many centuries had required the use of water or wine. In ancient times the ceremony was to propitiate the gods. The ritual has continued into modern times, with the cracking of a bottle of champagne on the bow of a ship by an invited female guest, to send it down the ways, a stock item in the newsreels of World War II.

In harbor, when ships assembled for review, or when important guests were visiting, a ship would be 'dressed' with flags flying from lines run from the tops of the masts. On great occasions, such as a visit from a head of state, or on a victorious arrival of a warship returning to port, the ship might also be 'manned', with sailors in dress uniform, standing on the yardarms. The traditions of dressing and manning have continued in modern navies into the twentieth century, with the men standing in dress uniform on the decks of modern carriers or submarines, together with signal flags flying from radar and radio masts. The visit of an admiral, whether of the same or other navy, would require both gun salutes and other forms of recognition. For instance, one print shows the crew of a ship's boat with raised oars in salute as the admiral's barge passes in a harbor.

Burial at sea was a custom often described in logs, journals and in other accounts. The body of the deceased would be sewn in a canvas shroud, and in some accounts, with a coin placed in the mouth, and weights such as shot or chain in the canvas to ensure that the body would sink. The last stitch by the sail maker might pass through the nose of the corpse. In the American Navy, the body would be placed on a grating or plank, covered with an American

1. Basil Hall, *Fragments of Voyages and Travels* (London, Edward Mixon, 1846) as cited in Leland P. Lovette, *Naval Customs, Traditions and Usage,* (Annapolis, MD: US Naval Institute Press, 1939) p. 47.
2. Leland P. Lovette, *Naval Customs, Traditions, and Usage,* p. 37.

'Naval Officers visiting'.
Collotype, *c.*1890.

During what might have been a naval review in the latter 19th century, a high ranking French officer mounts
the gangway to the ship while his longboat prepares to give way to the waiting American boat, also bearing a
high ranking naval officer. In the distance, a British officer approaches, while in the foreground, men in a small
motor-launch watch the proceedings. The receiving ship is firing a salute. The number of guns fired depended
on the rank of the officers being welcomed aboard; for example, an admiral would mean a salute of 17 guns.

flag, and laid on the railing while the last services were read. In many cases, from the Episcopal
prayer book, the words would be read out: '...we therefore commit this body to the deep, to
be turned into corruption, looking for the resurrection of the body, when the sea shall give
up her dead, and the life of the world to come...' As the words were read, a line under the
plank would be lifted, the body would be tipped over, and the flag gently pulled back.[3]

Visitors aboard naval ships would be received with ceremony, fully spelled out in naval
regulations. The origin of the custom of saluting with guns is said to originate from the
principle that a gun, once fired, could not be fired for some time. Thus a ship firing its
guns in salute would be demonstrating to another ship or to port authorities that it was
rendering itself powerless, at least for several minutes.[4]

In the American Navy the number of detonations in each gun salute, the type of uniform
to be worn, and the explicit 'side honors' such as manning the ship, to be shown in

3. Lovette, p. 39.
4. Lovette, pp. 26-27.

Deck Scene on a British Ship, c.1870.

In this deck scene aboard HMS *Royal Oak*, officers, seamen and marines are all assembled in dress uniform. A highly decorated, bare-headed officer appears to be handing what may be orders to another high ranking but less highly decorated officer.

recognition of various classes of important visitors, were all set in advance. Thus a visit from the President or former President of the United States, the president of a foreign republic, or any foreign sovereign or member of a royal family, would rate a twenty-one gun salute, greeting by officers and men in full dress uniform, with the yards or rails manned. Vice-Presidents, Secretaries of State or the Navy, and any Ambassador would be greeted with nineteen guns, full dress uniforms, and eight side boys at attention. And as one proceeded down to lesser ranking officials, shorter salutes would be fired — for example, Admirals, Generals, and Vice-Admirals would each be entitled to a seventeen gun salute. The interval between the firing of guns would be five seconds, and all officers and men on deck would stand at attention during the salute. Ranking guests would be welcomed aboard with an honor guard and the piping of a bosun's whistle.[5]

When a ship of the US Navy called at a foreign port, strict protocols governed the visit of officers from the ship to other ships in port which flew an American flag, including merchant ships and yachts. The visiting officer would gather specific categories of information, including the name and nationality of the vessel, the name of the owner if a yacht, and the tonnage and cargo of merchant ships. Other details about the ship's recent voyage and future plans would all be collected, as part of the officer's regular intelligence duties. All such visits would be subject to any local rules as to quarantine.[6]

On long uneventful voyages between ports of call, without encounters with other ships, the opportunity for marking the passage of time with ceremonies would decline. Aboard naval vessels, every Sunday would be marked by a moment of religious services, often followed by a reading of the Articles of War. In the Royal Navy, celebrations of the monarch's

5. Lovette, pp. 96–98, citing from the 'Rules, Regulations, and Instructions for the Naval Service of the United States, 1818.'
6. Lovette, pp. 342–43, 'Regulations and Instructions for Boarding Officers.'

'Crossing the Line' Ceremony. Pencil and watercolor, 19th century.

This original watercolor of a Crossing the Line ceremony depicts Neptune's chariot drawn by two men in leopard costumes. The rituals surrounding the initiation have been traced back to the 17th century and some are thought to have their origin in guild initiations from the late Middle Ages.

birthday and Christmas would provide two annual events that required the issuance of an extra allowance of grog and a holiday from work. In the American Navy, Independence Day on 4 July, would rank with Christmas as an event worth noting. If such an event fell on a visit to port, officers and local dignitaries might be invited aboard. In the early days of American independence, British visitors were sometimes uncomfortable at the 4 July celebrations, as noted in more than one journal.

The drinking of toasts with grog became quite ritualized aboard British ships. In addition to the toast to 'sweethearts and wives', on Saturday nights, noted in both the American and British navies, the British specified other ceremonial toasts on the other nights of the week. On Sunday, sailors toasted 'Absent friends'; on Mondays, 'Our ships at sea'; on Tuesdays, 'Our men'; on Wednesdays, 'Ourselves'; on Thursdays, 'A bloody war and quick promotion', or 'A bloody war or a sickly season', or sometimes, 'the King' and on Fridays, 'A willing foe and plenty of sea room'.[7]

Sundays, annual holidays, visitors from other ships or from ashore, and occasional diplomatic missions of naval officers would all provide fairly sedate and serious moments of recognition of the passage of time. Prayer meetings, and the raising and lowering of the national flag, served on both British and American naval ships as solemn moments at which the crew would gather.

More outlandish were the customs surrounding 'Crossing the Line'.

Crossing the Line

Crossing the Line ceremonies matched the initiation ceremonies of many medieval guilds, and by the sixteenth century, a pattern of customs had emerged in European shipping to provide a 'baptism' for all sailors aboard who had not previously crossed the Equator. The ritual had become quite elaborate by the eighteenth and nineteenth century, marked in Britain, France, the United States, and in the merchant fleets and navies of other European

7. James Pack, *Nelson's Blood*, p.178; and Lovette, p.121, citing Commander W.N.T. Beckett, *A Few Naval Customs, Expressions, Traditions, and Superstitions,* 2nd edition, (Portsmouth, England: Gieves, Ltd., no date).

'Crossing the Line', USN Pensacola, 1890.

The *Pensacola* was a screw steamer launched in 1859. She saw combat action in the Civil War. In 1890, the year of this ceremony, she cruised along the coast of Africa and returned to New York in May of that year. Here is photographic proof of what is seen in many prints and paintings of the inventive and imaginative costumes of Neptune and his court.

countries by similar customs. The night before the Equator was approached, 'Neptune', usually the oldest sailor who had crossed the equator the most, would hail the ship, and announce the ceremony to take place the next day. Officers who had not crossed before were sometimes allowed to pay their way out of the ceremony, the money to be used to purchase extra beer or grog for the crew.

On the day of the ceremony, Neptune and his retinue would come over the bows of the ship and take over the deck. The retinue might consist, among others, of Neptune, 'Davy Jones' or the Devil, two 'Bears', men dressed in skins who would pull Neptune's chariot, a 'Barber' and a 'Doctor'. Often Neptune was accompanied by Amphritrite, the wife of Triton or Neptune, usually a young sailor dressed up with a wig and outlandish female clothing. The addition of the Barber and the practice of a mock shaving of the victims first occurred about 1750 in the British navy and appeared regularly thereafter in illustrations, while the Doctor appeared around 1800.[8]

The ritual of shaving by the Barber included a foul mixture of some form of soap, and the mock shaving with either an ugly notched piece of metal, or a wooden oversized razor. The 'Doctor' would conduct an examination and force some unpleasant pills on the victims, often washed down with water forcibly administered through speaking trumpets. The victims would then be ducked in a large canvas tub at the feet of Neptune. In some ceremonies, Neptune, acting as a judge, would require of each initiate that he would swear, on an atlas, that he would ensure that such a ceremony always be carried out on any future voyage at which he crossed the line.

Neptune himself was often made up to look as he might in Baroque art: naked from the waist up, with long hair and a long beard, often made of unravelled rope, swabs, seaweed or sheepskin. Often he sported a crown, and whatever clothes he wore would be soaking wet, on the assumption he had just come from the depths of the sea. Usually Neptune carried a trident or spear, sometimes with a large fish impaled on it. Amphritrite, the queen, sometimes carried a doll, who might have a marlin spike for a teething ring. Sometimes she would hold a fish, as a substitute for a baby.

In the more elaborate ceremonies, other sailors might be made up as Neptune's servants, as nymphs or maids, and Neptune might be accompanied by a bottle-bearer and sword-bearer. The chariot on which he was drawn on deck could be a gun-carriage, a tub, or in some cases, the ship's fire-pump. After a mock sighting of the altitude of the sun to determine if the ship was crossing the equator, taken through a glass bottle, Neptune 'took

8. The description of the typical crossing the line ceremony is derived from Henning Henningsen, *Crossing the Equator* (Copenhagen, Munksgaard, 1961), pp. 57-59.

'Baptême Sous Les Tropiques'.
Hand colored aquatint. 1834.

In this print of a French Crossing the Line ceremony, the unfortunate initiate is given a good hosing as Neptune and the other celebrants look on. There were many similarities between the French, British and American versions of this ritual. A print of this ritual is dated in the 1690s. A later edition in the Collection was dated at the end of the 18th century.

over command' of the ship. At this point, the sailors who had not previously crossed the line had their names called out from a list and were brought before Neptune for their 'trial'.

After the trial, the victim was blindfolded, perched on a plank over the tub, forced through the mock shaving, then ducked over into the tub of water. At this point, the victim was often hosed or had buckets of water poured on him. Members of the crew who were roundly disliked or very unpopular would be given extra duckings, and would be subjected to various other tortures such as a rough haircut, taking pills made from sheep dung, or suffering the application of after-shave lotion made of white paint or chalk.[9] A certificate of baptism would excuse the sailor from such ceremonies in the future.

9. Henningsen, pp. 66–75.

English Settlement   *Bay of Omara.*

Nagasaki. View from the Road to Mogi Bay. 1862

'*Nagasaki – View from the Road to Mogi Bay*'.
Charles Cooper King. Watercolor.

This 1862 watercolor by Charles Cooper King, Royal Marine Artillery, of the general area of Nagasaki, combined with the watercolor 'Map of Fortifications of Nagasaki Habor' showing the number of guns, gun positions and the state of readiness, make it apparent that he was conducting an intelligence gathering mission.

Diplomacy

American and British naval officers were often called upon to serve as diplomatic representatives of their country, either informally, or sometimes, with quite formal appointments. Several items in the Collection surround the famous visit of Commodore Matthew Calbraith Perry to Japan in 1853 which lead to the Treaty of Kanagawa in 1854, opening that country to contact with the United States. An American attempt by Commodore James Biddle in 1846 had failed to break Japanese isolation.

A remarkable letter in the Collection from Commodore Perry to his wife, written 14 December, 1853 aboard the USS *Mississippi* at Madeira, gives insights into his state of mind as he was on his way to Japan.

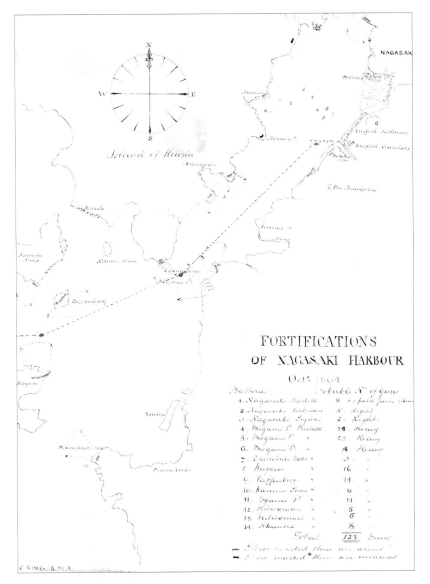

'Map of Fortifications of Nagasaki Harbour'.
Charles Cooper King. Watercolor.

Charles Cooper King prepared this detailed map of the fortification of Nagasaki harbor in 1864 showing the location of some 125 guns. The chart gives the operational capacity, the range of fire and angles of coverage of the weapons. Often ceremonial visits served to gather such military intelligence.

… it is to be hoped that Cap. McCluney on the *Powhatan* will soon follow me and that I may reach Japan by the 1st of May next… I still continue to anticipate success and look forward with much anxiety for the time when I shall enter upon the experiment of overcoming the restrictions which they seem so determined to enforce.... so far as the action of the President and his Cabinet have had to do with getting me aways and in vesting me with extraordinary powers, both diplomatic & naval, I ought to be satisfied, But the mal administration of the affairs connected with the equipment of the vessels has been very discreditable. nor can I be certain when the other ships are to be sent to me, or in fact whether they will be sent at all but I must do the best I can with what means they do send me.[10]

10. Holographic (handwritten and hand-signed) letter in the WH Collection, Matthew Calbraith Perry to Jane Perry, 14 December, 1852.

'Landing of Commodore Perry, Officers & Men of the Squadron.'
Artist − Heine. Lithograph, *c.*1855.

Following up on his discussions commenced in 1853, Commodore Perry returned to Japan and landed at Yokohama, 8 March, 1854 to meet the Imperial Commissioners. After three weeks of negotiations, he concluded a treaty of peace and amity with Japan. Note the number of American warships at anchor in the distance. After about two and a half centuries of isolation, this was the beginning of the opening of Japan to the western world.

As it turned out, other vessels joined Perry's *Mississippi* − the side-wheel steamer *Susquehanna* and the twenty-gun sloops *Plymouth* and *Saratoga*. The small fleet proved sufficient to impress the Japanese and to begin the process of opening up Japan to modern trade.

Perry and other officers had frequently combined visits to ports of call, the showing of the American flag, with other missions, such as the Anti-Slavery Squadron off the West African Coast in the 1840s, and many visits to South America, Europe, and the Far East throughout the nineteenth century. Exercising strict protocol in visits ashore, showing the power of US warships, while conducting peacetime expeditions or visits, required that naval officers be gentlemen not only in manners, but in education, knowledge of the world, and in respect for international customs.

The tradition of naval officers serving as diplomatic representatives continued into the twentieth century and to the present. Part of the job of naval officers in both the British and American navies has been to act as diplomats in many situations. Whether the negotiating of a treaty took place in the chambers of a local potentate, as in negotiations

Perry Scroll.
Japanese. Watercolor, mid-19th century.

Japanese artists painted a number of scrolls depicting the initial landing of Commodore Perry in Japan. This one shows a larger-than-life size Perry landing with his officers and men for a formal meeting with the two Princes, representing the Emperor, and the governor of Uraga. Perry delivered a letter from the American President.

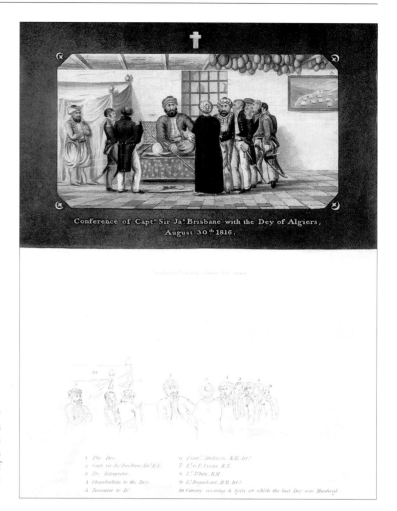

Conference, Captain Sir James Brisbane with the Dey of Algiers.
Hand-colored aquatint engraving.

This conference on 30 April, 1816 shows the diplomatic work of naval officers. The individuals, including the Dey's staff and the British officers are identified in an accompanying legend, which notes that the canopy conceals the sofa on which the Dey was later murdered. Activities of the Algerian corsairs continued off and on until the French took over the North African Coast in the 1830s.

The Signing and Sealing of the Treaty of Nanking.
Steel engraving.

This signing ceremony aboard a British warship, 29 August, 1842 was imposed upon the Chinese after their defeat in the first Opium War. The Chinese paid a 21 million pound indemnity and agreed to open their ports to the drug trade. They also ceded a lease to Hong Kong to the British under the treaty. The picture shows officers, diplomats and Chinese authorities meeting next to the implements of British power, the weapons of the gun deck.

The Great International Naval Review.
Chromolithograph.

This was held in New York Harbor in 1893 to celebrate the 400th Anniversary of Columbus discovering America. Another purpose of this American-hosted review was to show the world that the United States aspired to become a major naval power. Among the ships of the New Navy in the review were the *Yorktown, Atlanta and Dolphin.*

with the Dey of Algiers in 1816, or aboard ship, as in the case when the British secured the Treaty of Nanking in 1833, naval officers played a crucial role in British diplomacy. Officers of other navies also served as auxiliaries to the diplomatic corps, as a print in the Collection of a French officer visiting the Island of Timor, under Portuguese control, demonstrates.

Still another form of 'gunboat diplomacy' was the holding of international naval reviews. Naval ships of many nations during time of peace would gather to steam together, all flying their national colors, with many of them fully 'dressed' with flags. One such naval review held in the New York harbor with the ostensible function of celebrating the 400th anniversary of the first voyage of Columbus across the Atlantic, also served to announce to the other naval powers that America's New Navy had joined the club. Powered by steam, built of steel, and carrying turret-mounted guns, the US New Navy of the 1880s and 1890s implemented the ideas of Alfred Thayer Mahan, the leading advocate of sea-power.

Voyages by ships of this growing modern fleet to foreign ports to 'show the flag' soon demonstrated that the US had become a world power to be reckoned with. Departing from a foreign port on such a voyage might require the firing of a salute by the guns aboard the ship sailing out, sometimes answered by shore batteries or by other ships in the harbour. A naval ship departing from a distant port of call on a homeward bound voyage might display a lengthy 'homeward bound pennant', a narrow ribbon-like streamer flown from an aft mast, as long as forty feet or more.[11] Such banners would be lengthened, the longer the ship had been away from home.

Even trips of exploration could serve the dual purpose of demonstrating a nation's sea power. Captain Cook's three voyages to the Pacific in the 1760s and 1770s, the American Wilkes expedition, 1838-1842, and the circumnavigation of USS *Constitution* in 1844-46 served to show the flag and develop contacts, as well as to gather scientific and oceanographic information. The voyage of HMS *Challenger*, a sail-and-steam screw corvette, in the period 1872-1876, was another notable scientific expedition. Each expedition had official artists aboard the ships, leaving many fine records in original art work and in prints of diplomatic (and some not so diplomatic) encounters with peoples in far-flung regions of the world.

Captain Cook's encounters ran the gamut from peaceful exchanges and invitations to feasts ashore, to fully-fledged battles as natives of the New Hebrides islands attacked with arrows, darts and stones. Cook himself was killed in the last of the expeditions, in 1779 in Hawaii.

In one interesting encounter on 8 September, 1845, the USS *Constitution* met with a British Squadron in the China Sea between Macao and the Philippines. Since the last news received by the American commander suggested that US-British disputes had led the two countries to the verge of war, he cleared his decks for action. With fully loaded guns, Commodore Percival received aboard a representative of British Admiral Sir Thomas Cochrane. Percival asked, 'Is it peace or war?' The surprised Royal Naval officer replied, 'Why, peace, of course.' The dangerous moment passed, and the Americans were able to provide the British ships with desperately-needed supplies including four tons of bread and many gallons of whisky. Soon, visits between the ships resulted in some serious merry-making among the crews.[12]

Another encounter between naval ships off Samoa in March 1889 almost led to war. In what some took to be divine intervention, war was averted by a typhoon. The storm sank three German warships and two US ships, the *Trenton* and the *Vandalia*, had their bottoms ripped out by reefs and had to be destroyed A third US ship, the *Nipsic* went aground and had to be refloated. A British vessel, HMS *Calliope* was able to steam out of the anchorage

11. A homeward bound pennant in the WH Collection, from the *Eliza Adams*, is over forty feet long.
12. Watercolor sketch by Lt. John B. Dale, USN. September, 1845. WH Collection.

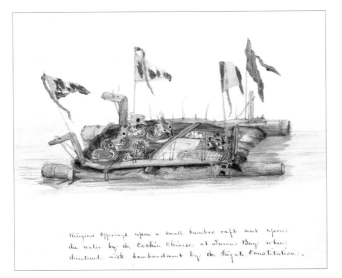

Dale Sketchbook: 'Religious Offerings upon a small bamboo raft sent upon the water by the Cochin Chinese at Turon Bay when threatened with bombardment by the Frigate Constitution.'

Lt. John B. Dale, who was the Fifth Lieutenant on the voyage of the USS *Constitution* circumnavigating the globe 1844-1846, kept a journal and created over eighty pencil and pen and ink drawings and watercolors. Dale wrote in his journal 'the day before the storm a singular "josh pigeon" or religious offering was taken up floating near the ship.' He further wrote 'whether this was committed to the deep by the poor fishermen of whom great numbers pass out and in the Bay every day to propitiate the Evil Spirits of the sea and to ward off the coming storm; or whether it was dispatched against the foreign "robbery ship", we are unable to decide.' The ship engaged in gunboat diplomacy, trying unsuccessfully to free a French clergyman, Fr. Lefevre, who was held hostage in Cochin China (Vietnam) in 1845.

Dale Sketchbook: Sugar Loaf Mountain.

One of the tasks during the US Exploring Expedition (1838-1842) was to take measurements and geodetic information. A small group, including Lt. John Dale, scaled Sugar Loaf Mountain at Rio de Janeiro without carrying along the instruments needed for taking the mountain's 'correct admeasurement'. Ordered by the expedition commander, Charles Wilkes, the chastened young men climbed Sugar Loaf again, this time lugging the proper apparatus.

From HMS Challenger. Sketch Book.

During the HMS *Challenger* Expedition, which conducted world-renowned scientific oceanographic research, B. Shephard painted a collection of watercolor sketches. A cooper, Shephard captured this scene as the men on the yardarms of HMS *Alfred* give three cheers for the *Challenger* on her way out of Halifax harbor, 19 May, 1873. The 2,300 ton corvette voyaged nearly 70,000 miles on her three and a half year round-the-world voyage, 1872-1876.

Samoan Hurricane of 1889.
Oil painting.

The Samoan hurricane of 1889 interrupted a moment of gunboat diplomacy that brought Germany and the United States close to blows. USS *Trenton* and USS *Vandalia* were so seriously damaged they were total losses. The US gunboat *Nipsic* was saved by beaching her. Three German warships were also completely destroyed but HMS *Calliope* survived by steaming to the open sea. The *Trenton* was the flagship of Rear Admiral L.A. Kimberly, commanding the Pacific Station. Following the storm, the three powers agreed to a tripartite protectorate over Samoa. In 1899, the islands were partitioned between and annexed by Germany and the United States.

and later provide assistance. The jurisdiction of the islands was peacefully settled with joint administration until 1899, when the islands were divided into American Samoa and Western Samoa, which remained a German colony until World War I.

Formal Parties Aboard

In addition to hosting formal visits from diplomats and naval officers from other nations, British and American naval ships often held dances, balls and large parties for visitors from shore, as well as less formal tours of the ship while in port. These occasions gave officers and men opportunities to show off their ship, and of course, would require that it be thoroughly cleaned up, with everything stowed in its proper place, and that the whole crew dress in their finest outfits. Ships visiting in ports sometimes even staged theatrical events, with rows of benches and chairs set up to accommodate a large audience. On some particularly noteworthy holidays, such as 4th July parties, the ship would be 'decked out' with bunting and American flags, and the ship's band would provide music for a formal dance. A lucky sailor might avail himself of the opportunity to make the acquaintance of a young lady of the port at such a gala event. In one illustration of such a party, we see an officer quietly chatting to some of the lady guests while he leans, in an attempt to appear nonchalant, on a cannon.

BALL SCENE ON BOARD THE MISSISSIPPI.

'Ball Scene on Board the USS Mississippi'.
Wood engraving.
Hand-colored.

On deck, naval officers in full dress uniforms gleaming with epaulets and braid, dance with ladies in evening gowns. The uniforms and gowns suggest a date in the mid-1850s. Bunting streaming from the masts could be for a Fourth of July celebration. One officer leans on the breech of a gun while he chats to the ladies. When in a port of call, a ship would reciprocate parties ashore with shipboard galas.

Decorating the ship and celebrating events such as Christmas and national holidays while at sea, even though no guests might come aboard, remained a tradition throughout the nineteenth century and to the present. Affixing holly to the topmast required some agility, and might be done even if there were no girls to come aboard for a kiss. Mess-captains, those who brought the meals from the galley to the separate mess-groups, would sometimes

Christmas Dinner.
Magazine illustration.

American sailors, about 1890, enjoy a special treat, plum-pudding.

Holly on the Masts, c.1885.
Chromolithograph.

Decorating the ship for holidays, especially Christmas, took many forms. Here, a young sailor, clinging with some confidence and bracing himself with a bare foot, ties holly to the top of the mainmast. He has already completed the decoration of the mast in the background.

Silver Basket.
Packet ship *Liverpool* – Captain Eldridge.

At the end of the maiden voyage of the packet ship *Liverpool* from New York to Liverpool in 1843, the passengers were so impressed they had this silver bowl appropriately engraved and presented it to Captain John Eldridge, 'a very popular commander.' The bowl was made in Birmingham and further engraved by Wordley and Mayer in Liverpool. The *Liverpool*, the first three-deck liner to be built, was laid down by Brown & Bell in New York and launched early in 1843. In its bows were ample and comfortable accommodations for the sailors: two 'cabins' – each thirty feet in length with plenty of light where they could read, sleep and mend their clothes without being cramped for room as they too often were on board merchant ships. Her figurehead was of Lord Liverpool carved by 'Dodge', probably the same artisan as one of the better known New York City figurehead carvers, Jeremiah Dodge, who by attribution also carved the figure 'Jack Tar'.

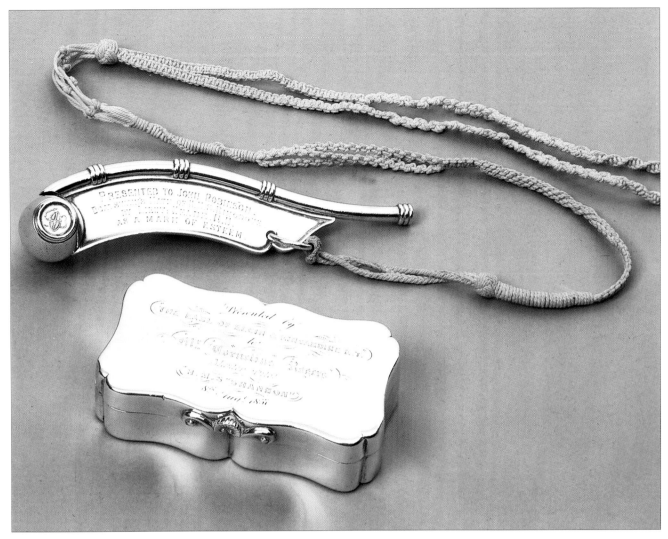

Bosun Whistle of J. Robinson, HMS Ringdove.
Snuff Box – Lord Elgin.

Silver gifts were presented in ceremonies to mark achievements of particular men and officers. Fine presentation items such as this bosun's whistle, given to Boatswain's Mate John Robinson of HMS *Ringdove* and the snuff box presented by Lord Elgin to Cornelius Ryan, Master Pilot of HMS *Shannon* (in India 1857) commemorated valor, skill or heroism. Robinson's whistle is engraved on one side: 'PRESENTED TO JOHN ROBINSON. BOATSWAIN'S MATE OF H.M.S. RINGDOVE BY LIEUT. HEANE. R.N. AS A MARK OF ESTEEM' and on the reverse is engraved a depiction of HMS *Ringdove*. The lanyard is a work of macramé art, combining nine different types of knots in a handsome display. Ryan was commended for successful piloting under dangerous circumstances. Lord Elgin, the donor of the box, was a diplomat and a son of Lord Elgin of Greek marble fame.

decorate the meals with flags on national holidays or sprigs of holly or other appropriate decoration at Christmas.

Traditions

Aboard both British and American naval ships, traditions ran deep. Some events and practices were governed by strictly established protocol such as the precise number of gun salutes required on different formal occasions, while other ceremonies were based on remembered traditions. Events in a ship's life, could lead to thousands attending a naval traditional ceremony, such as at the launching of HMS *Trafalgar* in 1841. Other ceremonies, governed

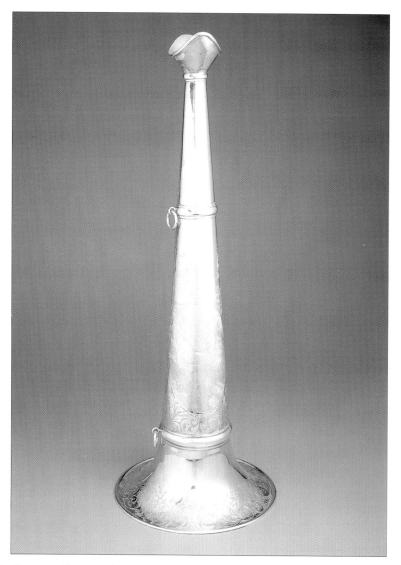

Silver Speaking Trumpet − Captain Robert Pierson − Steamship Philadelphia.

Captain Robert Pierson of the steamship *Philadelphia* performed so admirably during a 'fearful gale of July 1850' that the passengers presented him with this beautifully engraved silver speaking trumpet. The inscription includes: 'with the hope that his life may be preserved for future usefulness continuing his trust in God who guides the whirlwind and directs the storm.' In one panel the sail and steam ship is engraved in a setting of high winds and lightning. The passengers were on their way from New York to Panama on the first leg of a trip to the newly-discovered gold fields in California.

by both informal custom and formal protocol included such events as the daily raising and lowering of the national flag, or a funeral at sea. Visitors to a ship broke the routine, and ship-visits became the occasions for appropriate salutes, decorations, and once in a while, a party that a shipboard artist might try to capture for posterity. Images of all such rituals help us come to understand how both American and British tars recognized the special moments aboard ship and ashore that stood out from the everyday routines.

Launching of HMS Trafalgar *in 1841.*
Hand-colored lithograph.

Keel laying, launching and stepping the masts of major ships could all be the occasion of major ceremonies. In this launching of HMS *Trafalgar* at the Woolwich Dock Yard, the ship has yet to have its masts stepped. The crowd of thousands includes men and women of all classes, sailors manning the yardarms of a ship, and others climbing aloft simply for a good view of the event. There are a number of side-wheel steamboats portrayed in the print.

THE PIRATES.—Drawn by M. Biard.—[See Page 463.]

The Pirates.
Hand-colored wood engraving.

In this illustration, published 20 July, 1861, the pirates deceive their prey by having a fiddler stand on a keg while a pirate disguised as a woman and a man in a top hat wave from the railing. The other desperadoes crouch out of sight with their weapons, ready to attack.

(Opposite) *'Abordage du Triton par le Corsaire le Hasard'.*
Steel engraving, hand-colored, *c.*1830.

Boarding scenes were often painted, as artists tried to catch the confusion of hand-to-hand combat when naval forces overcame pirates or when two navies clashed at sea. In this French print, more than forty men struggle with boarding axes, pistols, muskets, lances, knives and their bare hands, while the smoke of the large guns obscures part of the deck.

CHAPTER NINE

Sailors Outside the Law

The very nature of sailing at sea granted a special kind of freedom from the laws which applied on land. Once a ship sailed over the horizon, it became a small and usually orderly fragment of the human social order, operating in isolation. Aboard naval ships, the rules and regulations, enforced through discipline bound the officers and men. Aboard merchant and whaling ships, the crew's obedience to the shipping articles of the ship's company, to government rules and regulations, and to the customs of the sea governed behavior. However, the reach of the laws imposed by governments was limited by those governments' powers to enforce the laws.

If the crew and officers undertook to break any laws which prevailed in the nation of their home port, or any other nation, their isolation at sea gave them a measure of freedom to do so. The laws of nations could have little effect on a rogue ship, and then only if another armed ship, serving as an enforcer, were to impose the will of a state. For such basic reasons, the history of the age of sail is full of stories of mutineers, pirates, smugglers, privateers and a wide variety of outlaws of the sea. Privateers were privately-owned armed merchant ships commissioned by a government to make war upon its enemies, earning a profit from any ships it might capture as 'prizes'. In the Caribbean, piracy flourished in the seventeenth and early eighteenth century. In waters off the Mediterranean coast of North Africa, warships continued to raid the ships of Christian nations throughout the 1820s. In other regions of the world, such as the South China Sea off south-east Asia, pirate activity continued well into the twentieth century. Many law-abiding seamen and officers who did not join in mutiny, piracy, smuggling or privateering found their lives often touched by the outlaws of the sea.

Pirates

The lives of pirates have been the subject of romantic fiction and great exaggeration. Fiction and fact are so interwoven in popular memory, that it has long been difficult to sort out one from the other. Throughout the nineteenth century, legend and fact often could not be distinguished in prose, poetry, song and art. However, several reliable primary sources, together with careful scholarly work in recent years, particularly by David Cordingly and Marcus Rediker, allow the modern reader to begin to separate fact from legend and fiction.

In the 1600s, French settlers on the island of Tortuga, off the north coast of the large island of Hispaniola in the Caribbean, made their living either on a few plantations, or hunting wild cows and wild boars in the rugged interior mountains. The hunters dried and smoked the meat into 'boucan', and they came to be known as 'buccaneers'. As the Spanish sought to impose control over the island, the buccaneers took up private raiding against the Spanish, and soon discovered that fortunes could be made by capturing treasure ships and, later, by raiding settlements on the Spanish 'Main', the mainland of Central and South America.

One Dutchman who had been sold into indentured servitude in the islands, took up travelling with the buccaneers in the 1670s, and later wrote a careful account of his adventures. Alex Oliver Exquemelin's *De Americanensche Zeerovers* was soon translated into German, Spanish, English, and other languages. The English edition, *Esquemeling, the Buccaneers of America* was first printed in 1684, and immediately became a best-seller, apparently starting the Western world's fascination with literature about pirates. Esquemeling (as the British spelled his name) inspired authors like Defoe, and later, Robert Louis Stevenson and others to write fanciful accounts of pirate adventures at sea. A twentieth-century edition of Esquemeling, brought out in 1923, faithfully provided a factual account of many early rogues of the sea.[1]

The buccaneers included men like François L'Olonnais, who raided the Spanish settlements of Lake Maracaibo in Venezuela, murdering inhabitants and holding others for ransom. The buccaneers, after a successful raid, would return to Tortuga with several hundred thousand pieces of eight, each worth the equivalent of some $23 in modern currency.[2]

According to the 'Articles of Association' these pirates established, they would divide the

1. William Swan Stallybrass, ed., *Esquemeling – The Buccaneers of America* (New York: E.P Dutton, 1923). The copy in the WH Collection is undated, but Dutton, in New York, and Routledge, in Britain, published the edition in 1923.
2. David Cordingly, *Under the Black Flag: The Romance and the Reality of Life Among the Pirates* (New York: Random House, 1995), pp. 35-36.

Wild Heroes of the Seas.
Wood engraving.

This illustration shows twelve separate prints which decorated an 1868 poster announcing the publication of a popular account of piracy by D.M. Kelsey. The illustrations covered a range of scenes, from Lieutenant Maynard defeating Blackbeard, a depiction of Sir Henry Morgan, the 'Great Buccaneer', to an oft-repeated legend, never substantiated, that pirates made their victims 'walk the plank'. The Kelsey book, however, in the romantic tradition of glorifying pirate actions, mixed fact and fiction in describing the 'Rogue Rovers of the Ocean'.

Piratical Barbarity.
Wood engraving with letterpress.

For passengers and crew alike, a continuing hazard of the sea remained attack from pirates. Here, Miss Lucretia Parker prays for her own life and the life of officers and crew, as pirates dispatch the last three surviving members of the crew of ten of the English sloop *Eliza Ann*, 12 March, 1825. Miss Parker's account of the tragedy was published as a broadside, with a 38-stanza verse that gave lurid details. The picture is at the moment reflected in these lines:

> Upon my bended knees to Him I raised
> My supplicate prayer, summissively did bow
> While steadfastly on me the Pirates' Chieftain gaz'd
> And for reasons most vile, withheld the fatal blow.

Ten coffins represent the murdered crew. After her rescue, Miss Parker's account, in the form of a broadside, made for exciting reading. The Pirate's vile reasons were never made explicit.

(Left) *Captain George Lowther and his Company at Port Mayo in the Gulph of Matique.*
Engraving.

On 14 September, 1723, a sloop, commanded by Captain George Lowther with thirty or forty pirates on board, captured the *Princess Galley* near Barbados. The pirates seized more than fifty-four ounces of gold, gun powder, pistols, gunner's stores, bosun's stores, two quarter deck guns, two swivel guns and eleven black slaves. Two seamen were forced to join the pirate crew – the surgeon's mate and the carpenter's mate. Two other members of the merchant ship's crew decided to join the pirates of their own accord. Shortly after this attack, officials sent a sloop to the island of Blanco to round up pirates. Lowther committed suicide and was found dead with a pistol by his side. In 1724, a Court of Admiralty was held at St Kitts and the remnants of Lowther's crew were put on trial. The two sailors from the *Princess Galley* who had voluntarily become pirates were reprieved. On 20 March, eleven pirates were hanged.

(Right) *Captain Edward England.*
Engraving.

Edward England was a notorious 18th century pirate operating in the Atlantic. In 1719 he sailed the West Coast of Africa in the *Royal James*, seizing nine ships, the captured vessels ranging from twelve guns to two guns and an average size of a crew of sixteen men.

ANN MILLS,
(Served on Board the Maidstone Frigate)

Ann Mills, pirate.
Engraving, 18th century.

The number of women who disguised themselves as men and went to sea as sailors appears to be relatively few although exact proof is very difficult. Two of the most famous women who became pirates were Ann Bonny and Mary Read. Mary Read enlisted aboard a man-of-war, then became a soldier and later sailed in a Dutch ship for the West Indies where she was captured by pirates and became one of them. Ann Bonny ran away to the Caribbean where she joined a band of pirates that included Mary Read. The leader of the band was Calico Jack Rackham. One day in 1720, Ann Bonny, Mary Read and Calico Jack were captured. They were imprisoned and tried at Jamaica where all three were sentenced to death. Rackham was hanged and the two women escaped the gallows because they were pregnant. Ann Mills went to sea as a common sailor about 1740 aboard the frigate *Maidstone* during the war of Austrian succession. The print shows her holding the cut-off head of a French enemy she had slain in hand-to-hand combat.

loot according to strict principles, with each individual pirate getting a single share, their elected captain five or six shares, and boys getting a half share. Any pirate who had lost a limb or an eye would receive a fixed compensation, for example 600 pieces of eight for a lost arm, prior to the division of the spoils. Esquemeling decried the fact that buccaneers spent their fortunes in a few days or weeks in the brothels and taverns of Tortuga. Only a few captains had the foresight to buy plantations or set themselves up as legitimate merchants, to settle into a more regular life on their vast loot.[3]

In the early eighteenth century, pirates entered their 'Golden Age', infesting the Atlantic Ocean and Caribbean Sea from 1699 to about 1724. In that year, the Royal Navy largely stamped them out. Sometimes the pirates of this period offered the crews of merchant ships the option of joining their own crews or death. Many chose to join, and the numbers of mutineers and captured crews soon swelled the total number of pirates into the thousands.

Two famous women pirates, Mary Read and Anne Bonny, sailed with the pirate crew of Captain John Rackham. They were captured and tried in Jamaica in 1720. Both women were pregnant when tried, and were thus reprieved from the hangman's noose, but Mary Read died in prison a few months after the trial. There is no record of what happened to Anne Bonny. Both women dressed in men's clothing, especially during engagements with other ships, and both had been raised as boys. Their stories suggest that among the pirates, and among ordinary merchant sailors, there may have been many more 'cross-dressing'

3. William Swan Stallybrass, ed., *Esquemeling – The Buccaneers of America* (New York: E.P Dutton, 1923), pp. 60 and 75.

Boarding a Ship.
Oval oil painting. Early 19th century.

This oil painting depicts a sailor and a Barbary corsair in hand-to-hand combat.

women, disguised as men, who were never found out.[4]

While the pirates of the Caribbean and South Atlantic coast were known as buccaneers, pirates of the Mediterranean were called corsairs. Corsairs usually sailed with commissions from the rulers of Moslem states on the northern coast of Africa, with permission to attack all Christian ships in the region. Despite the efforts of European navies, and beginning in 1803, the United States Navy, to suppress these 'Barbary Pirates', they continued their depredations until 1816, when a combined Anglo-Dutch fleet bombarded Algiers. Scattered activities of corsairs continued to harass shipping until the French began their conquest of the region in the 1830s and 1840s.[5]

The exploits of the United States Navy in engaging the Barbary Pirates led to several heroic paintings of the battles. In the Collection, a watercolor of the *Louisa* of Philadelphia, reminds one of French privateers in the Mediterranean. Captain William Bainbridge ran the US frigate *Philadelphia* onto a reef in pursuit of corsairs off the North African coast, 31 October, 1803. She could not be worked free. When attacked by Tripolitan forces, the *Philadelphia* could not bring her guns to bear and Bainbridge surrendered. On 16 February, 1804, leading a group of eighty volunteers disguised as Maltese sailors in *Intrepid*, which

4. Cordingly, pp. 56–65.
5. Cordingly, xviii.

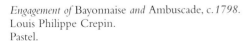

Louisa *of Philadelphia by Antoine Roux, père (Sr.).*

This armed letter-of-marque brig flying the American flag dealt with French privateers out of Algesiras near Gibraltar in 1800. Under the leadership of a daring young first mate, the vessel repelled the privateers' attack witnessed by thousands ashore at Gibraltar. The adventure was recounted in Fenimore Cooper's *The History of the Navy.* The watercolor, painted by Antoine Roux, Sr. in Marseille, probably dates from before 1806.

Engagement of Bayonnaise *and* Ambuscade, *c.1798.*
Louis Philippe Crepin.
Pastel.

This attack by the French privateer *Bayonnaise* on the British privateer *Ambuscade*, during the Napoleonic Wars, shows a typical tactic of boarding. Crossing the bowsprit of the attacking vessel across the deck of the victim, raiders would use it as a pathway to attack. Here the attack on the *Ambuscade* is in full fury with the French the eventual winners of this engagement. This was a study for a large oil painting of a full view of both vessels now hanging in the Musée de la Marine in Paris.

Preparation for War to Defend Commerce.
Engraving, hand colored, *c.*1800.

To help protect American commerce, especially against depredations of Barbary pirates, merchants in various coastal American cities raised subscriptions to build warships. The frigate *Philadelphia* was built in the Humphrey's Yard near Old Swedes Church in Philadelphia and launched in 1799. The *Philadelphia*, under the command of Captain William Bainbridge and while pursuing a Tripolitan ship, ran aground on a reef. Being unable to train her guns properly to fight, Bainbridge surrendered his ship. The Tripolitans later freed her and moved her inside Tripoli Harbor. He and the crew spent nineteen months in Bashaw's Prison.

carried a Mediterranean rig, Stephen Decatur set fire to *Philadelphia* in the harbor of Tripoli. Admiral Nelson called the raid 'the most daring naval exploit of the age.'

In the Far East, pirates abounded in the waters of the South China Sea and the islands of the East Indies. The earliest American 'China Traders' from Salem, Massachusetts, sought the protection of US naval forces in raiding and dispersing the settlements of the pirates of the region. A log in the Collection details the 1832 punitive raid by the US frigate *Potomac* on Quallah Battoo, in retribution for an earlier lethal attack by pirates based there on the US merchant ship *Friendship*, engaged in the Sumatra pepper trade out of Salem. The American warship bombarded the town, which contained several fortified wooden compounds, effectively wiping out the stronghold by killing some 150 natives and burning out the forts and town.[6]

6. See also James Duncan Phillips, *Pepper and Pirates: Adventures in the Sumatra Pepper Trade of Salem* (Boston: Houghton Mifflin, 1949), pp. 91-102.

Burning of the Frigate Philadelphia.
Oil painting. Early 19th century.

In this image, the raiding US volunteers aboard the Mediterranean-rigged *Intrepid* can be seen as they set fire to the US frigate *Philadelphia*, 16 February, 1804. For his leadership in the raid, Stephen Decatur was promoted to the rank of Captain, the youngest man ever to achieve that rank in the US Navy.

Action of Quallah Battoo, As Seen From The Potomac… *Feb. 5, 1832.*
Aquatint. (Illustration opp. p.120 'Voyage of the United States Frigate *Potomac'.* Reynolds. New York: Harper & Brothers. 1835.)

Malay nations of Quallah Battoo in 1831 plundered a Salem trader *Friendship* and murdered part of her crew. The US Frigate *Potomac* was sent on a punitive expedition.

Wiert Adels.
Mezzotint engraving. Latter 18th century.

This engraving of Wiert Adels was done by the mezzotint master Charles Howard Hodges (1764-1837) after a drawing by Jacobus Perkois (1756-1804). The text on the print reads (translated from the Dutch): 'Steersman of the Dutch koff "The Blossoming Blossom", which sailed from this shore, after the French had captured his ship, by great bravura he made himself master and brought the ship into Hellevoet on the 5th of August.' He was actually steersman for a ship which was bringing grain from the Baltic port of Libau. A Duinkerk privateer seized his ship on the 1st of August. By this act of 'great bravura' he managed to seize the chief of the privateers and throw him overboard. Thus he managed to bring his ship into Hellevoetsluis.

Nicolaas Jarry.
Engraving. Latter 18th century.

This engraving of Nicolas (or Nicolaas) Jarry was done by Pieter Willem Jan van Megan (1750-1785) and Matheus de Sallieth (1749-1791) also after a drawing by Jacobus Perkois. The text reads (translated from Dutch): 'Nicolaas Jarry Captain of the Vlissingen privateer "The Vlissinger."' Jarry was also a folk hero, having seized more than fifty vessels in the course of a colorful career. After taking five prizes in January 1783, he was about to seize a sixth when another English frigate came alongside. In order to spare his crew from destruction he ran up the flag but just at that moment he received a deadly wound. After two painful days, he died.

Privateers

During time of war, an armed ship, fitted out by a private owner, would serve as type of contract warrior. A privateer was issued a license. Under the agreement, a privateer would seize merchant ships of the enemy, and be entitled to a proportion of the value of the ship and cargo, with a set proportion returning to the sovereign whose flag the ship flew. Some merchant ships would be granted 'letters of marque and reprisal', which allowed them to seize ships of their nation's enemy if they encountered them in the course of their regular trading.[7]

A privateer would be operating, in one sense, within the law, while a pirate, with no such agreement, operated beyond the law. Yet in practice, the two types of marauding at sea could be very similar – some seventeenth century buccaneers sailed under agreements with the

7. The distinction between privateers and merchant ships under letters of marque and reprisal is detailed in David J. Starkey, *British Privateering Enterprise in the Eighteenth Century*, (Exeter, University of Exeter Press, 1990), pp. 19-31.

Pigou *and* L'Aventure.
Oil Painting, *c.*1793.

In 1793, England and France went to war. The French privateer *L'Aventure*, stopped the Philadelphia-built ship, *Pigou*, on her way to Mauritius, probably claiming she was carrying English goods. One way or another, *Pigou* made two voyages to Canton, China in the latter 1790s. Her captain on one voyage was Richard Dale who had been John Paul Jones' First Lieutenant in the victory of *Bonhomme Richard* over the HMS *Serapis* in the American Revolution. On another voyage her master was John Green, Jr., a son of the captain of the *Empress of China*, the first American flag vessel to reach China (1784).

French government or with the governments of island colonies; often privateers would continue to operate during time of peace, technically acting as pirates, yet they would sometimes be protected by the nation or colony under whose flag they operated.

The famous pirate Henry Morgan (1635-1688) operated as a privateer against the Spanish, under a commission granted by the Colonial Council of Jamaica. Although the Spanish had authorized attacks on British possessions in the Caribbean, Britain and Spain were officially at peace during the period of Morgan's raids on Panama and his other depredations against the Spanish in 1670-71. The British, to preserve good relations with the Spanish, had Morgan arrested and brought to Britain. But after two years, he was knighted, returned to the Caribbean, and was appointed Lieutenant Governor of Jamaica. Whether Morgan was a

PAUL JONES THE PIRATE

'Paul Jones, The Pirate'.
Engraving, c.1800.

A naval hero to the Americans, the British saw John Paul Jones as little more than a pirate, especially for his lightning raids against British ports. This picture was clearly a form of propaganda as Jones never employed the skull and crossbones as an emblem. Jones started life as a sailor by the name of John Paul in Scotland. After an altercation in the West Indies where he claimed he killed a man in self-defense, he changed his name to John Paul Jones.

privateer, a pirate, or a respected citizen was not only a matter of national viewpoint, but subject to the changing state of Spanish-British relations.[8]

The line between pirates and private naval forces, which could enlist in the support of a national cause, remained blurred in many other periods of conflict as well. During the American Revolution, a French privateer *Calonne*, captained by an Irishman, Luke Ryan, seized a merchant brig, *Nancy,* of Aberdeen. Ryan was captured by a British ship and taken to London for trial on the charge of piracy. His case was complex, for he had served for a period as a privateer for the British. Although convicted of piracy, it was because he was Irish and therefore a British subject. The British court sentenced him to hang, and he was awaiting execution when the Treaty of Paris ended the Revolutionary War. A few days later, Ryan and members of his crew were pardoned. He was never able to collect his prize moneys from the French, however, and died in debtors' prison in 1789.[9]

Jean Lafitte, who maintained a fleet of pirate ships operating off the Gulf Coast in the 1810s from Barataria Bay, was suspected of complicity with the British and was attacked by US Naval forces during the War of 1812. However, he volunteered his forces to assist in the United States' defeat of the British at the Battle of New Orleans in 1815. After the war, he moved his headquarters outside of US jurisdiction, to Galveston Bay in Texas, and died there about 1825. Like others, Lafitte was defined as pirate or as patriotic freebooter, depending on one's national

8. Cordingly, pp. 42-55.
9. Donald A. Petrie, 'The Piracy Trial of Luke Ryan,' *The American Neptune* (Summer, 1995) pp. 185–294.

USS Kearsarge *vs. CSS* Alabama.
Chromolithograph, *c.*1880.

The *Alabama*, a screw sloop with sails, was built for the Confederate government by an English shipbuilding company in Liverpool. Fitted out as a cruiser, she was commanded by Captain Raphael Semmes. She successfully cruised for twenty-one months, capturing sixty-nine vessels worth six and a half million dollars. Having to leave the neutral port of Cherbourg, France, she steamed out 19 June, 1864 and was met by the *Kearsage*. After an hour's battle, the spirited and deadly cannonading of the *Kearsage* sank the *Alabama*.

viewpoint, and also depending upon the politics of the moment.

During the Civil War in the United States, the British outfitted several ships for the Confederate Navy, which the Union side defined as 'British Pirate ships'. Thus the *Alabama*, finally tracked down and defeated by the USS *Kearsage* off the coast of France, was treated in the Northern press, as the 'Pirate *Alabama*'. The privateer *Savannah*, operating out of Charleston, South Carolina, was captured by the US brig *Perry*, and the crew brought to New York where they were tried for piracy. The trial resulted in a hung jury, and the prisoners were later quietly traded for captured Union troops.[10]

Maritime nations agreed at the Treaty of Paris of 1856 to declare privateering illegal, but the Confederate States of America were not a party to that treaty. Privateering had played a significant part in many wars in the age of sail, particularly for Americans in the American Revolution and the War of 1812.

10 Ernest A. McKay, 'Privateer or Pirate,' *Seaport: New York's History Magazine*, Fall 1997, pp. 16-21.

Smugglers

The distinction between a merchant ship and a smuggler, like that between privateer and pirate, was after all, a distinction imposed by one nation and often rejected or ignored by others. Under a range of policies collectively called 'mercantilism' by historians, each of the eighteenth century European empires tried to restrict trade with its colonies and among them, to ships of their own empire. Laws would prohibit the manufacture of certain goods in the colonies that could be produced in the home country, and import duties on goods would effectively bar them from some colonies. Thus, the British imposed high duties on sugar imported to New England from Spanish or French colonies in the Caribbean. Perfectly respectable Dutch or British merchants would trade to Hispaniola, and be regarded by the Spanish as a smuggler. In the British colonies of North America, as well as in the Caribbean colonies, British subjects often ignored the rules imposed by Spain and France prohibiting their ships from trading with their possessions.

Even within the empires, rules and regulations imposed by the European power would frequently be ignored. John Hancock, who signed the Declaration of Independence so boldly, was proud to be known as the most important 'Sugar Smuggler' in Boston. The colonists' protests against the Tea Act with the 'Boston Tea Party', as well as similar raids dumping East India Company Tea overboard in other ports along the Atlantic Seaboard in 1773, led to the closing of the Port of Boston. Such clashes lead up to the War of Independence.

The British issued explicit rules regarding the imports of 'spirits, tea, tobacco, or snuff' to the British Isles. A set of Acts of Parliament, compiled and issued in 1807, spelled out the specifics. With exceptions for small amounts to be used by crews and officers for their own personal needs, all such commodities aboard ships within a few miles of the coasts of Britain or the Channel Islands had to be properly documented, or be subject to seizure and confiscation. Ships at anchor, or 'hovering' near the coast, were to be regarded as 'runners of foreign goods'.[11]

Smuggling during the eighteenth century was no minor infringement confined to a few outcasts of the sea. Rather, because of the strict mercantilist rules imposed by France, Britain, and Spain, the natural flow of trade between markets was severely constricted. The rules were regularly violated. While the ruling power would regard such violations as smuggling, traders recognized that in order to make a profit they would have to ignore the laws, bribe port officials, and carry goods from areas where they could be purchased cheaply and sell them where they were dear. The dividing line between a legitimate trader and a smuggler, like that between privateer and pirate, remained a matter of viewpoint.

Although the Chinese empire in the nineteenth century prohibited the importation of opium, only a few other foreign products, such as ginseng and silver specie, could find a market in China. British and French merchants traded opium for silk, porcelain, and other Chinese products. British traders and the Royal Navy enforced the right to trade freely in that commodity in the Opium Wars of 1839-42 and 1856-60. What was smuggling from the Chinese viewpoint was free trade from the European viewpoint.

11. *Abstracts of Acts of Parliament empowering officers and men in his majesty's service to seize smuggling vessels and smuggled goods.* 1807, p. 15. Pamphlet, in WH Collection.

Slave Traders

In the seventeenth and eighteenth century, Spain prohibited Spanish ships from engaging in the trade in slaves from Africa to their islands. However, they granted the 'Asiento', the privilege to trade in this human cargo to their islands, to British and other foreign traders. Thus, the slave trade for British and Colonial American traders was a perfectly legal business in the eighteenth century during periods of peace, from the point of view of both Spain and Britain. In the late eighteenth century, British reformers pressed to outlaw the practice, partly on moral grounds. Whig politicians also hoped to diminish the power of Tories, some of whose support came from families with large estates in the British West Indies, dependent on a supply of new slaves from Africa to maintain their holdings.

The Americans outlawed the slave trade in 1807, and the British in 1808, and henceforth, what had been a legal merchant trade became a dangerous, illegal, and even more frightfully inhumane form of smuggling. After peace was restored at the end of the Napoleonic wars and the War of 1812, both the British and the American navies sent forces to the coast of Africa to attempt to interdict the continuing trade. Both the Royal Navy and the American West African Squadron became international enforcers of the growing European disapproval of the slave trade. The American Congress declared the slave trade piracy in the 1820s, as the approved punishment. However, the United States hanged none of the slave traders they caught until 1861.[12]

Most of the Spanish colonies had declared their independence by the 1820s, and the new republics soon abolished slavery. Spain still held Cuba, Puerto Rico, and Santo Domingo, and retained slavery there until the 1870s. The planters on those islands still eagerly sought slaves. Spain agreed to allow both British and American ships to stop suspected slave trading vessels flying the flags of Spain. Denmark, Holland and other European powers, as well as most of the independent republics of the Western Hemisphere, also agreed to allow ships flying their flags to be stopped by British or American naval ships on suspicion of slave trading. Even Portugal, which allowed slavery in Brazil until 1888, agreed to the outlawing of the international slave trade across the Atlantic, and permitted British and American ships to inspect Portuguese ships for slave smuggling.

If such a ship were carrying slaves, the naval officers would impound the ship, sometimes turn over the officers and crew to a representative of the government of the nation whose flag they flew, and then free any slaves aboard. A slave ship might carry several hundred slaves, purchased at trading stations along the coast of West Africa, from as many as a dozen different trading stations scattered along several hundred miles of African coast, and it was impossible to return them individually to their home villages or regions.

The Royal Navy deposited most of its 'recaptives' in Sierra Leone, a colony established for freed slaves from Britain and for American blacks who had fought on the British side in the American Revolution. By the early 1800s, the settlement at Freetown, Sierra Leone, was beginning to expand with landings of recaptives.

12. Rodney Carlisle, *Prologue to Liberation: A History of Black People in America* (Appleton Century Crofts, 1971).

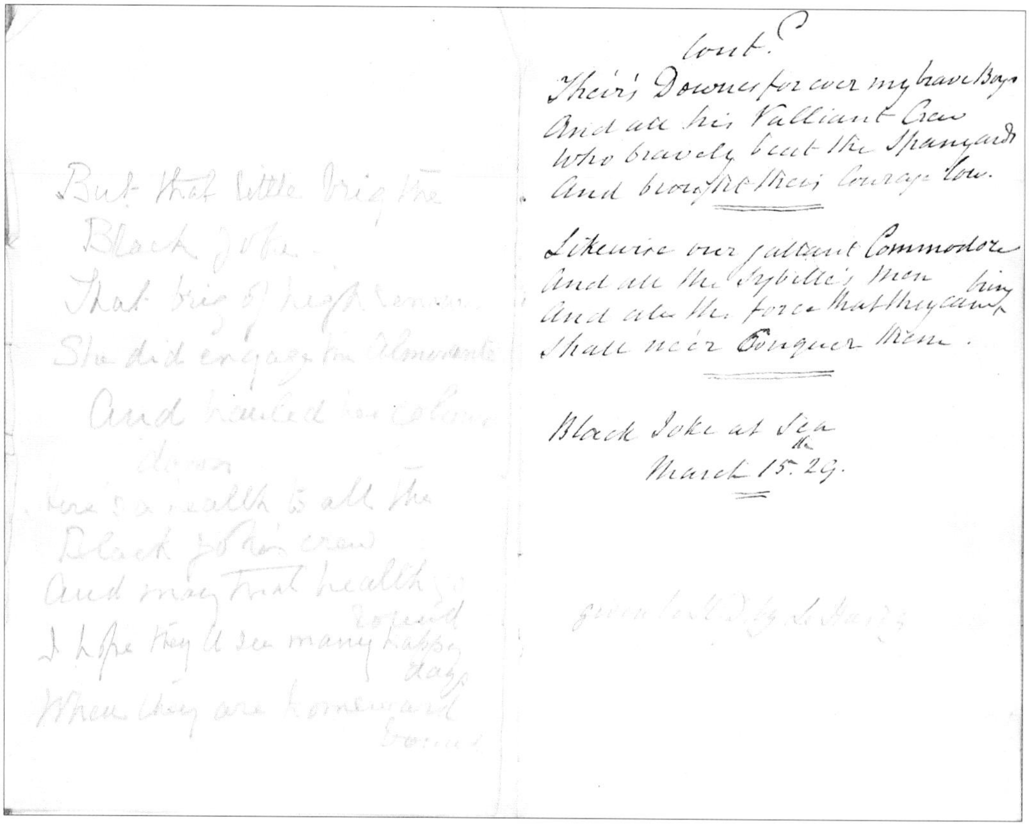

Log of HMS Black Joke.

The smooth log of the *Black Joke* provides a full account of the engagement shown opposite. Manned with only fifty-seven officers and crew, the ship subdued the Spanish slaver *El Almirante* with eighty officers and men aboard, freeing 467 slaves. The British officers and men divided a reward fee for the slaves released at Sierra Leone. (WH Collection)

[Handwritten log, left column:]

But that little brig the
Black Joke.
That brig of high renown
She did engage the Almirante
And hauled her colours down
Here's a health to all the
Black Joke's crew
And may [find?] health
I hope they'll see many happy days
When they are homeward bound

[Handwritten log, right column:]

cont.
Their's Downes for ever my brave Boys
And all his Valliant Crew
Who bravely beat the Spaniard
And brought their courage low.

Likewise our gallant Commodore
And all the Sybille's men
And all the force that they can bring
Shall ne'er Conquer them.

Black Joke at Sea
March 15th 29.

In the 1830s and 1840s, the US Navy's West African Squadron, once commanded by Commodore Matthew C. Perry, made a practice of taking its recaptives to the colony of Liberia, next to Sierra Leone. Liberia had been established by the American Colonization Society as a haven for freed American slaves and the Society struggled to maintain the colony through the period 1821-1848. In 1848, Liberia became an independent republic, and the fledgling nation also worked to stop the slave trade. Recaptives from slave ships landed in Liberia settled on the outskirts of the capital city of Monrovia, in a location the older settlers from America called 'Congotown', after the diverse Africans who settled there.

For both the American Navy and the Royal Navy, however, interdiction of the slave trade in the period 1820s through the 1850s was a difficult and dangerous mission. The coast of Africa was plagued with disease, especially malaria, that added to the other perils of the sea. Slave trading ships were often well armed, and sometimes fought back when cornered. More often, they would simply try to out-sail any warship they encountered and escape over the horizon.

HMS *Black Joke*

The British, American, and even the Liberian governments would use captured slave ships, emptied of their slave cargoes and outfitted as pursuit vessels, as part of the enforcement fleets against the slavers. The British at first sold the captured slave ships at auction, allowing some of them to be purchased by naval officers to augment the naval ships they already commanded. The officers hoped to increase their prize money, so such private investments sometimes returned a profit.[13]

One such captured brig, the *Black Joke*, sailed under Royal Navy colors, with Lieutenant Henry Downes in command. The brig, manned with fifty-seven officers and crew, served as a 'tender' to the HMS *Sybille* which headed a British anti-slavery squadron operating

13. W.E.F. Ward, *The Royal Navy and the Slavers* (New York: Pantheon, 1969), p. 128.

HM brig Black Joke *engaging the Spanish slave brig* El Almirante *in the Bight of Benin, 1 February, 1829.*
Hand-colored aquatint.

This highly accurate hand-colored etching depicts the engagement between the *Black Joke* and the slaver *El Almirante*. The *Black Joke* had been purchased at auction by the commander of the Royal Navy squadron and converted from its prior role as a transport for slaves, into an adjunct to the ant-slavery force. *El Almirante* carried ten 18-pounder cannon, the *Black Joke* only one long 18 pounder and a 12 pounder carronade. After a thirty-one hour chase and a close action of one hour and twenty minutes, the *Black Joke*, despite its lighter armament, bested the slave ship. The entry in the smooth log of the *Black Joke* shows that during the battle, the two ships were sometimes 'within a biscuit's throw' of each other.

along the coast of what is now the nation of Nigeria, in the late 1820s. On 1 February, 1829, Downes led a successful thirty-one hour chase and an eighty minute battle against the Spanish slave ship, the *Almirante*. The *Almirante*, crewed with eighty officers and men, carried 467 slaves, ten eighteen-pounder guns, and four long nine-pounders. The *Almirante* had the smaller *Black Joke* well out-gunned, as the British brig only carried one long eighteen-pounder, one twelve-pounder carronade, and a small pivot gun mounted on the rail.

A fine print in the Collection depicts the engagement. The Collection also includes the smooth log of the station duty for 1827-1829 of the *Black Joke*, kept by Lieutenant Downes. After ordering 'sweeps' or oars in the chase, and following the slave ship all night, the crew were able to maneuver the *Black Joke* to within close gunshot range of the slaver. The story of the overnight chase and gun duel with the Almirante is best told in Lieutenant Downes' own words:

> ... am 6:30 a heavy squall. Brig well tried stood on her legs like a Briton. ...daylight saw a brig SSE 8 or 9 miles standing to the southward and a press of sail made all sail in chase. 9:30 out sweeps which were kept going till nearly sunset. At noon we c[oul]d make out chase distinctly to be the Almirante. Between 4 and 5 o'clock fired several shot to bring her to. 5:30 chase loose and gave us his broadside and stood away from us. [We] kept firing at him until dusk and kept co[mpany] with him till daylight. He trying evry possible maneuver to steal away.
>
> Daylight light aires. Almirante and Black Joke nearly becalmed within 1 1/2 mile of each other. ...in the course of the night we repeatedly passed each other within musket shot, but did not exchange shots during the night. At 130 o'clock in the afternoon a light breeze sprung up, when on hauling to the wind on the [starboard] tack brought the chase into our wake, tacked to take up a position on his [aft] quarter. We passed each other within half gunshot...
>
> Tacked again and caged away, then under all plain sail, royals, flying jib, etc. When he saw that we had the best of, and were nearing, him, he swung round, up colours and gave his broadside. [We] gave him three cheers, hoisted the Union Jack at the fore, the blue ensign at main and blue ensign at peak and kept the pivot gun/18pdr/and carronade 12 pdr at work at him; small arms men ordered to lay as flat as flounders; kept caging away to near him, he weaving and working at us with his round and grape.
>
> At about 3:30 we were so close to him that I gave orders 'stand by to board', when the breeze failed us and we were unable to put alongside; our position c[oul]d not be better, being within Biscuit's throw of his Taffrail, and with the pivot gun and small arms, sweeping away every one who showed his head. After having 13 killed and 15 wounded one of their men got on to the Taffrail and hailed to us they had had 'enough'. Sent officers ... to take charge of him – Black Joke one killed, 6 wounded.

The aquatint faithfully captures the details of the engagement, even to the flying of the blue ensigns, the gun on the taffrail, and the engagement at close quarters. The event became instant legend, with one of the crew aboard working up a song to commemorate the event:

Song by Thomas Earon, one of the *Black Joke's* Crew on 1 Feb 1829

Come all you gallant sailors bold
And listen to my song
The truth to you I'll tell
Although not very long.

It is of a Noble brig my boys
The Black Joke is her name
Commanded by bold Downes
A man of well known fame.

It was on the first of February
As you must understand
Along the Coast of Africa
Not very far from land.

We cruised about the Leagus (Lagos)
And their we did espy
A Brig with Spanish Colours
Which proved our enemy.

And now the time arrived
To show ourselves like men
For sweeping of our Vessel
It was our full design.

And as we came up to her
We gave to her a gun
Old Neptune sat upon the waves
A laughing at the fun

Be cool and steady my brave boys
Our Captain he did say
Before this day is ended
We will show them British play.

Although their force is greater
We ne'er shall yield to them
For ere the setting of the sun
Their colours we'll pull down.

Our men as bold as lions
Unto their Quarters flew
With courage bold undaunted
We hoisted Colours blue.

Like hearts of oak we boarded her
She tried to get away
Soon thirty of her bravest men
Upon her decks did lay.

And as the battle raged
In dismal and surprize
The Spanyards fled from their quarters
And aloud for mercy cried.

Give us our lives and liberty
From you we ask no more
The Brig and all her slaves
And also of grate store.

Ther's Downes for ever my brave boys
And all his Valiant crew
Who bravely beat the Spaniards
And brought their courage low.

Likewise our gallant Commodore
And all the Sybille's men
And all the force that they can bring
Shall ne'er conquer them.

Black Joke at Sea, 15 March, [18]29

Another verse, on a separate sheet included in the log book, appeared to represent a drinking toast in honor of the event, perhaps composed by Lieutenant Downes himself, to respond to the crew's song:

But that little brig the Black Joke
That brig of high renown
She did engage the Almirante
And hauled her colours down

Heres health to all the Black Joke's crew
And may that health go round
I hope they'll see many happy days
When they are homeward bound.

The fact that Lieutenant Downes carefully noted down the lyrics of the song and the words of the rhyming toast, hints at the part spontaneous poetry and song played in the day to day life of sailors. Downes' own account and the song are both strongly flavored with British naval pride.

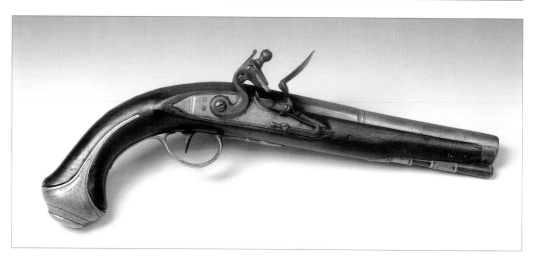

Pistol.

For close action, pistols and cutlasses were used. This brass mounted, English naval officer's pistol by Ketland, *c*.1785, of the type made for American naval officers (as well as English) was sold through the Ketland Company's Philadelphia office.

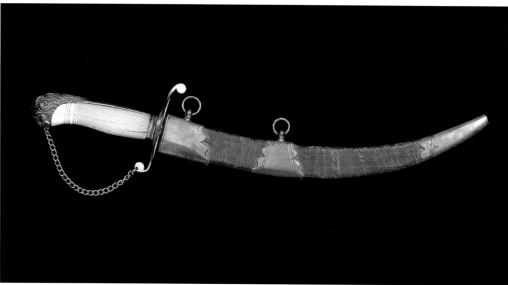

Curved-bladed British Dirk.

After 1800 this lion pommel was increasingly favored in the Royal Navy. After about 1805 fewer fighting (straight-bladed dirks) were produced. Most navies replaced the style with curved-bladed dirks. Apparently the fanciful symbolism of the Turkish Vassal States of North Africa, against whom American and British warships had fought, influenced the design. (See illustration Chapter One, page 30, of Midshipman John William Finch who is wearing one.)

Mutinies and Mutineers

Hundreds of mutinies aboard slave ships and dozens aboard merchant ships were testimony to the conditions faced by slaves, exploited merchant seamen, and sometimes, by naval seamen.

On 23 December, 1787, HMS *Bounty* set out from Spithead in Britain, bound for the Pacific, with the mission to collect breadfruit plants from the Society Islands and to transport them to the West Indies. It was hoped that breadfruit would provide a cheap and ready food for the slave population in the islands. The ship was commanded by an ambitious thirty-three year old, Lieutenant William Bligh. His command was noted for frequent floggings and a starvation diet, leading to a mutiny 27 April, 1789, led by his second in command, Fletcher Christian. The mutineers put Bligh and eighteen others adrift in a small launch. Bligh navigated the small overloaded craft over 3,000 miles from the Tonga group of islands westward to Timor, one of the great feats of seamanship of the eighteenth century.

Ten of the mutineers were discovered living in Tahiti, and they were arrested and brought to trial. The whereabouts of the *Bounty* was not discovered until 1808, when an American ship discovered some white residents on Pitcairn island, including one survivor and the descendants of the mutineers and their Polynesian wives.

In the Royal Navy, two massive mutinies in 1797 in fleets anchored at Spithead and at the Nore, resulted in negotiations to improve conditions for British sailors. Both mutinies seemed

Mutineers Turning Bligh Adrift.
Hand-colored mezzotint. Late 18th century.

On 28 April, 1789, a group of mutineers, led by Second-in-Command Fletcher Christian, seized control of HMS *Bounty* and set Lieutenant Bligh and eighteen companions adrift in the ship's launch. The launch, twenty-two feet long and six feet nine inches wide, could barely hold the group. Subsisting on meager rations and a limited water supply, Lieutenant William Bligh, in one of the great feats of navigation, guided the small boat some 3,600 miles across the Pacific Ocean from the Tonga Islands to Timor. In the print, a mutineer tosses a sword to Bligh. The purpose of the voyage was to bring breadfruit trees from the South Pacific to the West Indies where they were to provide a cheap food supply for slaves. Bligh published two accounts of his voyage and of the mutiny in 1790 and in 1792, examples of which are in the WH Collection.

to reflect the influence of ideas from the French Revolution, yet at the same time, it was clear that the mutineers sought only to improve conditions and pay, not to strike against the British monarchy or the crown.

Among the hundreds of mutinies aboard slave-ships, few records have survived, simply because the mutineers, if successful, would slaughter the crew and attempt to return the ship to Africa. In a few cases, however, mutinies aboard slavers came to the attention of the Anglo-American world. Perhaps the best known case is that of the schooner *Amistad*, which was carrying forty-nine slaves, originally from Sierra Leone in West Africa, from the port of Havana to Puerto Principe in Cuba in 1839. On the night of 1 July, the slaves seized control of the ship, killing the crew and sparing the two Spanish slave-owners aboard. Joseph Cinque, the leader of the slaves, ordered the Spaniards to sail to Sierra Leone. They obeyed during the day, sailing east, but at night, would secretly reverse course to the west. After two months of a zig-zag course, the ship was taken by the USS *Washington* off New York, and the slaves were brought to New London, Connecticut for trial. In a famous trial, the mutineers were defended by former US President John Quincy Adams, who argued they had not committed a crime, as their enslavement was illegal, and that they had simply fought for their natural right to be free. In February 1840, the US Supreme Court sustained a lower court opinion, freeing the mutineers. With funds provided by abolitionists, the group returned to West Africa.

RICHARD PARKER,
tendering the List of Grievances to Vice Admiral Buckner.

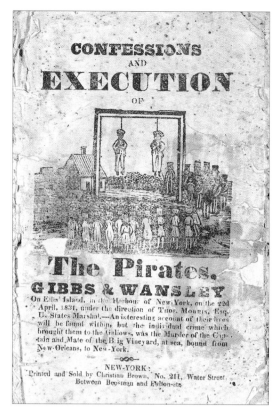

(Left) *Trial of Richard Parker.*
Engraving, late 18th century.

Of great concern to the British Admiralty were the mutinies at Spithead and The Nore in 1797. Lack of timely and sufficient pay, insufficiency of leave time and various other pent-up frustrations and grievances of the British tar led to the widespread mutinies at these two naval locations. The demands of those at Spithead, primarily about pay, were resolved and met. In this print the leader of the mutinous sailors at The Nore, Richard Parker, is depicted handing over a list of grievances to Vice-Admiral Buckner. The authorities took a much less sympathetic view – the mutineers were not successful like their Spithead brethren and a number of them, including Parker, were sentenced to death and hanged.

(Right) *Confessions and Executions of the Pirates Gibbs & Wansley. Chap-book.*

This pamphlet details the execution of the two pirates and gives a detailed confession by one of them. In his confession Gibbs claimed his real name was James Jeffers and that he had been raised in a respectacle family, then squandered his inheritance. After serving in the US Navy during the War of 1812, he joined a group of privateers sailing under the Colombian flag on the ship *Maria*. Dissatisfied with their take, the crew mutinied and 'declared war on all nations', hoisting the black flag of piracy. After capturing many ships and murdering their entire crews, the pirates were finally captured. Both men were hanged on Ellis Island in New York, 22 April, 1831, attended by a large crowd, as illustrated on the first page.

Another famous mutiny was that aboard USS *Somers* in 1842. Three men – Samuel Cromwell, Elisha Small, and midshipman Philip Spencer – were tried and executed by the Captain. They were allegedly the ringleaders of a plot to mutiny, murder the captain and other officers, and to seize the warship for piracy. Spencer was the son of John C. Spencer, the Secretary of War under President John Tyler, making the episode an immediate sensation. In order to clear his name of any wrong-doing in the decision to hang the mutineers, Captain Alexander Slidell Mackenzie demanded a court-martial. After a two-month trial, Mackenzie was acquitted. The story of the mutiny became the basis for the novel *Billy Budd* by Melville, and the action became an argument for the creation of the US Naval Academy in 1845, to instill professional values and training in the young officers of the US Navy.

THE U. S. BRIG-OF-WAR SOMERS.

Lith. & Pub. by N. Currier 2 Spruce St. New York.

The US Man-of-War Somers.
*c.*1843. Hand-colored lithograph.

This print depicts the hanging of two of the mutineers aboard the USS *Somers*, in 1842. This was the first mutiny aboard a US naval ship. This case was made controversial by the fact that the leader of the mutiny was nineteen year old midshipman Philip Spencer, the son of the US Secretary of War, John C. Spencer. According to Captain Alexander Slidell MacKenzie, Spencer and his co-mutineers, apparently guided by a romantic notion of taking the ship into piracy, were plotting to seize control by armed force. The two men shown here hanging from the starboard yardarm of the ship would be the bosun's mate, Samuel Cromwell, and seaman, Elisha Small. As a midshipman, Spencer would be hanged from the port side. On 31 March, 1843, Captain MacKenzie was acquitted at a court-martial of charges of murdering the three young men.

Outlaws of the Sea

When a sailing vessel left port, enforcement of law became a matter of naval armament. All nations recognized as a crime, mutiny against a captain appointed by the owner of a merchant ship or against superior naval officers. Yet other crimes at sea depended on national viewpoint. One nation's privateers would be viewed as buccaneers or pirates by another, during the Wars for Empire between Spain, France, and Britain, during the American Revolution, and during the American Civil War. The corsairs appointed by the Beys of Algiers or Tripoli to harry Christian enemies, were common pirates from the European and American point of view. British sugar merchants were smugglers from the Spanish viewpoint, and Colonial American sugar importers who evaded British customs were regarded as smugglers by the British. Slave traders who operated under the Asiento in the mid-eighteenth century were legitimate businessmen, although engaged in a despicable trade which came under more and more moral criticism. Their successors, after the British and American governments declared the slave trade illegal, were outlaws to be hunted down and driven from the sea. And mutineers against such slavers, as in the court case of the *Amistad*, were themselves freedom-fighters.

Enforcement of national laws by one or another of the naval powers added to the natural perils of the sea faced by outlaw seamen in the age of sail. Artists sought to capture, in prints and paintings, the outlaws, their adventures, and the naval forces who sought them out.

CHAPTER TEN

Perils of the Sea

The hazards of life at sea were so much a part of the seaman's life and many of those hazards were so appalling and held such morbid appeal, that they rapidly became part of folklore and popular culture. The moment of farewell when a sailor departed from his wife or girlfriend, the subject of so much art and song, was made even more bittersweet by the fact that everyone knew the sailor might not return. Many ships sailed over the horizon never to be heard from again; others collided, burned, ran aground, or simply developed leaks that pumping could not contain. In such cases a few survivors might return to tell of the loss of their shipmates after dramatic rescues at sea, hopeless days in lifeboats, or stranding on some inhospitable shore.

In the late eighteenth and much of the nineteenth century, various artists and writers presented the hazards of the sea with romantic, emotional overtones. Artists, writers, lyricists, and the public seemed to revel in how such risks made one feel – horrified, fascinated,

(Above) *Oil painting, 1836.* D. Wright.

In this shipwreck off chalk cliffs, probably Dover, crew members are being rescued by an early type of rescue-car rigged from the mast. Others wait their turn in the rigging, while a few try to swim through the surf to shore.

(Opposite) *'All Hands to the Pumps'*.

Weakened and leaky hulls were no match for high seas, as British reformer Samuel Plimsoll pointed out. Here, in an 1884 painting reproduced in William Randolph Hearst's color magazine section of the *Journal American* in 1905, we see some of the crew manning the pumps bringing water from below to run over the deck to the scuppers. The situation is desperate, as green water breaks over the rail, and a boy in the rigging points to another roller coming on. On the arms of some of the five sailors manning the pumps, tattooed crosses and anchors echo their faith and their hope for a safe harbor.

Sailor with Hook.
By Rhoades, 1875. Watercolor.

This original portrait of a rugged sailor with a hook in place of an amputated hand varies the stock elements of ship captains' portraits. Instead of a pose with a view through the window to the ship, here the view from a barren upstairs room looks over urban chimney tops. A hook instead of telescope or sextant, a ship model on a shelf, and a sea chest combine to suggest a life at sea resulting in a major injury.

depressed, saddened, or distressed. One commentator in 1849, even as he included a few anecdotes, self-consciously commented that his pen 'revolts at the revival of those fearful tales, those wholesale disasters, however eagerly they were once licked up by the public press, through that mania of the age for tales of aggravated horrors.'[1]

That 'mania of the age' was reflected in the production of hundreds of pictures and dozens of passages in book and song that played on the themes of the sailor lost at sea. Such works repeated the figure of seamen's wives turned widows by the perils of the sea. One oft-quoted poem by William Cowper (1731-1800), 'The Castaway' described a lonely death at sea.

> *He shouted: nor his friends had failed*
> *To check the vessel's course,*
> *But so the furious blast prevailed,*
> *That pitiless perforce,*
> *They left their outcast mate behind,*
> *And scudded still before the wind.*
>
> *At length, his transient respite past,*
> *His comrades, who before*
> *Had heard his voice in every blast,*
> *Could catch the sound no more:*
> *For then, by toil subdued, he drank*
> *The stifling wave, and then he sank.*

Richard Henry Dana, Jr. commented on the particular psychological horror of drowning at sea. 'When a man falls overboard at sea and is lost, there is a suddenness in the event and a difficulty in realizing it, which give to it an air of awful mystery... At sea, the man is near you – at your side – you hear his voice, and in an instant he is gone, and nothing but a vacancy shows his loss.'[2]

1. Lieut. A.F. Kynaston, R.N., *Casualties Afloat with Practical Suggestions for Their Prevention and Remedy* (London: Trelawney Saunders, 1849), p. 116.
2. Richard Henry Dana Jr., *Two Years Before the Mast*, pp. 40–41.

The Blind Sailor.
Hand-colored mezzotint.
Dated 24 June, 1793.

Hazards of the sea could be depicted through their effects on the survivors, as here a lady drops a coin into the extended hat of a blind sailor, while another lady (perhaps her mother) and a daughter look on in sympathy. The somber British illustration is published with a six-stanza verse in which the sailor accounts for his wounds. It was for his king, he says, that he lost both his nose and his eyesight as his vessel blew up during a sea battle with Spain.

Yet risk had another side. Literature and art played on the theme of how lives at risk made for heightened adventure. The great sea novels of Defoe, Smollett and Melville drew pathos and thrills from the very precarious nature of the sailing life. Through such writings, the public perceived sailors as risk-takers, living on the edge of survival; the sailor's very daredevil life style made him at once attractive to women, and envied by men whose lives were less colorful and dangerous. Yet for those actually engaged in taking the risks, the drudgery, cold, and ever-closeness of death hardly seemed romantic or colorful. Dana's own narrative sold as an adventure yarn as well as a tract advocating reform and care for the seaman, yet he made it clear that risking of life under miserable conditions held little appeal, and he urged his readers to turn from romance to the issue of 'what can be done for sailors, as they are, – men to be fed, and clothed, and lodged, for whom laws must be made and executed...'[3]

The death of sailors, especially when a whole ship went down with scores or hundreds of victims, generated another genre of art that has survived in collections and museums: memorabilia or commemorative art. Statues, ceramics, engraved silverware, as well as paintings and poetry, all depicted such tragedies, sometimes giving particulars as to date, condition, and numbers of victims. The function of memorial art was to provide a visual reminder, a souvenir of the event, so the tragic loss of life would not be forgotten. Medals were struck for ships, officers, and men who had assisted in rescues at sea; such medals and commemorative presentation items form a special category of artwork that put in three dimensional form, the same sentiments captured in memorial poetry and testimonial.

As a memorial poem, William Cowper's 'Loss of the Royal George' was still recited nearly a century after it was written. HMS *Royal George* was an English first-rate man of war of 100 guns. When she was being heeled over at Spithead to expose part of her side for the fitting of a valve below water, she suddenly capsized, 29 August, 1782. Admiral Kempenfelt and 800 sailors, marines, and visitors drowned.

3. Dana, pp.405-406.
4. William Cowper, *Collected Works*, 'Loss of the Royal George'. Among the 'visitors' were many prostitutes. (See discussion of prostitutes aboard ships in harbor in Chapter 6.)

Toll for the Brave!	*His sword was in its sheath,*	*But Kempenfeldt is gone*
The brave that are no more!	*His fingers held the pen*	*His victories are o'er;*
All sunk beneath the wave	*When Kempenfeldt went down*	*And he and his eight hundred*
Fast by their native shore!	*With twice four hundred men.*	*Shall plough the wave no more.*[4]

(Opposite) *Man Overboard.*
Watercolor. Mid-19th century.

This watercolor captures a moment of action in the rescue of a man overboard. One ship's boat, on the port side, shoves off, while the other is being lowered unevenly by sailors and marines. Passengers and crew observe from the stern of the ship, and other crew members watch from aloft as the swimmer makes for the life-buoy. The buoy was designed with two floats and a raised marker which could be illuminated at night so that victims and would-be rescuers could spot it above the wave tops. The sailor fell overboard from HMS *St Vincent* on her passage to Lisbon, December 1848.

The Sinking of the Ship Janson.
Watercolor. Artist: J. Mooy, *c.*1820.

The Ship *Janson* of Providence, Rhode Island, had arrived at Texel Road off New Dieppe from Batavia with a valuable cargo of coffee and rice. Starting from the right the watercolor shows three stages: 1) anchored amid drift ice that stove in the bow, 2) the ship is sinking and the crew is making efforts to abandon ship, 3) the ship is about to disappear. According to one report, nothing was saved but 'all hands' and the stern boat. The ship's pet monkey is running up the rigging of the main mast as the ship is about to sink completely.

In the memorial tradition, painting after painting of ships at risk in storms or wrecked at sea, of sailors clinging to lifeboats or floating spars come down to us from the era, giving visual details of such tragedies. Often, artists worked from their imagination rather than experience, taking artistic liberties in capturing a famous episode; even so, such works make the dangers and horrors of death at sea as vivid today as they did a century or two ago.

In the age of reforms through the nineteenth century, secular and religious advocates of seamen, naval officers, inventors, and a few courageous politicians attempted to reduce some of the risks of ordinary sea travel, turning from horrified fascination to a more rational and practical approach to risk-reduction, following the advice of advocates like Dana to take up practical concerns rather than dwelling on morbid topics or adventure. They began to ask what one could do about the risks in order to make life for seamen safer. Some worked to address the problem of risk in a logical and specific way, attempting to improve lifesaving services, provide funding for lighthouses and shore rescue crews, to develop lifesaving buoys,

HMS Orestes *from Hathorn scrapbook.*
Watercolor.

Remaining crew members aboard the wave-battered HMS *Orestes*, a sloop of 18 guns launched in 1824, attempt to chop down the foremast for the ship to ride more easily. This watercolor was found in a scrapbook of Captain George Hathorn, RN.

and to prevent overloading. Some reformers focused on drunkenness aboard ship, the cause of many accidents, drownings, and fatal fights. And drunkenness led to poverty for sailors and their families, draining their limited money away.

In 1841, Charles Ellms published a work which combined accounts of shipwrecks with an analysis of how they might be prevented. An early example of the genre (other writers emulated the same format later), he used the morbid fascination with shipwrecks to attract publishing interest and readership then presented suggestions for prevention and reform.[5]

In 1849, Lieutenant Kynaston, an officer in the British Royal Navy, developed a study of methods for rescuing sailors from death through drowning overboard. In his opening passages, he placed the work in the larger context of rational reform: 'To disarm our Channel of many of its terrors, and to reduce the number of shipwrecks in general, the energies of the British Government and the inventive genius of private individuals have been frequently directed...'[6] Some of the successes went beyond the construction of lighthouses, harbors, and lifeboats, he

5. Charles Ellms, *Shipwrecks and Disasters at Sea, Or Historical Narratives of the Most Noted Calamities, and Providential deliverances from Fire and Famine, on the Ocean, with a sketch of the Various Expedients for Preserving the Lives of Mariners by the Aid of Life Boats, Life Preservers, &c.* New York: Edwards, 1841.

6. Kynaston, p. v.

'Sailor and Sailor Boy Shipwrecked'.
Colored lithograph, *c.*1840.

Blue water sailors, young and old, faced death every day. A constant peril was shipwreck from storm or reef. Here is a romanticized depiction of a young boy who had bid his mother goodbye, gone to sea and was drowned by shipwreck.

noted, by 'striking at the causes which have been proved by subsequent investigation to have led to disaster.' He described many episodes, including several involving the use of life-buoys with lighted lanterns fueled by pitch to allow swimmers to find them. Kynaston, in the spirit of reform, devoted a whole chapter to drunkenness, and the degree to which it contributed to fatality at sea, by men becoming careless, fighting, attempting to swim to shore when anchored too far out, and from losing the ability to swim when inebriated.

Yet even in this reform-minded and 'scientific' study, centered around practical matters of ship handling during emergencies, Kynaston continued to play on emotions. For example, describing the fate of a small boy who fell overboard at night during a celebration of crossing

Three Shipwrecked Sailors.
Oil painting, American, 19th century.

Shipwrecked from storm or reef were perils of everyday life for a sailor at sea. This folk art painting shows a man waving a white cloth to a passing vessel for help, another man is praying, and the third is forlornly bemoaning his fate. A fully-dressed woman lies dead in a grotto while another woman starts to climb on to the rock ledge. For good measure a large dog is also in the picture. If there is a mysterious message in this painting, the reader is asked to fathom it. Certainly it is about life and death and possible salvation. The work was once owned by the noted American pop-art artist, Andy Warhol..

the equator, he tugged at the heartstrings in the same manner as did romantic poets like William Cowper decades earlier.

Echoing a romantic illustration chosen for the frontispiece of the book, Kynaston used the image of the floating buoy as grave marker. He described the aftermath of a sailor who had drowned with a reference to the picture: 'the sea-birds who had shrieked his dirge, had long since abandoned it for their ocean roost; and the lifebuoy, floating on the surface, may have been as a headstone to mark the site of the sailor's grave.'[7] Even though colored with such allusions, the work included practical details regarding the use of lifebuoys, dinghies, surfboats, lifeboat slings, signal lights, and waist-nets. Specific maneuvers of the ship with different wind force and when sailing at different angles to the wind were all detailed in a practical manner. Kynaston, like other authors in the mid-nineteenth century, liberally sprinkled his work with quotes from William Cowper's 'Castaway' and 'Loss of the Royal George'.

Concern with overloaded ships culminated in a movement led by Member of Parliament Samuel Plimsoll that called on the social conscience of the British people, with an appeal that focused on the plight of widows and orphans. Like other reformers who had preceded him

7. Kynaston, p. 143.

233

in attacking the issue of safety at sea, Plimsoll was personally appalled at popular unconcern with the plight of sailors, and sought to win support through emotion and sympathy.

> Now there are many hundreds of lives lost annually by shipwreck, and as to the far greater part of them, they are lost from causes which are easily preventible. I may say further, that they would not be lost if the same care was taken of our sailors by the law as is taken of the rest of our fellow-subjects.[8]

Plimsoll saw the greed of shipowners and their lack of concern to send out seaworthy ships as a primary cause of the loss of life, and he fought to pass legislation in Parliament, against the opposition of powerful shipping interests and their friends in government. He sought to require that ships not be loaded dangerously deep in the water. Many ships, he reported, went to sea with rotten timbers and hulls.

Plimsoll further stated:

8. Samuel Plimsoll, MP, *Our Seamen: An Appeal* (London: Virtue and Co., 1873), p. B.

'Room for one More'. Chromolithograph, c.1875.

Newspapers, reformist or 'muckraking' magazines and brochures supported Plimsoll's criticisms of shipowners and their dangerous practices. In this *Puck Magazine* cartoon, the captain of an overcrowded trans-Atlantic passenger ship keeps the gangway open as he shouts, 'Room for one more', while Death, his feet encased in coffins, cries out 'I Shall Soon Be On Board'. Death's luggage is marked 'Disease and Accidents' and a piece of funeral crape waves from his undertaker's top hat. To the left, another over-burdened vessel is already on its way to doom.

CAPTAIN OF OVERCROWDED STEAMER—"Room For One More."
DEATH—"I Shall Soon Be On Board."

'*Mate Sound the Pump, Morning Noon & Night*'. Wall plaque, pink lustre earthenware, Sunderland, *c*.1850.

The wording on the plaque was of critical importance to the survivability of the ship and those aboard her. It was imperative to know the depth of water in the well of the ship to determine if pumping was necessary. Here was a token of life at sea that could be an everyday reminder at home of the perils of the sea.

> A great number of ships are regularly sent to sea in such rotten and otherwise ill-provided state that they can only reach their destination through fine weather, and a large number are so overloaded that it is nearly impossible for them also to reach their destination if the voyage is at all rough. And I can show you that from these two causes alone ... rather more than a full half of our losses arise.[9]

Plimsoll, like the far less influential Kynaston, liberally sprinkled his work of practical reform advocacy, with specific anecdotes of sailors lost at sea, and their widows left stranded without resources, starving and freezing in lonely garret rooms.

Gradually, an awareness grew among the traveling public and among legislators that the economics of shipping did not lead shipowners to take care of their ships, to provide adequate lifeboats, to load them safely, or even to maintain them so as to survive a moderately heavy sea or storm. Yet public pressure did little to make sailing and early sail-and-steam vessels any safer. The literature of the sea, journals and logs, and accident reports continue to tell, well into the twentieth century, of overloaded ships, improperly stored or equipped life boats, worn rigging and engines, and rotten or rusty hulls.

The violence of the sea in a storm was a true peril, and escapes from the raging winds resulted in many kinds of artifacts. *Ex Voto* pictures painted at the request of thankful sailors, commemorating the survival of a life-threatening moment at sea, attributed to prayer to particular saints or to the Virgin Mary, could be donated to a church for public display. As tokens of thanks for deliverance from death, medals would be cut, silverware engraved, or secular paintings or drawings made depicting the storm, fire, or other peril.

Just as the popular culture of the twentieth century continues to remember the loss of the

9. Plimsoll, p. B.

235

Titanic (1912) and the Lusitania (1915), so in the eighteenth and nineteenth century, a number of great ship losses at sea were well known, and memorialized in art, song, and literature. Of the thousands of disasters at sea, a few dozen generated copy after copy of paintings, prints, published reports, and extensive discussion in the public press. Several of those more famous episodes are represented by art work and documentation in the Henderson Collection.

Commemorative Art, Selected Major Shipwrecks or Near Disasters

Shipwreck	Lives lost	Location in collection	Date	Artifacts
Centaur	200[?]	Mid Atlantic	9/16/1782	Painting, Pamphlet
Kent	82	Bay of Biscay	3/1/1825	Pastel
Philadelphia		Caribbean	1850	Presentation Silver Speaking Trumpet
Jessie Stevens		Atlantic	12/4/1852	Medal
Vesta-Arctic	300	Cape Race, Nfd.	9/27/1854	2 Lithographs
Rutledge	138	North Atlantic	2/19/1856	Lithograph
Atlantic	535	Mars Head, N.S	4/2/1873	Lithograph
Strathmore		Crozet Is.	1875	Medal

Many kinds of items in the Collection echo the same themes, often giving dates, numbers lost at sea, the names of officers, and the causes of the tragedy. A fine silver speaking trumpet serves as both a memorial and a presentation item to a hero who saved lives of gold seekers during a storm in 1850 on the way to Chagres in Panama. On one side of the trumpet the engraving appears to depict women and children aboard ship being told some sad news by a man; while in another scene, the paddle steamer Philadelphia fights through raging seas. The inscription gives details:

> To CAPT. ROBERT PIERSON, this trumpet is most respectfully presented by the passengers of the steamship Philadelphia on a voyage from N.Y to Chagres for his fidelity during the fearful gale of July 1850 with the hope that his life may be preserved for future usefulness continuing his trust in God who guides the whirlwind and directs the storm.

Particularly poignant was the story of HMS Centaur, which was accompanying British troopships back to England from the West Indies. A group of survivors made their way in a small boat over 250 leagues at sea (about 750 nautical miles) to the Azores in 1782 after their ship was dismasted and left sinking from hurricane damage. A print by R. Dodd, copied by an unknown Chinese artist, depicts the moment when the overloaded pinnace with twelve survivors began to lose sight of the doomed ship, which sank with all hands save the occupants of the boat. In his own account, Captain John Inglefield described the disaster:

Collision between the US side-wheel steamer Arctic *and the French propellor-driven* Vesta.
Hand-colored lithograph.

The American steamer *Arctic* on a homeward bound voyage from Liverpool, 27 September, 1854, collided, in a dense fog off Newfoundland, with the French ship *Vesta*. As the *Arctic* slowly sank over a period of five hours, the passengers attempted to abandon ship. However, some 300 lives were lost.

> In the evening of the 16th of September, when the fatal gale came on, the ship was prepared for the worst weather usually met with in those latitudes; the mainsail was reefed and set, the top-gallant masts struck, and the mizen-yard lowered down, though at that time it did not blow very strong. Towards midnight it blew a gale of wind, and the ship made so much water that I was obliged to turn all hands up to spell the pumps.[10]

After the pumps failed, many of the men rushed into the small pinnace and Inglefield joined them. He was later criticized for abandoning the remainder of his crew to their deaths, and for this reason he wrote out the detailed narrative explaining the wreck and his survival.

> The boat falling astern, became exposed to the sea, and we endeavoured to pull her bow round... but in the attempt she was nearly filled; the sea ran too high, and the only probability of living was keeping her before the wind. It was then that I became sensible how little, if any thing, better our condition was than that of those who remained in the ship; at best, it appeared to be only a prolongation of a miserable existence. We were altogether twelve in number, in a leaky boat, with one of the gunwales stove, in nearly the middle of the Western Ocean, without compass, without quadrant, without sail, without great coat or cloak; all very thinly clothed, in a gale of wind, with a great sea running![11]

10. John Nicholson Inglefield, *Capt. Inglefield's Narrative, concerning the Loss of His majesty's ship the Centaur, of Seventy four guns; and the miraculous preservation of the pinnace, in a traverse of near 300 leagues on the Great western ocean.* (A new edition, corrected. London for John Murray and A. Donaldson, 1783), pp. 5-6. Spelling modernized.
11. Inglefield, pp. 26-27.

'Preservation of Captain Inglefield'.
Oil painting, *c*.1785.

This Chinese painting, based on an English print by Dodd, captures the moment in 1782 when Captain Inglefield abandoned the HMS *Centaur* as it was sinking in mid-Atlantic. At this moment, his men jury-rig a blanket as a sail and move off through the heavy swells. After making landfall in the Azores, Inglefield had to answer for abandoning many other men aboard ship, who all perished, so he published a complete narrative of the adventure to help explain and justify his actions. The artist depicts the desperate moment, with men bailing the overloaded boat, and the doomed ship wallowing in the sea under storm-heavy skies.

It was this moment that the artist captured in his painting, showing the overloaded pinnace. The narrative points out that the pinnace was out of sight of the ship when a sail was improvised; the artist took a bit of liberty with the timing to capture the whole poignant scene.

> ... It was now five o'clock in the evening and in half an hour we lost sight of the ship. Before it was dark, a blanket was discovered in the boat. This was immediately bent to one of the stretchers, and under it as a sail we scudded all night, in expectation of being swallowed up by every wave, it being with great difficulty that we could sometimes clear the boat of the water before the return of the next great sea...[12]

Through careful navigation and with considerable luck, the small boat, with fresh water and its supply of a few biscuits exhausted, came in sight of the Azores, and eleven men survived. The British public was at once horrified and morbidly interested in the details of all such tragedies, and Captain Inglefield's account ran through more than one edition.

Later, the stories of other ships depicted in the Collection, the *John Rutledge*, the *Atlantic* and the *Huron*, each attracted newspaper and magazine exposés, investigations, and public outrage, and the attention of artists, engravers, and print makers.

The *John Rutledge* was an American packet steamer that sailed from Liverpool for New

Death of Lord Nelson.
Hand-colored engraving.
Artist: A.W. Devis. Engraver: Wm. Bromley.

This 1812 print was a serious effort to recreate the actual death scene of Lord Nelson, 21 October, 1805. An accompanying text explains the identities of eleven of the fourteen witnesses, giving their rank in 1805, as well as their rank at the time of publication of the print. Officers, a surgeon and his assistant, a valet, purser, chaplain, steward and carpenter are all identified by name. The painter, A.W. Devis, went aboard and had the eleven witnesses sit for portraits in the precise location they occupied when Nelson died. Such fidelity to historical accuracy was rare.

York, with over 100 immigrants from the British Isles. Passing through ice fields in the North Atlantic, on 19 February, 1856, the ship hit an iceberg, stoving in the bow.

Pumping soon proved inadequate to keep up with the flow, and about midnight, passengers and crew abandoned ship. Although the crew launched five lifeboats, passengers and crew had insufficient clothing for the bitter cold. Nine days later, a steamer *en route* from Le Havre to New York found a single lifeboat with a lone survivor, a man named Nye. The boats had drifted apart; as people died, Nye explained, the survivors threw them over the side of the boat. But as the strong died, only Nye survived, and he was too weak to dispose of the last four bodies in his lifeboat. No other survivors were ever found.

The loss of the *Atlantic* resulted from poor navigation and seamanship. The 2,376-ton White Star liner ran aground twenty-two miles from Halifax, Nova Scotia in a blinding storm, 2 April, 1873. Some twenty sailors swam ashore, and soon life savers were able to rig

Snuff and patch boxes, early 19th century.

Many decorated snuff and patch boxes commemorated Nelson's victory and carried patriotic mottoes. Items of a wide variety of types proliferated in honor of Nelson after Trafalgar.

a line from the rocky crags to a mast of the ship. As a consequence, some 422 passengers and crew were saved, with dozens of brave actions by crew and officers. However, a later investigation suspended the license of the ship's master, Captain J.A. Williams, due to his careless navigation and high speed in dangerous waters.

The US naval steamer *Huron* was on a surveying mission off the coast of North Carolina, when it foundered in a gale, 24 November, 1877. Only one lifeboat and a few swimmers made it to shore, with the loss of 104 men. The ship, rigged as a three-masted schooner, was also driven by a steam engine, and had been constructed in Chester, Pennsylvania by John Roach and Sons. The company asserted that the ship was extremely seaworthy, with a double hull, strongly riveted iron decking, and built to explicit US Navy specifications for a sloop of war. A court of inquiry found the captain and navigator responsible for the wreck, and agreed the ship was seaworthy; both officers had been killed in the wreck.

While sailing on a merchant or passenger ship entailed risks which could have been moderated with a greater concern for safety, naval vessels by definition meant sailors risked their lives for their country and sailed into harm's way. Great sea battles which involved thousands of sailors and major ships of the line caught the popular imagination and public

John Crawford.
Engraving.

The text accompanying this 1797 print by E. Orme explains that John Crawford of Sunderland, Durham climbed to the Main Top Gallant Mast to nail the Ensign to the Mast of Lord Duncan's ship, after the flag had been shot away by the Dutch, under Admiral de Winter on 11 October, 1797. Replacing the flag was essential, lest the enemy think Lord Duncan had signaled surrender by voluntarily hauling down the Ensign, 'striking the colors'. This original print representing an authentic incident was later copied by various print pirates, British and American, with patriotic sentiments.

'The True American Sailor'.
Mid-nineteenth century. Lithograph.

The American print publisher, N. Currier, sometimes borrowed themes and ideas from already popular prints. Labeling this heroic incident as 'The True American Sailor' was particularly ironic in light of the fact that the original incident involved a British sailor in the late eighteenth century. During the heat of battle, it was essential that a ship's flag stay aloft, otherwise the enemy might take its absence as a signal of surrender.

memory. In fact, the death of Nelson and the Battle of Trafalgar on 21 October, 1805, for the British, became a subject of repeated motifs in art, sculpture, silverware, pottery, patch- and snuff-boxes, and even in the renaming of London landmarks with Nelson's Column and Trafalgar Square. Hero worship in this case became a hallmark of British culture ever since.[13]

For Americans, certain battles and individual ship-to-ship engagements also stood out, with popular memory and memorials focusing on both naval heroes (mostly officers) and on the spectacle of ship-to-ship warfare. Through the period from 1750 to 1910, many major wars put British or American sailors at risk:

13. Lily Lambert McCarthy, *Remembering Nelson,* Greenwich, CN: Privately Printed, 1995. This work describes a collection devoted to Nelson memorabilia.

'*Farragut Aboard the* Hartford'.
Chromolithograph, *c.*1880.

As the USS *Hartford* ran into Mobile Bay past the Confederate ironclad *Tennessee*, several gunboats and a number of mines on 5 August, 1864, Admiral David G. Farragut issued the order, 'Damn the Torpedoes! Full Speed Ahead.' This print captures the heat of the battle as the guns fire practically muzzle to muzzle. By this action the last major port of the Confederacy's Gulf Coast was effectively closed.

WAR	DURATION	BELLIGERENT STATES
Seven Years War	1756-1763	Britain, Prussia v. France, Austria, Spain, Russia
American Revolution	1776-1783	Britain v. US, France
French Revolution	1793-1802	Britain, Austria, Prussia, v. France
Quasi War with France	1798-1801	US v. France
Napoleonic Wars	1803-1815	France, Spain
Barbary Wars	1801-1805	US v. Barbary States
War of 1812	1812-1815	US v. Britain
Mexican–American War	1846-1848	US v. Mexico
Crimean War	1853-1856	Britain, France, Turkey, Sardinia v. Russia
US Civil War	1861-1865	Union v. Confederacy
Spanish American War	1898	US v. Spain

Note regarding duration: In wars with more than two belligerents, the year-span reflects British or US participation.

Victory of the British on the Glorious First of June 1794.
Hand–colored Stipple engraving.

This stylized commemorative print, published in 1795 by Daniel Orme, historical engraver to His Majesty, attempted to capture a deck scene during the battle. However, the Royal Academy artist, M. Brown, historical painter to the Duke and Duchess of York, was either too tasteful or too inexperienced to depict a battle scene with much realism. Here, a single trickle of blood from a small wound on the breast of an officer stains his otherwise immaculate uniform. Other officers, also without smudges to their splendid uniforms, bear the symbols of their office, such as swords and speaking trumpets, and stand about with their backs to the action, as if posed. A boy bears a speaking trumpet, perhaps that of the fallen officer. Heroic depictions of victories, such as this one, over the French by the British fleet under the command of Lord Howe, were key to British national pride in the 18th and 19th century.

US Frigate United States *vs. HM Frigate* Macedonian. Thomas Birch (1779-1851).

In this 1813 oil painting the US Frigate *United States* under the command of Stephen Decatur defeats HM Frigate *Macedonian*, 25 October, 1812. Together with four other naval engagements late in 1812, this US victory over the British heartened Americans to fight on. Here, the Frigate *United States*, on the right, is only lightly damaged, while the *Macedonian* is shrouded in shadow, its sails and rigging shattered. The British flag is visible in the debris. Representative of a Dutch tradition of maritime art depicting heroic actions and ship engagements, such paintings give a feel for one of the perils of the sea – naval battles. Like the 1794 British victory of the 'Glorious First of June', American naval victories were a source of patriotic pride.

Each of these wars saw a number of major naval incidents or battles, most memorialized in paintings, then in prints, as well as described in official and unofficial reports. Like disasters at sea, many battles resulted in the casting of medals and the production of ceramics, silverware, and other types of three-dimensional memorials.

Naval Engagements Depicted in Henderson Collection (Partial Listing)

Engagement/Battle	Year	War
Bonhomme Richard v. *Serapis*	1779	American Revolution
L'Aventure v. *Pigou*	1793	French Revolutionary
First of June	1794	French Revolutionary
Blanche v. *Le Pique*		French Revolutionary
Battle of the Nile	1798	French Revolutionary
Ambuscade v. *Bayonnaise*	1798	French Revolutionary
Burning of *Philadelphia*	1804	Barbary Wars
Louisa v. Algerine privateers	1800	Barbary Wars
Trafalgar	1805	Napoleonic Wars
USS *Constitution* v. *Guerriere*	1812	War of 1812
USS *President, Congress* v. *Curlew*	1813	War of 1812
United States v. *Macedonian*	1812	War of 1812
USS *Chesapeake* v. *Shannon*	1813	War of 1812
USS *Enterprise* v. *Boxer*	1813	War of 1812
Mobile Bay	1864	US Civil War
Kearsage v. *Alabama*	1864	US Civil War
USS *Maine*	1898	pre-Spanish-Am. War
Manila Bay	1898	Spanish American War
Santiago de Cuba	1898	Spanish American War

USS Constitution *and HMS* Guerriere.
Oil painting attributed to Thomas Chambers, *c.*1840.

This colorful oil represents the battle of the USS *Constitution* and HMS *Guerriere* on 19 August, 1812. *Guerriere* in the foreground, is dismasted and defeated. A fortunate vessel, *Constitution* gained the nickname 'Old Ironsides' in this action when the enemy shot glanced ineffectually off her hull. This single ship victory early on in the war was a psychological lift to the Americans. The *Constitution* was one of the first frigates in the United States Navy. Rated at forty-four guns, she was launched at Boston in 1797 with a revolutionary design by Joshua Humphreys of Philadelphia. The United States declared war on Great Britain 18 June, 1812. One of the leading causes was the impressment of American sailors from American vessels over a number of years. In a number of actions, the *Constitution* was never defeated. She is still in commission and is the oldest American vessel afloat – in Boston Harbor, Massachusetts.

'*Interesting chace* [sic] *and excape* [sic] *of His Majesty's Sloop* Curlew *from two American Frigates, M. Head Esq. Captain'.*
By S. H. Laston. Watercolor, *c.*1813.

This watercolor, probably by a British sailor aboard the *Curlew*, depicts the escape of the sloop (brig) *Curlew* from the US Frigate *President* and the US Frigate *Congress* in 1813. The American side is shown by entries in a log of the *President* dated 3 May, 1813. 'Discovered two strange sail... at three the chase made signals hoisted an English ensign and pendant. The *Congress* in company – in chase of a Brig – five – all sails set in chase. Eight – lost sight of the chase – *Congress* in company.'

John Paul Jones.
Mezzotint, late 18th century.

American naval hero John Paul Jones was celebrated for his daring raids on Britain during the American Revolution and the victory of *Bonhomme Richard* over HMS *Serapis*, 23 September, 1779. It was in this battle that Jones uttered the immortal words, 'I have not yet begun to fight'.

Portrait Print of Isaac Hull.
Mezzotint, *c*.1813.

This print of Isaac Hull commemorates his command of USS *Constitution* during its engagement with HMS *Guerriere*. The miniature depiction of the battle at the bottom of the Hull portrait shows men in action and in the water.

Many of the perils of the sea were much less dramatic than the risk of war. Disease, accidents at sea, fires, fights, drowning, and the possibility of running out of food or water all haunted the life of seamen. Ships' logs, journals, narrative accounts, as well as the art left by sailor-artists and professionals, often reported causes of death among both ordinary seamen and officers of an extensive and disheartening variety.

Beyond the great causes of fatality that included disease, storms and war, the range of possibilities was staggering. Reformer Samuel Plimsoll traced thousands of deaths to the simple cause of unseaworthy and rotten-bottomed ships. In time of war, merchant ships encountered privateers and full scale sea-battles might result; in peacetime, pirates roamed certain regions of the world at different periods, as discussed in the previous chapter. The individual sailor, as distinct from a whole crew, ran dozens of personal risks: falling from aloft to be crushed on deck; being struck by falling block and tackle; falling overboard to drown. All or some of a crew might be cast adrift in a ship's boat after their ship was wrecked to die of thirst or hunger. Going ashore for water or food in remote regions sometimes entailed the risk of native hostility or attack while moored in an apparently safe bay or inlet. Even

REEFING TOPSAILS.

Reefing Topsails.
Hand-colored aquatint.

Simply doing the daily work on a sailing vessel could be risky. This 1832 print by W.J. Huggins shows six men in a high wind trying simultaneously to hold on for their lives and to furl a sail. Their expressions, the hat lost to the wind, and the flapping sail, all tell of the hazard.

in regular maritime ports of call, a seaman might be mugged, be stabbed or shot in a fight, or suffer an accident. Some died from poisonous liquor or food ashore.

Hazards that produced dramatic incidents were the ones that tended to be more frequently depicted. Men being killed by sharks or whales received disproportionate coverage in art and literature compared to the hundreds of thousands dying from disease. Similarly, only a few thousand sailors ever died from freezing to death when their ship became locked in Arctic or Antarctic ice, yet paintings of such dramatic strandings are far more common than depictions of the ravages of common causes of death such as scurvy, smallpox, yellow fever, pneumonia, venereal disease or malaria. Like so many other aspects of life at sea, it was the relatively unusual or dramatic which often earned the attention of artists, the attention of memorialists, and the fascination of the public.

Storms at sea and great naval battles naturally caught the popular imagination far more than disease. It was nearly impossible to depict the conditions that would cause ill health, especially when the action of microbes and vitamins was so ill-understood, compared to the visual qualities of a turbulent sea, a raging storm, or a man-of-war in action. Some rare pictures of daily conditions provide oblique evidence of some of the less glamorous, but nevertheless powerful causes of mortality. Pictures of lifebuoys, rescue equipment, surfboats and ships' boats testify to the high risk of ordinary drowning; pictures of maimed and broken sailors ashore suggest the consequences of many of the common causes of death and injury.

Survival at sea required not only a seaworthy ship, but adequate stores of water and supplies. Throughout the logs and journals of various officers, the concern with finding water and transporting refilled casks to the vessel occurs again and again. The ordinary task of rowing a boat ashore and loading water or the more spectacular method of cutting ice from Antarctic icebergs for melting aboard ship became a subject of several journal sketches, paintings, prints, journal entries, and log notations.

A youth rescued from a shark. Hand-colored engraving based on John S. Copley's 'Watson and the Shark'. Late 19th century.

Another hazard was attack by shark, whether on the high seas or in coastal waters. The nearly-drowning youth is rescued by a crew with mixed emotions of fear, horror and courage. One points with pity. Two of the men reach for the boy, while another stabs at the shark with a boat hook. The crew includes a black man. Elements of the story are captured by the background, with a harbor, lighthouse and ship at anchor. The print is based on a real episode in Havana Harbor originally recorded in an oil painting by John Singleton Copley, 1778. In later years Watson became the Lord Mayor of London.

Although statistics might reveal disease as the most common cause of fatality among seamen, finding depictions of this particular everyday risk in art and artifact is even more difficult than finding visual evidence of the life and death matters of drowning, water supply, and food. Advertisements for cures of venereal disease sometimes took a curious form, especially as its mere mention was somewhat taboo. One such handbill from Philadelphia resembled a banknote, which would entitle the bearer to a cure 'of a certain disease, without Mercury or Balsam.' Embellished with symbols of the sea, it was clear that the handbill was directed to sailors who feared the adage, 'one night with Venus, a lifetime with Mercury.'

'The Newcastle *Sending a Surgeon on Board the Barque* Westbury'. Watercolor, *c.*1870.

Professional medical care at sea was rare. In this watercolor, the captain's wife, Mrs Cook, met with an accident on the voyage from London to Bushire in 1870. A boat crew, including one black man, rowed the surgeon from the passing *Newcastle*. The grateful captain of the *Westbury* expresses his appreciation with signal flags flying 'Accept my best wishes'. The anxious crew on the *Newcastle* watch from the deck of their ship as the boat makes its way through heavy seas.

Ridding a ship of rats.
Colored woodcut, *c*.1870.

This Japanese woodcut depicts a more mundane peril of the sea, disease-carrying rats. Here a few Caucasian sailors chase the rats with sticks and smoke from a coal-scuttle, while a passenger gives directions.

In the eighteenth and early nineteenth century, diseases were little understood and few medicines existed to treat them effectively. Sailors' journals give only rare references to venereal disease; more common and more fatal were 'fevers' which would cover a range of illnesses from the common cold through pneumonia, intestinal symptoms, smallpox, malaria, yellow fever, and a host of unknown diseases which would strike down sailors aboard ship, far from even the primitive medicine found ashore in the period. The medicines carried aboard ships make it clear how futile most treatments would be. It appears that in the earlier days many of the medicines were used to 'tighten one up or loosen one up.' Methods of ridding a ship of rats, whose lice sometimes carried plague, were rarely depicted; a nineteenth century Japanese woodcut captures such an incident.

Lack of fresh fruit and vegetables on long sea voyages brought scurvy, a result of Vitamin C deficiency. Edward Strother, a member of the London College of Physicians, prepared a book of health suggestions for travelers in 1729, which mixed what we now know to be good ideas with some very poor advice. Under the topic of scurvy he opined that sea air was full of salt which could create great disorders in one's stomach. He said that blood was thus poisoned and one should use antacids from the vegetable kingdom such as 'scurvy grass, Water cresses (and) Pepperwort.' While such herbs might have provided some Vitamin C, in another passage, he warned against citrus fruit:

> Some sailors content themselves with eating oranges and do Feats with them; however it is hardly possible that some sensible Damages will be done by this Method as soon as ever he recovers his Health; and therefore it is more advisable to act more safely although more slowly.[14]

14. Edward Strother, *The Practical Physicians for Travellers, Whether By Sea or Land,* (London 1729), pp. 114-115.

'*Loss of the* Kent'.
Pastel, *c.*1830.

One of the better known shipwrecks by fire in the first half of the nineteenth century was that of the East Indiaman *Kent* bound from England to Bengal and China. On the night of 28 February, 1827, a violent gale in the Bay of Biscay buffeted the vessel. An officer checking the stowage of casks in the hold dropped a light which ignited spirits from a stoved cask. The flames enveloped various sections of the lower portion of the vessel. On board were over 600 people including about 350 soldiers accompanied by about 100 women and children, 20 private passengers and a crew, including officers, of 148 men. The captain, to fight the fire, ordered the lower deck to be scuttled. They faced death by fire or death by water. A sail was sighted and flags of distress were instantly hoisted and minute guns fired. She was the *Cambria*, a small brig of 200 tons bound for Vera Cruz. Boats were lowered with occupancy for women and children first. Many were saved by lowering themselves by a rope hanging from the spanker boom. Miraculously, only eighty-two perished.

James Lind, who served as surgeon aboard HMS *Salisbury*, was shocked at the huge casualties from scurvy which had occurred during a voyage around the world in 1740-44 by Commodore Anson. In 1747, Lind made a controlled dietary experiment, discovering that the juice of oranges and lemons could serve as a specific against the disease. He published his experimental findings in a *Treatise of the Scurvy*, in 1753.

Captain James Cook (1728-79), a largely self-educated officer who came up through the ranks in the British Navy, gave intelligent attention to the cleanliness of the ship and the living conditions of the crew. Like Lind, he experimented with various anti-scorbutic items for the diet, including 'sour krout' (pickled cabbage), 'portable dried soup', malt, and the juice of oranges and lemons as well as scurvy grass. The voyage of HMS *Endeavor* demonstrated the success of his ideas. The ship left Plymouth on 25 August, 1768, called at Madeira and Rio de Janeiro, rounded Cape Horn and reached Tahiti on 10 April, 1769. The whole voyage was made without a single case of scurvy, an unheard-of achievement at that time.

Even with the experiments of Lind and Cook, however, it took decades for the Royal Navy to address and solve the problem of scurvy. It was not until 1795 that the issue of lemon juice was officially adopted in the Royal Navy. Soon, however, the British substituted

USS Richmond. 'Loose Cannon', c.1867. Wood engraving.

The expression, a 'loose cannon on a rolling deck' derives from incidents just like this in which a cannon could break loose in a storm, roll from bulwark to bulwark, and smash everything in its path. The risk to life and limb is shown in this print of a 'Pet Parrott' gun on board USS *Richmond*. This is a page from *Harper's Weekly* for 14 May, 1864.

lime juice (which was lower in Vitamin C than lemon juice), because limes were grown in their own West Indian islands, while lemon juice had to be imported from groves in the Mediterranean. Scurvy was effectively conquered by about 1800.

Injuries would often result in death, but even if the accident victim recovered, he might lose an arm or a leg. Amputation was the common treatment for broken or lacerated limbs; the survival of the image of peg-legged sailors either as beggars in the streets or as cooks aboard ships was no artistic conceit. Sailors broke their legs from falls aboard ship and/or crushed them in battle actions. Rolling loose cannon, heavy masses of timber, or falling cargo in the hold could so mangle a leg that there was often little recourse but amputation. Aboard most merchant ships, the master served as the doctor, aided perhaps by the ship's carpenter, whose wood saw came in handy as a surgeon's tool.

The peg leg and the eye-patch became immortalized in popular memory through art and literature. For the common sailor amputee with a wooden leg, nearly the only shipboard job he could take on would be that of cook, where he would not be required to go aloft or to work on the pitching deck.

As in other areas of the life of the seaman, the surviving art and artifact from the period 1750-1910 tends to give emphasis to the dramatic and heart-rending events, not the ordinary hazards and risks. Even so, the many perils of the sea were real. Today, a sense of the risks to the life of Jack Tar can be gained by a balanced look at art and accounts, ranging from memorials of battles and shipwrecks, through depictions of everyday work and conditions, to pictures of the maimed survivors of life at sea.

The Souvenir: Peg-legged Sailor – 'Pray Remember Me'.
Watercolor, early 19th century.

This small souvenir opens like a book to reveal a watercolor picture of a pitiful sailor with a broken peg-leg. Amputation was common for battle injuries and limbs crushed in maritime accidents. Peg-legged sailors, like sailors blinded in one or both eyes, testified to the hazards of the mariner's life.

Philadelphia Floating Church of the Redeemer.

Floating churches were built on the East Coast to woo mariners from a life of sin to a more Christian way of life. In 1848, a group of Philadelphia Episcopalians built a floating church and moored it in the Delaware River. In 1850 she sank; refloated in Philadelphia, she was later towed across the Delaware and set ashore to become a church in Camden, New Jersey. Later the church was consumed by flames.

Chapter Eleven
Symbols and Religion

Over and over in their craft work, in sketches, and in the tools they made, sailors repeated many motifs, some imbued with special significance derived from the sailing life. In our search for the inner life of Jack Tar through artifacts and art he left behind, the sometimes commonplace and sometimes mysterious symbols hold out tantalizing hints. It is rewarding for the modern collector to discover the same motif carved into whale ivory, whale bone, wood, decorating a document, or sketched into a log or journal. Seeing these motifs repeated so many times, we can only speculate about the special appeal they may have had for sailing men, what meanings they conveyed, and what fears, hopes, and longings lay behind them.

Some of the symbols and repeated motifs clearly spoke of women left behind, whether sweetheart, wife, or mother. Hearts were a traditional motif ashore, associated in folk art with the major events of life, including birth, marriage, and death. English and other European settlers brought the motif to America in the colonial period. One of the earliest known examples in America was a gravestone carved in Charlestown, Massachusetts, in 1674. In early American folk art, including the art of the Pennsylvania Dutch and the work of English, Swiss, and French immigrants to the colonies, hearts were ubiquitous. Hearts would adorn utilitarian objects, and decorate crafted items that were made with great care and highly prized,

(Above) *An Illustration from an American Tattoo Design Book (about 112 designs) 1890.*

Pages from rare tattoo books like these help identify the popular themes of the era. Most of the designs of this book are marked with the price for customers, ranging from $4.00 for George Washington to 15 cents for a fouled anchor and 10 cents for a cross.

Sewing box decorated with stars, diamonds, hearts, etc.

Sailors' crafts in gifts for their girlfriends, wives, and mothers, often utilized a range of symbols, some drawn from shore life, others from the sea. This fine sewing box is inlaid with exotic wood, whale ivory, and crushed abalone in the form of hearts, stars, diamonds, flower petals, trees and wreaths. Etched in the plaque on top is 'T. NICKERSON'. A 'Thomas Nickerson' was listed as first mate on the whaler *Samuel Wright* of Salem, Massachusetts, during 1833-36. Perhaps this is the same Thomas Nickerson (1805-1883) who was aboard the whale ship *Essex* when she was struck and sunk by a whale in 1820. Inside, separate spindles carry spools of different colored thread that can be pulled through the holes in the inlaid wooden hearts and diamonds.

Wooden box with inlays.

This elegant wooden box was designed to hold a swift, or wool winder. Note the inlays of hearts, diamonds and stars.

Wooden picture frame with carved heart, cross, anchor, seam rubber, bodkin, serving mallet, snuff spoon.

This grouping of sailor handcrafted items all contain hearts. The wooden frame with cross, anchor, and heart reflects Faith, Hope and Love (Charity). The serving mallet for winding mar-line around a rope and the sailmaker's seam rubber both had very practical ship-board uses. The fine whale ivory bodkin combines a tortoise shell heart and a hand while the snuff spoon has two cutout hearts. It is interesting to note the combination of utility and sentimental decoration – a pining for love of a woman.

celebrating life's milestones.[1] Hearts were particularly common in clock-cases, and in love-tokens and gifts given during courtship, such as rolling pins and boxes. The heart showed up on baptismal certificates, in quilts, and of course, on valentines. So it was fully in the tradition of these shore-side crafts that the sailor adorned gifts for his women-folk with hearts. The sailor in his craftwork made items from whale ivory or whale bone, such as bodkins, busks, and pie-crimpers, decorated wooden boxes and other gifts which repeatedly bore the heart symbol.

In searching for motifs to decorate hand-made gifts, the sailor borrowed liberally from religion and from patriotic art, as well as from established folk art traditions, reaching into his imagination, his memory, and scouring the ship for existing symbols to emulate. Magazines, newspapers, religious tracts, books, and the handicraft of other sailors aboard ship could all provide ideas from which the sailor might draw as he designed his craft work. Stars, diamond-shapes, tear-drop shapes, and more elaborate patriotic eagles, escutcheons, and flags carved from whale ivory adorned some carefully carved wooden objects. From the

1. Cynthia V.A. Schaffner and Susan Klein, *Folk Hearts: A Celebration of the Heart Motif in American Folk Art* (New York: Knopf, 1984), pp. 3-4.

Wooden Slavic plaque: God Bless Our Home.

This carved wooden Slavic plaque reads: 'God Bless our Home', while the delicate carving picks up the common symbols of a cross, anchor and heart representing Faith, Hope and Charity.

eighteenth century, some such surviving inlaid work is quite crude, while later nineteenth century work sometimes reflects the perfection of the skills, particularly among the whalers on long voyages. Among reproduced motifs, which may have been copied from illustrated books or papers, were themes such as leaves and floral designs, similar to those used in cemeteries, and vines and grapes, representing Bacchus and wine, or perhaps good luck. From mythology, figures such as Pegasus, the winged horse, or Neptune and his retinue could provide still other ideas for the more ambitious carver. The horse, reputedly a symbol of lust and longing, occurred over and over in the scrimshander's work on jagging wheels or pie-crimpers, as did the snake.[2]

Delicately carved feminine hands, a frequent motif among craftsmen ashore, although less widespread than the heart, repeatedly appeared in the art of sailors, sometimes in unexpected places, among the items the sailor himself would use on a daily basis. The beckets, holding the macramé handles used on sea chests, were sometimes in the form of a life-sized woman's hand, grasping the loop of rope. Smaller delicate hands adorned earrings and canes, and are found in tattoo books. A lady's hand, like a heart, could serve as a reminder of a woman left behind, or it could convey a deeper sense of contact, a reminder of the grasping of one hand by another, an intimate yet entirely proper representation of the physical contact between individuals. An open hand could well convey a meaning of beneficence and generosity, while an extended hand could represent either an invitation or protection.[3]

More direct evidence of the sailor's thoughts dwelling on the girl or wife who would get the gift was the common practice of carving or inlaying her name or initials into the gift itself. While only a relatively small

Plaque with heart, cross, American eagle, and Masonic motif.

A carved wooden plaque has a wealth of symbols: Masonic square and dividers, anchors, an American eagle and the combined cross, anchor, and heart, also carving representing Scottish thistles.

Cemetery Gate.

This gate from a cemetery may have marked the grave of a sea captain in Nantucket. Apparently the lower portion of the gate was produced by a foundry in some quantity. The top section, with raised name, here 'L.D. Collins', with a shield for the inscription of a date, was separately cast to order and bolted on the lower section. The anchor served to denote a life at sea, now at an end. The neo-gothic quatrefoil design, which was a stylized Christian cross, served as a frame on the outside. The laurel wreath, surrounding the anchor, served as a symbol of valor, or heroism. For mariners who were fortunate enough to live out their last days ashore, such a gate could represent the end of a long life at sea.

number of pieces of scrimshaw have been traced to particular identified sailors, the presence of wives' names on a few have helped in that historical detective work.[4] Carved or painted anchors, whaling lances, and compasses, symbols of sea-life itself, would appear on items destined to be taken ashore as well as used aboard, as mementos of a particular voyage or of years at sea. Just as in paintings and engravings, in which the subject holding an instrument such as a telescope or sextant would convey his rank and occupation aboard, a lance or a stylized whale might denote a whaler, or a compass rose or a ship's wheel might well denote sailing the trackless ocean.

The anchor as a symbol conveyed more than simply a reminder of sailing life. An anchor would only be used when a ship was not sailing, but in a harbor, bay, off-shore anchorage, or other relatively shallow stopping point. As such, it conveyed an implicit meaning – here was the device which held a ship to the land, which represented the beginning or end of a voyage, not the lonely and dangerous passage on the high seas, but the safety of harbor and port.

Anchors, often wrapped in a length of line, or 'fouled', occur over and over. Anchors adorn carved boxes, printed work such as song sheets and title pages of nautical books, sketches in logs, and decorated documents.[5] Oversized anchors shown ashore in prints or in such documents suggest, in an oblique and symbolic way, a voyage which has ended. A depiction of an anchor on a tavern sign, or on a commercial product would mean simply that the place or thing was to be associated with the sailing life, and yet, with the most solid and land-connected aspect of that life.

2. Michael McManus, *A Treasury of American Scrimshaw* (New York: Penguin, 1994), p. 130.
3. McManus, p. 124.
4. McManus, pp. 90-111.
5. Anchors on title pages were extremely common. One example from a rare book in the Collection is William Berrian, *The Sailor's Manual of Devotion* (New York: John Gray, 1857.)

Tattooist Chest.

The hand-decorated inside lid of this American tattooist chest shows the prevalence of patriotic themes in tattooing in the late 19th century. The British and US flags and clasped hands suggest Anglo-American friendship. Note the sailing ship, snakes, stars, cannon and cannon balls.

6. C.H. Fellowes, *The Tattoo Book*, Princeton, NJ: Pyne Press, 1971, p.vii, 5-7. The body of this work is a tattoo catalog discovered in 1966, including designs from the period 1898-1910. The Henderson Collection includes a tattoo catalog from about a decade earlier.

Tattoo Art

The work of tattooing is mostly lost to later generations, for the art itself would be buried on land or at sea when the man bearing the living canvas died. Yet from tattoo-parlor books, some prints showing tattoos, and from some photographs early in the twentieth century, a later generation can glean a sense of what this art form conveyed.

Sometimes, an engraving or print of a stylized sailor, will show a simple anchor on the back of the hand. In the Collection, the earliest print showing an anchor tattooed on a hand is English and dated 1791. Such a symbol, suggesting hope, also served as a signal to everyone who met the sailor ashore, of exactly what his profession was. Two sailors, even when dressed in civilian garb or decked out for church, when meeting for the first time, might spy the anchor. Like a secret handclasp or badge of a club, the small tattoo on the back of the hand would be a silent signal of solidarity, giving a sense of camaraderie at the bottom of the social ladder.

In the late eighteenth century tattooing came rather rapidly into the world of the sailor, after the return of Captain Cook from the South Pacific, where sailors had encountered the lively art of tattooing among the Polynesians. A few sailors had been captured and forcibly tattooed, while others had a few decorations voluntarily made while visiting the islands. One account of the forcible tattooing brought the custom to public attention, *A Narrative of the Shipwreck, Captivity and Suffering of Horace Holden and Benjamin Nute*.[6]

Aboard ships, the custom spread widely in the nineteenth century. The reasons may be simple. Sometimes there was little material available upon which an artist could perform his work; a tattoo could not be stolen from its owner; as artists learned the work, the

Illustrations from an American Tattoo Design Book (about 112 designs), c. 1890.

Pages from rare tattoo books like these help identify the popular themes of the era. Most of the designs of this book are marked with the price for customers, ranging from $4.00 for George Washington to 15 cents for a fouled anchor and 10 cents for a cross.

Examples depicted: 'Jack's Last Port'; George Washington with anchor and cross; Our Navy and clasped hands; US warship, believed to be USS *Chicago*, c.1890; American eagle, clasped hands, cross, anchor, and heart; sailor in hammock dreaming of an angel.

materials were present on many occasions: needles, ink, and the 'canvas' itself. Once a sailor had a tattoo, he never need worry about losing it as he moved from ship to ship, something that could not be said of any other piece of art work or personal adornment. So when tattoos were introduced into the Atlantic culture of sailors, they fitted perfectly into the lifestyle, needs, and into the folk art traditions that had already developed.

Finding exact and reliable evidence of the kinds of tattoo art the ordinary sailor of the mid-nineteenth century displayed on his skin is no easy matter. To know this art form, we must look at the rarely-preserved tattoo-sample books and sample-cards which shop owners provided to sailors.

From the tattoo sample-books, we see that shipboard artists and those who set up tattoo parlors ashore later in the nineteenth century soon began to replicate many of the themes that had become common in the older three-dimensional craft work of sailors, including: patriotism, naval events and ships, women with hour-glass figures presented as 'liberty' or as a goddess, and a wide variety of personal messages of love and devotion to the girls and mothers left behind. Tattoo art became the repository for more than a century of existing sailor-craft themes.

Examining early sample books, many of the ancient themes and symbols show up along with some new ones: personal initials, hearts, clasped hands with and without wedding rings, representations of particular naval ships, flags, cowgirls, Liberty, stylized sailing ships, George Washington, crosses with garlands and crosses alone, flags with shields and arrows, goddesses such as Ceres or Aphrodite, Neptune and his attendants, representations of the sailor's departure copied from the classic engravings, and fouled anchors. Now and then an identifiable particular ship, such as the 1880s USS *Chicago* or the 1890s USS *Maine* help us now to estimate the time frame of the tattoo sample collection.

Various legends surrounded the meaning of the tattooed cross. Some have asserted that Christian sailors wore a cross to ensure that they would receive a proper burial if they died

Tattoo – 'The Sailor's Return'.

Another tattoo illustration captures the traditional theme of 'The Sailor's Return', with ship, loving couple and a waiting home. Samuel F. O'Reilly was the inventor of an electric tattoo machine that spread world-wide.

British Seaman on the gun deck of a British man-of-war receiving a tattoo.
Chromolithograph, late 19th century.

Working by the light of the gun port a sailor tattoo artist embellishes a fellow sailor with patriotic emblems: crown and flags – traditional themes in British sailor art.

in a foreign port. More superstitious sailors may have believed that a tattooed cross would prevent their body from being devoured by fish if buried at sea.

The tattoo books help define some of the symbols that caught on in the folk culture of the sailor as tattoo work gave every sailor the chance to carry with him some personally chosen decoration. Because tattoos fitted so well into the demands of sailing life, with their permanence, portability, and availability of materials, sailors could conveniently capture those elements of art with which they most closely identified. For such reasons, it is no surprise that female figures, patriotic emblems, ship-names, and the embellished anchor became so common. In the late nineteenth century, mores, custom and even naval regulation appeared to prevent sailors from indulging in tattoos that depicted lascivious women, but among early twentieth century sailors, the women in tattoo art began to look more and more the pin-up girls in the popular press. Like the craft work, however, tattoo art was not made for a later generation but for its owner and each example had a life span limited by that owner. The catalogs, sample-books and sample-cards, and some prints and photographs, therefore, remain as collectibles, providing us now with only an elusive suggestion of the richness of the art form.

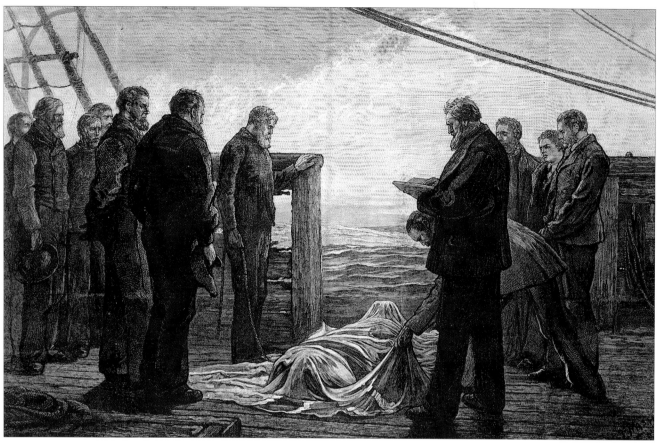

Harper's Weekly, *31 March, 1877*.
Wood engraving.
'Therefore we commit his body to the Deep'.

This rather faithful depiction of a burial at sea shows one sailor with a line beneath the board on which the body rests, while another grasps the flag, so that when the wrapped body is tipped over, the flag will be retained. The captain reads the service, and the other sailors, heads bowed, think their own thoughts at this solemn moment.

(Opposite) *Burial at Sea.*
Watercolor.

In a tragic explosion in 1881 off Punta Arenas, HMS *Doterel*, a screw sloop launched in 1880, of 1,130 tons, sank to the bottom of the sea. This funeral ceremony, after the fact, is attended by boats from HMS *Champion* (on the left) and HMS *Turquoise* in the Straits of Magellan.

Death and Religion

For the sailor, always facing the perils of the sea, thoughts of death and dying were never far away. Symbols of the afterlife abounded: death's-head, crosses, and from time to time, stylized representations of devils. The death's-head, so famous as the symbol of pirate flags, was common on the headstones of graveyards ashore. In some older log books, a captain might enter a small skull and crossbones or outline his entry in black to indicate those days on which a sailor had been killed at sea, just as a whaling captain might stamp in his log a stylized outline of a whale on those days when one or more were killed.

A death's-head in a log served as the briefest notation of a life lost that day. The burial ceremony aboard ship, with the disposal of a weighted and canvas-wrapped body over the side, was a sad and solemn occasion, with a reading of the service from a book of prayer. Many travellers or seamen who kept a journal or diary, when witnessing a burial at sea, would offer a brief description. The Hodge Diary included his attendance 28 December, 1797 at John Alkison's burial. And in 1799, Hodge noted men lost overboard in September and November.

As we look at death's-head, and then at crosses, angels, devils, and quotations from the Bible carved or cut out by sailors, the question naturally arises: were the sailors truly religious, or were they simply echoing motifs because they were common in the culture? Scholars disagree about the degree of piety of sailors, perhaps more reflective of the divergence of opinion among the commentators than among their subjects. Sunday church services were common, but did the holding of a service mean that sailors were pious? Those who believe such services simply represented men going through the motions have ample evidence to support their view.

Dr Beers rather dryly noted the matter of fact saying of prayers at a burial at sea in his journal for 18 April, 1824:

> The dead body of a seaman was committed to the deep yesterday and today another is to undergo the same ceremony. The corpse is sewed up in a hammock with 2 or 3 heavy shot, then placed on a board which is inclined until the body slips off.[7]

7. Journal of Dr Samuel Beers, entry for April, 1824, in WH Collection.

Even worse than a funeral at sea was the loss of a man overboard. The Hodge Diary, the Hill letters, and practically every logbook or seaman's journal notes from the nineteenth century, remarks upon attendance at church services and funerals, but frequently such contemporary documents reflect skepticism about the genuine effect or feeling of the sailors in attendance. In 1834, in his account of his voyage before the mast, Dana noted:

> If there is anything which irritates sailors and makes them feel hardly used, it is being deprived of their Sabbath. Not that they would always, or indeed generally, spend it religiously, but it is their only day of rest.[8]

Dana was not the only one to observe that the most important part of the Sabbath celebration for sailors was not religious service, but the respite from work. In 1824, Dr Samuel Beers witnessed a service and clearly doubted any positive effects:

> A sermon was delivered today by our chaplin which to use a very poetic expression what it contained was like 'an idiot's frivolous dream'. The effusions of this man's oratory and the beaming rays of the sun beating on the bare heads of his hearers would probably cooperate in producing idiotism.[9]

Shore leave on a Sabbath was not always a search for a church service, but simply a chance to escape from the confines of the ship, and perhaps to scout out opportunities for more ribald pleasures ashore. The struggle between sin and salvation, between blasphemy and prayer, between cavorting and converting became ever more prominent in the nineteenth century, with the efforts of missionaries and preachers to affect the lives of sailors.

In the merchant and naval fleets of Britain, the United States, and nations of Europe, religious leaders and congregations worked hard through the rest of the century to convert the wayward sailor. The 'Bethel' movement began in London in the years 1816–1817, growing out of the Methodist-led revival movement there which hoped to make converts out of the hard-drinking, swearing and

THE FLOATING CHURCH OF OUR SAVIOUR, FOR SEAMEN

The Floating Church of Our Saviour, For Seamen.
Built for the Young Men's Church Missionary Society, New York, 15 February, 1844.

One of several floating churches built in the United States. The floating church movement, like the Bethel church movement more broadly, had its beginnings in Britain. Designed to attract seamen and make them comfortable, such churches in New York, Philadelphia, London and elsewhere served the spiritual needs of transient sailors.

The Chapel for Seamen (aboard a ship).

From about 1816 onward, missionary societies and church groups worked to bring religion to the seamen of the Anglo-American seagoing world. This Chapel for Seamen opened aboard a ship in the Port of London, 18 March, 1818, and was the earliest floating chapel for seamen.

roughneck sailors returning from the Napoleonic wars, many of whom were destitute or maimed. A symbol of the movement to establish seamen's churches was a Bethel Flag designed by one Zebedee Rogers, depicting a cross and a dove and a star of Bethlehem on a blue background. The symbols represented Christmas, Easter, and the Pentecost. The symbols of the Bethel movement, shown on its flag, spread as various churches around Britain and later, around the world, established special meeting places for seamen, and 'bethel' churches were soon found in many ports.[10]

A close scholarly study of the Bethel mission movement by Roald Kverndal suggests that it was quite successful, at least as measured by its rapid world-wide expansion. Yet the mere founding of churches and social centers is external to the man; was Jack Tar really beginning to have faith? That question is more perplexing. Every sailor convert was under pressure from his ship mates to return to his earlier life style, for as Kverndal noted, 'there could be no basic compatibility between a Christian walk of faith and a model of manhood which had to prove itself by bouts of confirmed depravity.'[11]

Ashore, the movement to minister to the social needs of sailors as well as their spiritual needs led to the creation of the Seaman's Home Societies in Britain in the 1820s and their rapid emulation in many port cities and in the United States. Several floating churches were constructed and are depicted in surviving prints and paintings. Two of the earliest

8. Dana, p. 74.
9. Journal of Samuel Beers, August, 1824, in WH Collection.
10. Roald Kverndal, *Seaman's Missions: Their Origin and Early Growth* (Pasadena, CA: William Carey Library, 1986), pp. 156–162.
11. Kverndal, p. 567.

were the 'Floating Chapel for Seamen', dedicated 4 May, 1818, in London, and the 'Floating Church of Our Saviour' launched in 1844 in New York Harbor. A second floating church in New York, the 'Floating Church of the Holy Comforter', was opened at the foot of Dey Street 11 October, 1846. Another floating church in the Delaware River, for sailors stopping in Philadelphia, was called the 'Floating Church of the Redeemer', consecrated 11 January, 1849. Constructed on a barge or on a pair of hulls, these churches could be moored at the docks amidst the coming and going of ocean-going ships, convenient for seamen.

The establishment of the Philadelphia church was stimulated by the creation of the New York floating churches a few years earlier. The Churchmen's Missionary Association for Seamen of the Port of Philadelphia raised the funds for the floating church on the Delaware River, which could hold 600 people. Less than two years after being launched, the church sank, due to defects in the twin hulls on which it was built. Refloated, the church was towed from one mooring to another, and in 1853, was towed across the river to Camden, New Jersey, where it was set ashore. There it became the Parish Church of St John's, but it later burned down. Meanwhile, the Association in Philadelphia rented a loft on Dock Street, and continued to hold services. The surviving institution is the 'Seaman's Church Institute of Philadelphia'.[12]

Among the reasons for constructing such floating churches and special seamen's churches ashore near the waterfront was the consideration that sailors might feel more welcome in such a setting, knowing it was constructed especially for them. The well-established congregations in churches on shore, may often have seemed unwelcoming to the transient sailors, with their rough manners, their distinctive clothing, and their rolling walk. 'The sight of a floating church,' wrote one supporter of the movement in 1848, 'carries the conviction to [the sailor's] mind that it was designed for him; and if landsmen should be there, he knows that they are the strangers, not he.'[13]

The Bethel church described in Melville's *Moby Dick* in New Bedford, Massachusetts, with its pulpit in the form of a ship's prow, still holds services, still mounting the same nautical decor. Bethel churches which held services for seaman were soon found throughout the world, many of which survive to this day. Charitable societies set them up in major cities, and missionaries established them in remote seaports. In the Collection is a letter from a Mr Thomson Mifsionary (*sic*), inviting the captain and crew of an American whaleship anchored in Papeete Bay, Tahiti, to Sunday services at the bethel chapel, 'abreast of the Frigate Grampus.'

Seamen's Missions and Bethel societies became so widespread that it is difficult to believe that nineteenth century sailors could avoid their influence. With boarding houses set up for sailors, well-established churches providing them with literature and services in nearly every major port, the average sailor was thoroughly exposed to religion by the 1840s and later.

The mission societies worked hard at interdicting the sailor's encounters with prostitutes,

12. Kverndal, pp. 507-508.
13. *An Appeal of the Churchmen's Missionary Association for Seamen at the Port of Philadelphia*. Philadelphia: Daniel Schnesk, 1848, p. 13.

Memorial with willows.

Willow trees were a recurrent symbol of mourning. The widow in funereal black, the ship, and the memorial convey a whole story of mortality and faith. The inscription reads:

To
the Memory of
Capt.
Atwell Richmond
Lost at Sea Jan. 7 1831.
In the 42nd Year
of his age.

Now wild despair in every eye
Beheld a watery grave.
O say my muse was no one nigh
His fellow men to save?

When lo! the strong increasing gale,
With rude and sudden sweep,
Before they'd time to reef a sail,
O'erwhelmed them in the deep.

crimps, tavern-keepers, and the other temptations of the port cities. Yet 'Sailortown vice' and the twin deities of 'Bacchus and Venus' were powerful opponents, and for every report of conversion or successful church attendance, the ministry continued to report 'backsliding' and defection from the church.[14]

There is hardly any way to measure, in retrospect, the degree to which the Bethel movement succeeded in bringing religion to sailors. The tension between heathen and Christian was a major theme in Melville's *Moby Dick*, accounting for the fact that the book was not accepted by the reading public in the United States until well into the twentieth century. Journals in the Collection, like that of Samuel Beers, who found the preacher inducing 'idiotism' reflect similar contemporary tension.

Despite Dr Beers' skepticism, depictions of prayer aboard ship, of devout services with bowed heads on the ships of many nations, and repeated depictions of funeral rites for sailors leave us with plenty of evidence that sailors in the nineteenth century aboard American, British, and other ships, encountered religion on a daily basis.

14. Kverndal, pp. 566–568.

267

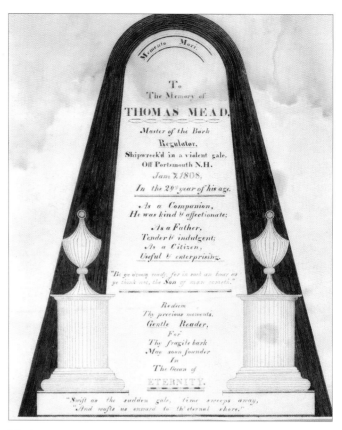

Memorial to Thomas Mead.

Memento mori messages like this were designed to remind the living of their own mortality and to draw lessons for those living ashore from the sudden and unexpected death of sailing men. The inscription reads:

Memento Mori
To
The Memory of
THOMAS MEAD,
Master of the Bark
Regulator,
Shipwreck'd in a violent gale,
Off Portsmouth N.H.
Jan. 7. 1808,
In the 29th year of his age.
As a Companion,
He was kind & affectionate;
As a Father,
Tender & indulgent;
As a Citizen,
Useful & enterprising.

"Be ye always ready, for in such an hour as
ye think not, the Son of man cometh."

Redeem
Thy precious moments,
Gentle Reader,
For
Thy fragile bark
May soon founder
In
The Ocean of
ETERNITY.

"Swift as the sudden gale, time sweeps away,
"And wafts us onward to th' eternal shore."

Passages from the Bible which related to sailing and sea were frequently quoted in logs, journals, and in religious material produced for sailors. *The Seaman's Companion*, printed in London in 1676, includes six sermons by John Flavell, based on six separate passages from the Bible, in the book of Acts, Psalms, Deuteronomy, and Luke.[15] Tracts, prayer books, and collections of sermons especially written for the sailor abounded in the nineteenth century, and such religious material, although rare, serves as testimony to the effort to bring sailors to religion.

In their crafts, sailors repeated many themes and motifs that reflected their thoughts of the afterlife, including crosses, angels, memorial urns, and weeping willows. The awful

15. John Flavell, *The Seaman's Companion*, London: Francis Titon, 1676.

Grazia Ricevuta della Vergine S.ta delle Grazie alla Bombarda Nom.ta il S.mo nome di Maria del Cap.e Paolo Mittelli sotto il giorno 7 giugno 1822 Stromboli

Ex Voto, *7 June, 1822.*
Watercolor gouache.

An art genre on the continent of Europe, the *Ex Voto* usually depicted a miraculous escape from catastrophe with a depiction of the Virgin Mary and Jesus to whom prayers had been offered and to whose intervention survival was attributed. Captain Paolo Mittelli commissioned this work after escaping bombardment from falling lava during an eruption of Stromboli off Italy in 1822.

mystery of death at sea seemed to haunt the minds of many sailor-craftsmen as they carved their work. Signs of crosses, angels, and devils give hints of those thoughts. Doves might symbolize the flight to heaven of the soul; the willow would signify loneliness and mourning, while vines and evergreens might represent life after death. Portuguese and Spanish sailors in the American whaling fleet sometimes carved detailed pictures of Christ on the Cross, perhaps reflecting a more devout group, or perhaps simply the Catholic cultural tradition of representing the crucifixion more graphically, with a bleeding body.[16]

We may imagine a sailor working as craftsman through the long hours of a slow watch. As he concentrated intently on shaping his work, did he think of the meanings conveyed by the symbols? When carving scrimshaw shapes for a gift, did he speculate about the woman to whom he would give the present, and dwell on what she would think when using it? When making a tool for himself, did he daydream of the hours he would later spend using it? And as he carved or painted the crosses or angels, did he echo in his heart the prayers and sermons he had heard through the Bethel movement and in the services aboard ship?

As we look at surviving artifacts, replete with hearts, crosses, anchors, hands, implements

16. McManus, pp. 133, 134. Despite the depiction of many religious motifs in the scrimshaw shown in his work, McManus concludes, 'The fact remains that religion played a very minor role on board except for burial at sea.'

Masonic Apron.

Captain Daniel Clifford Payson left this masonic apron among his effects at the time of his death by drowning in the mouth of the Mississippi in 1827. The handwritten legend gives the details of his membership in a Newburyport masonic lodge. The apron and the explanation help document masonry among American seafarers.

of the sea, and mysterious emblems of masonry, navigation, astronomy, ancient mythology, and motifs from Christianity, we may glimpse more deeply into the inner thoughts of the sailor. We can only guess whether the sailor's intense concentration focused on making the shape to match perfectly the ideal form, or penetrated more deeply to the meaning of the symbol he carved or drew.

Behind those objects and images, were hours of carving, sketching, and handling of everyday objects by Jack Tar, never far from his concerns of loneliness for women, hard work, rigorous punishment, and the constant perils of the sea that could bring him to face eternity at any moment.

Be it known to all men present, that Benjamin Block, of the Parish of St Catherines, having a desire to become a member of the ancient Fraternity of Masons, hitherto comply'd with the usual ceremonies. Viz. having his Shirt-flaps cut and marked with divers mysteries signs, and tangents — it now only remains — to fix on the bandage — and prepare the red hot poker, (for which purposes the proper Officers, are now attending) and the initiation is complete.

Harke'e Mr Wigsby — mind what I say, I have consented to have my main sheets cut and hack'd about, in a pretty stile, and Poll will swear enough about that, when she comes to over-hawl my rigging, but D—n me, if you offer to blind fold me, or to heave in sight any of your red hot pokers, may I never weigh anchor again. — If I don't upset every Man Jack of you. —

MAKING a SAILOR a FREE MASON.

Cartoon: 'Making a Sailor a Free Mason'.

A number of maritime handicraft items contain masonic symbols. This cartoon parody of a masonic initiation ceremony plays on the sailor's use of nautical jargon when ashore. In fact, many British and American mariners (most of whom were officers) were masons and some would draw on the ceremonies and emblems of the order when crafting items from wood or other materials.

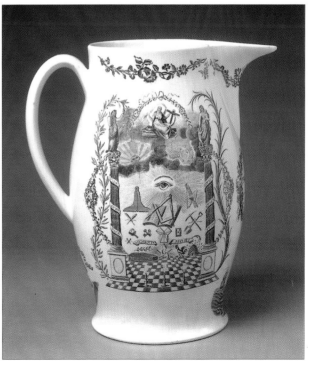

English Creamware Jug – 'The Mary' – with Masonic Symbols.

This English creamware baluster-shaped jug (probably Liverpool, *c.*1803), transfer printed in black with painted enamel colors, displays a design incorporating many Masonic symbols including Hope and the eye representing the Supreme Being. Many sea captains were members of Masonic Lodges and decorated their artifacts with Masonic symbols. On the reverse is an American brig inscribed 'The Mary'.

'USS Georgia Cruice (sic) Around the World'. Souvenir.

The 'USS Georgia' departed Hampton Roads 16 December, 1907, with fifteen other battleships and auxiliary vessels on the first leg of an around-the-world cruise of the 'Great White Fleet'. President Theodore Roosevelt conceived of the voyage as a way of demonstrating America's arrival as a naval power. This embroidered panel shows a photograph of the sailor/purchaser visiting in Yokohama in late October; in early November the squadron was in Amoy, China, where this embroidered souvenir was probably created. A painting of the Great White Fleet is also depicted. On 22 February, 1909, an unprecedented voyage of 14,000 men covering 46,000 miles was completed at Hampton Roads.

CHAPTER TWELVE

Epilogue

B
y the turn of the twentieth century, life had changed for the average British and American seaman who sailed the oceans of the world. No longer threatened with press gangs, rarely experiencing the trickery of crimps, and now living amongst advocates of temperance, reform, and social progress, the sailor faced a different world than his forebears had in 1750 or 1800. Although wind-driven wooden merchant sailing ships still plied coastal waters and fishing grounds, the major merchant routes were dominated by steel-hulled, steam-propelled ships. By 1900, more and more steamships carried no sails at all. Steam turbines, diesel engines, and powerful new and larger ships started to dominate the seaways. Large coal-smoke belching freighters supplanted the sailing merchantmen, and vast new passenger liners, like floating palaces, captured the sea routes from Liverpool to New York and criss-crossed the oceans of the world.

In some ways, the life of Jack Tar still reflected much of the tradition that had developed over the prior century and a half. In the United States and British navies, sailors knew of the heritage that lay behind them, with its heroes, with its protocols and practices of port-calls, and its rich rituals and customs. Small arms drill, saluting the flag, attending Sunday services, burials at sea, holiday celebrations, all carried patterns of the past.

Reformers had made progress against abuses. Of great relief to Jack Tar was the suspension of impressment in England after 1815. The United States did not have impressment. A milestone in punishment in the American Navy was the abolition of flogging in 1850.[1] Two decades later in England, the use of the cat-o'-nine-tails was suspended in peacetime and altogether in 1879.[2] However, not all was smooth sailing. For

(Above) '*He cometh not*'. Photograph.

For sailors, no matter when they go to sea, there is always the possibility that they may not return which is so poignantly depicted in this photograph.

1. Dennis J. Ringle, *Life in Mr. Lincoln's Navy* (Annapolis, MD: Naval Institute Press, 1998), p. 101 and Harold D. Langley, *Social Reform in the United States Navy, 1798-1862* (Chicago: University of Illinois Press, 1967), p. 117.
2. J.R. Hill, *The Oxford Illustrated History of the Royal Navy* (Oxford, NY: Oxford University Press, 1995), p. 265.

instance, in 1859, British naval authorities were faced with low morale and a disruptive situation. To alleviate these circumstances the government enacted five Navy Discipline Acts or amendments during the 1860s and other ameliorating actions were taken.[3] In both the British and American navies in the 1860s and '70s there was a transformation of the conditions of the ordinary sailor.

One of the major reasons for these changes was the transition from sail to steam. This change led to widespread effects on the living conditions of the sailors. Eventually, damp and dark wooden walls became steel with heating and lighting. Because of steam, fresh water was possible. Fresh water could take the place of foul-smelling and problematic drinking water and of salt water for washing clothes.[4] The machinery for steam engines and new auxiliary equipment required engineers. Engineering required special training. Great advances were made in gunnery and this necessitated special training.[5] With the requirement for specialists came a need for a new type of sailor, one with more ability and potential to learn new skills than in the sailing days. To attract this type, both the British and the American navies became aware of the necessity of improving their images and conditions of the sailor: doing away with corporal punishment, better pay, better pensions, a chance for a professional, lifelong career and better leave policy.

In 1880, corporal punishment was officially made illegal by the British authorities.[6] Flogging was replaced with confinement. By 1880 there were numerous indications in England of success in attracting sufficient numbers of high caliber and better quality seamen.

There were claims that the American Navy was a major attraction for Englishmen. For many decades, the number of foreign sailors aboard American flag vessels had been a concern of the federal government. For instance, at some point during the Civil War aboard Admiral Farragut's flag ship, USS *Hartford*, the crew was 35% foreign, the USS *Cairo* was 33%, the USS *Louisiana* was 28%, and the USS *Kearsarge* was 21%. Most of these foreigners were Northern Europeans especially from Ireland.[7] One author, Professor Peter Karstan, stated that in 1878, 60% of the enlisted men in the American Navy were foreign-born.[8]

On the officer front, many British officers after the Napoleonic Wars for many years were faced with economic and promotion problems.[9] There were too many officers and too few billets.

During the nineteenth century, a sailor's social status and the way he saw his position in society changed very little until the last quarter of the century. After years of public indifference, in the 1890s the British sailor suddenly became fashionable. At this time in the United States there were growing efforts to improve the lot of the sailor and build up America as a world naval power.

Although flogging and some other cruel punishments had long been abandoned in both navies, strict discipline aboard ships and the expectation of obedience to orders continued to be the rule. While conditions in merchant ships lagged behind, the sadistic cruelty of near-psychopathic ship captains that Dana and his contemporaries had decried became rare. Advocates such as the members of the American Seamen's Friend Society in the United

3. Eugene L. Rasor, *Reform in the Royal Navy* (Connecticut: Archon Books, 1976), p. 14.

4. Dennis J. Ringle, *Life in Mr. Lincoln's Navy* (Annapolis, MD: Naval Institute Press, 1998), pp. 8, 109.

5. Eugene L. Rasor, *Reform in the Royal Navy* (Connecticut: Archon Books, 1976), p. 34.

6. Ibid. p. 48.

7. Dennis J. Ringle, *Life in Mr. Lincoln's Navy* (Annapolis, MD: Naval Institute Press, 1998), pp. 17-18.

8. Eugene L. Rasor, *Reform in the Royal Navy* (Connecticut: Archon Books, 1976), p. 27 and W. Jeffrey Bolster, *Black Jacks* (Cambridge, MA: Harvard University Press, 1997), p. 224.

9. Anthony J. Watts, *The Royal Navy: An Illustrated History*, (Annapolis, MD: Naval Institute Press, 1994), p. 9.

U. S. Sailors Life "Cleaning Up".

U. S. Sailors Life "Assisting the Cook."

U. S. Sailors Life "Sewing Class".

U. S. Sailors Life "Sport aboard Ship."

U. S. Sailors Life "A Boxing Match."

U. S. Sailors Life "Music on Board."

'Day to Day Life Aboard'.
Postcards. *c.*1900

Through the centuries some things remain basically the same for those who go to sea. These six postcards dating from about 1900 depict: 1) 'Cleaning Up' – swabbing the deck; 2) 'Assisting the Cook' – peeling potatoes; 3) 'Sewing Class' – making and mending; 4) 'Sport Aboard Ship' – gambling; 5) 'A Boxing Match' – only gloves have been added; 6) 'Music on Board' – music was perennial.

States[10] and Samuel Plimsoll in Britain fought for safety and improved working conditions. Labor unions worked to raise wages and improve the lot of merchant sailors. The British continued to serve grog aboard ships of the Royal Navy well into the twentieth century, although the more strait-laced American Navy had banned alcohol on its ships much earlier.

Postcards and photographs had replaced prints and hand-crafted souvenirs in some exotic ports; yet in the harbor towns, bars, brothels and street girls continued to beckon to the

10. Dennis J. Ringle, *Life in Mr. Lincoln's Navy* (Annapolis, MD: Naval Institute Press, 1998), p. 3.

Model of the Battleship USS Massachusetts.

Today one would call this creation 'folk art' and it was probably done by a sailor. Note the large number of miniature sailors aboard. The actual battleship, *Massachusetts*, was launched at William Cramp & Sons' shipyard at Philadelphia in 1893. With the possibility of war with Spain in March 1898, she was assigned to the Flying Squadron for defense of the Eastern seaboard. She participated in shelling fortifications at Santiago, Cuba. Early in July 1898 she helped the Battleship *Texas* force the Spanish cruiser *Reina Mercedes* to beach and surrender. In later years she was a member of the North Atlantic Squadron, a training ship for Naval Academy midshipmen and subsequently for Naval Reserve gunnery training. She finished her days as a target ship.

visiting sailor. And the women left behind at home still haunted the sailor's memory. Tattoos of hearts on the arm or chest, with the wife's or girlfriend's name or initials entwined, gradually came to replace the lovingly carved heart in wood, or whale-ivory, or inlaid abalone shell. Some of the motifs of earlier crafts survived well into the twentieth century, with the heart, cross, and anchor constant reminders of maritime traditions. Lighthouses, stars, flags, weeping willows, mothers, angels, masonic emblems, and many other symbols and signs were repeated from year to year, decade to decade, surviving on their own as bearers of tradition and the culture of the sea.

With the construction of the ABCD ships and the beginning of the New Navy in the 1880s, the United States Navy began to supplant ironclad wooden hulls and sails with steel

LOCATION OF THE MAINE—HAVANA HARBOR.

RECOVERING THE DEAD BODIES.

Copyrighted 1898 by Kurz & Allison, 267-269 Wabash Ave., Chicago.

Launched 1890.   Blown up 1898.
Draught, 21 ft. 6 in. 6,682 tons. Speed
17 knots. 9,293 H. P. Cost, $3,000,000.

DESTRUCTION OF THE U. S. BATTLESHIP MAINE

In Havana Harbor, February 15th 1898, 9:40 P. M.

Armament, 4-10 in. breech-loading
Rifles; 14 rapid fire Guns; 4 revolving
Cannons; 4 Gatlings; 7 Torpedo Tubes;
Officers and Crew, 450;   Killed and
Drowned, 266.

'Destruction of the U.S. Battleship Maine'.
Print.

In 1895, a recurrent revolt against Spanish rule broke out in Cuba. The battleship *Maine* entered Havana Harbor to protect American lives and interests in January 1898. She was rent by a terrific explosion on 15 February, 1898. The exact cause of the explosion is still debated. At that time the American press called for war-like actions against Spain claiming Spanish sabotage by a mine. The United States, in essence, declared war on Spain on 21 April, 1898. 'Remember the Maine' became a popular slogan.

ships and steam power.[11] After the mysterious explosion that sank the battleship *Maine* on 15 February, 1898, in Havana Harbor,[12] the United States demonstrated the power of the modernized fleet in the brief Spanish-American War. The overwhelming victory of Commodore George Dewey over Spain's Asiatic fleet in Manila Bay, 1 May, 1898 and of Commodore Winfield Scott Schley over another Spanish fleet outside Santiago Bay, Cuba on 3 July proved the efficacy of the modern ships. Under the treaty of peace with Spain, the United States gained an instant empire: the islands of Guam, Puerto Rico and the Philippines.[13]

To protect these far-flung territories, the United States soon began to exercise its naval strength, in the arms race, vying with Germany to take second place after the Royal Navy.

11. Jack Sweetman, *American Naval History: An Illustrated Chronology* (Annapolis, MD: Naval Institute Press, 1984), pp. 96, 99.
12. Thomas B. Allen, 'Remember the Maine?' (*The National Geographic*, Feb. 1998), pp. 92-109.
13. Jack Sweetman, *American Naval History: An Illustrated Chronology* (Annapolis, MD: Naval Institute Press, 1984), pp. 103-111.

'Battle of Manila Bay, 1 May, 1898'.
Print.

On 25 April, 1898, Congress declared that a state of war had existed with Spain since 21 April. The Secretary of the Navy cabled Commodore Dewey, commanding the Asiatic Squadron at Hong Kong, to proceed to the Philippine Islands and commence operations against the Spanish fleet. On 1 May, 1898, with Commodore Dewey aboard his flagship USS *Olympia*, his squadron steamed into Manila Bay and gained complete victory over the Spanish Fleet located there. With this victory, Dewey became one of the great national heroes in American naval history. In 1899, he was elevated to the rank of 'Admiral of the Navy' – no other officer has ever attained that prestigious position.

14. Robert A. Hart, *The Great White Fleet* (Boston: Little, Brown and Company, 1965), p. 26.
15. Jack Sweetman, *American Naval History: An Illustrated Chronology* (Annapolis, MD: Naval Institute Press, 1984), p. 119.

In 1907-1909, US President Theodore Roosevelt, a forceful proponent of a strong navy, sent the 'Great White Fleet' on a world tour.[14] Reminiscent of the gunboat diplomacy of Matthew C. Perry in opening Japan to western trade, and echoing earlier around-the-world cruises of British and American naval ships, the Great White Fleet carried the American flag to foreign ports and demonstrated the emergence of a new World Power. Meanwhile, construction crews and engineers worked against great odds to build the Panama Canal, so that the United States would never again have to race its warships around Cape Horn to defend one of its coasts.[15]

By 1910, the life of Jack Tar had changed greatly, and the era of sail and sail-and-steam had come to an end. Aircraft, wireless telegraphy, and submarines would make the next naval war – just over the horizon – very different from those that had gone before.

Even so, in the first decade of the twentieth century, echoes of the age of sail could still be heard and seen in the art, in the memories, in the customs, and in the day-to-day lives

Items produced to commemorate Admiral Dewey's victory over the Spanish fleet at Manila Bay.

With the annihilation of the Spanish fleet at Manila Bay, George Dewey became hero of the day. A countless number of hero-worship items were produced. One such is the printed textile 'The Hero of Manila. Admiral Dewey.' Also shown is a signed photograph of Dewey in his uniform of 'Admiral of the Navy', to which rank he was elevated in 1899 and to this day is the only officer ever to have held that position. The lid of the cut crystal pitcher is engraved 'GD' 'USS Olympia' and is believed to be his own personal water pitcher.

of sailors. Crossing the line ceremonies, often considerably softened from the harsh initiation rites of an earlier century, now involved passengers aboard liners and freighters as well as new crew members. Ships still saluted each other with guns; officers were still piped aboard by bosun's whistle; in the US Navy, black men still served as stewards and cooks[16] and stood in the rear of group photographs. Aboard ship in the long watches of the night, sailors still dreamed of the wives and sweethearts and the cozy homes left behind, and old salts who had taken up the sea in the age of Melville retold stories of windjammers, high seas, and the days before diesel and steam. Mariners still faced the perils of the sea, when storms, reefs, shallow water, collision, fire, and fatefully, icebergs, continued to threaten their lives.

As the age of sail drew to a close, the art and artifact, the crafts, the prints and the pictures started to find their own perilous way down through the years. Passed on as traces of an age, they went from parlor and heirloom, and from shipping office, to storage trunk and

16. W. Jeffrey Bolster, *Black Jacks* (Cambridge, MA: Harvard University Press, 1997), p. 223

'Spinning a Yarn'.

One thing that has not changed through the centuries: as long as sailors sail the seven seas, they will always have long yarns to swap.

dusty attic, then to junk shop and antique dealer, and on to auction houses, and thence to museums, archives, and into the carefully assembled holdings of many private collectors. Some valuable items were lost, destroyed in fires and the bombing raids of later wars, and others were simply thrown out amidst accumulated rubbish, unrecognized for the silent messages they carried of their origin. What has survived to our times, when carefully sorted and viewed with sensitivity, can represent a window on the age of sail and sail-and-steam. Through that window, we catch glimpses of a way of life that is now long vanished.

In these bits and pieces we hope we can still see Jack Tar as he was, in his motives, his punishments and perils, his emotions, his hopes, and his prayers. The search will continue, and collectors will always be part of that search.

Bibliography

Secondary works either cited in the text or forming part of the background information.
Rare books in the Henderson Collection are included in this listing.

Abbott, Charles. *Treatise of the Law Relative to Merchant Ships and Seamen.* Charles Abbott of Inner Temple, second American (edition) from the Third London Edition with annotations, by Joseph Story, Esq. Newburyport: Edward Little & Co, 1810. (Henry Phelps, New York, October 1817)

Allen, Oliver. *The Seafarers: The Windjammers.* Alexandria, VA: Time-Life Books, 1978.

Altoff, Gerard T. *Amongst My Best Men: African-Americans and the War of 1812.* Put in Bay, OH; The Perry Group, 1966.

Baddeley, John. *Nautical Antiques and Collectables.* London: Sotheby's Publications, 1993.

Banks, Steven. *Handicrafts of the Sailor.* David & Charles, Newton Abbot, UK, 1974.

Barker, M.H. *Greenwich Hospital.* London 1826.

Bassett, Fletcher S. *Legends and Superstions of the Sea and of Sailors in all Lands and at all Times.* London: Low, Marston, Searle, & Rivington, 1885.

Bauer, K. Jack. *A Maritime History of the United States: The Role of America's Seas and Waterways.* Columbia, SC: University of SC Press, 1988.

Baynham, Henry. *Before the Mast: Naval Ratings of the 19th Century.* London: Arrow, 1972.

Baynham, Henry. *From the Lower Deck: the Old Navy, 1780-1840.* London: Hutchinson, 1969.

Beck, Horace. *Folklore and the Sea.* Lexington, MA: The Mystic Seaport Museum, 1983.

Berrian, William. *The Sailor's Manual of Devotion.* New York: John Gray, 1857.

Bishop, Robert. *Folk Art in American Life.* New York: Museum of American Folk Art, Viking Studio Books, 1995.

Bligh, William. *Lt. Wm. Bligh's voyage in the Bounty's Launch from the ship to Tofua and from thence to Timor.* 1790.

Bligh, William. *An Account of the Mutiny on the Bounty.* 1792.

Bolster, W. Jeffrey. *Black Jacks: African American Seamen in the Age of Sail.* Cambridge, MA: Harvard University Press, 1997.

Botting, Douglass. *The Seafarers: The Pirates.* Alexandria, VA: Time-Life Books, 1978.

Branch-Johnson, W. *The English Prison Hulks.* London: Christopher Johnson, 1957.

Browne, J. Ross. *Etchings of a Whaling Cruise and with notes of a Sojourn on the Island of Zanzibar, to which is appended a brief history of the whale fishery, its past and present condition.* New York: Harper and Brothers, 1846.

Bradford, James C. (ed.). *Command under Sail: Makers of the American Naval Tradition, 1775-1850.* Annapolis: United States Naval Institute Press, 1985.

Carlisle, Rodney. *Prologue to Liberation: A History of Black People in America.* New York: Appleton Century Crofts, 1970.

Carlisle, Rodney. *Where the Fleet Begins: A History of the David Taylor Research Center.* Washington: Naval Historical Center, 1998.

Chapman, Captain C. *All About Ships.* London: Edward Colyer, 1869.

Clark, William H. *Ships and Sailors: The Story of our Merchant Marine.* Boston: L.C. Page, 1938.

Clary, James. *Superstitions of the Sea.* St. Clair, MICH: Maritime History in Art, 1994.

Colcord, Joanna C. *Roll and Go, Songs of American Sailormen.* Brooklyn, NY: Bobbs-Merrill, 1924.

Colledge, J.J. *Ships of the Royal Navy.* Annapolis, MD: United States Naval Institute Press, 1987.

Cooper, J. Finamore. *Naval History of the United States,* Vol. 1 & 2, Philadelphia, Lea and Blanchard, 1839.

Cordingly, David. *Under the Black Flag: The Romance and the Reality of Life Among the Pirates.* New York: Random House, 1995.

Cowper, William. *Collected Works.* London: William Pickering, 1851.

Cranz, Jacqueline L. *American Nautical Art and Antiques.* New York: Crown, 1975.

Creighton, Margaret S. *Dogwatch and Liberty Days: Seafaring Life in the Nineteenth Century.* Salem, Mass. Peabody Museum, 1982.

Creighton, Margaret and Lisa Norling. *Iron Men, Wooden Women: Gender and Seafaring in the Atlantic World, 1700-1920.* Baltimore, MD, Johns Hopkins University Press, 1996.

Crossman, Carl. *The Decorative Arts of the China Trade.* Woodbridge Antique Collectors' Club, 1991.

Cruikshank, G. *The Progress of a Midshipman.* London 1821.

Dana, Richard Henry, Jr. *Two Years Before the Mast.* New York: Harper and Brothers, 1840.

Dana, Richard Henry, Jr. *The Seaman's Manual.* London: Edward Moxon, 1868.

DePauw, Linda Grant. *Seafaring Women.* Boston: Houghton-Mifflin, 1982.

Dibden, Charles. *A Collection of songs, selected from the works of Mr Dibden.* London, 1790.

Dugan, James. *The Great Mutiny.* London: Andre Deutsch, 1966.

Ellms, Charles. *Ocean.* New York: Edwards, 1841.

Fellowes, C.H. *The Tattoo Book.* Princeton, NJ: Pyne Press, 1971.

Flavell, John. *The Seaman's Companion.* London: Francis Titon, 1676.

Flayderman, E. Norman. *Scrimshaw and Scrimshanders Whales and Whalemen.* New Milford, CN: N. Flayderman & Co., Inc., 1972.

Foucault, Michel. *Discipline and Punish: The Birth of the Prison.* (Translated by Alan Sheridan). New York, Vintage Books, 1977.

Frank, Stuart M. *Dictionary of Scrimshaw Artists.* Mystic, CN: Mystic Seaport Museum, 1991.

Frank, Stuart M. *More Scrimshaw Artists.* Mystic, CN: Mystic Seaport Museum, 1998.

French, Joseph Lewis (ed.). *Great Seas Stories.* New York: Tudor Publishing Co, 1943.

Frere-Cook, Gervis (ed.). *The Decorative Arts of the Mariner.* Boston: Little Brown, 1966.

Goldsmith-Carter, George. *Sailors, Sailors.* London: Paul Hamlin 1966.

Griffiths, Anselm John (Captain). *Observations on some Points of Seamanship, with practical hints on naval oeconomuy, &c, &c.* Cheltenham: Hadley, 1824.

Grossman, Anne Chotzinoff and Lisa Grossman Thomas. *Lobscouse and Spotted Dog.* New York: Norton, 1997.

Haine, Edgar A. *Disaster at Sea.* East Brunswick, NJ: Cornwall Publishers, 1983.

Hart, Robert A. *The Great White Fleet.* Boston: Little Brown & Co., 1965.

Heck, J.G. *J.G. Heck's Iconographic Encyclopaedia.* New York: R. Garrique, 1851.

Heinl, Robert Debs, Jr. *Soldiers of the Sea: The United States Marine Corps, 1775-1962.* Annapolis: United States Naval Institute Press, 1962.

Heinl, Robert Debs, Jr. *Dictionary of Military and Naval Quotations.* Annapolis, MD: United States Naval Institute Press, 1966.

Hellman, Nina, and Norman Brouwer. *A Mariner's Fancy: The Whaleman's Art of Scrimshaw.* New York: South Street Seaport Museum, 1992.

Henningsen, Henning. *Crossing the Equator.* Copenhagen, Munksgaard, 1961.

Hill, J.R. *The Oxford Illustrated History of the Royal Navy.* New York: Oxford University Press, 1995.

Howe, Henry. *Life and Death on the Ocean: A collection of extraordinary adventures in the form of personal narratives.* Cincinnati: Henry Howe, 1856.

Hugill, Stan. *Shanties from the Seven Seas.* Mystic, CN: Mystic Seaport Museum, 1994.

Hutchinson, J.R. *The Press Gang Afloat and Ashore.* New York, 1914.

Huxham, John. *An Essay on Fevers, To which is now added a dissertation on the Malignant, Ulcerous Sore-Throat.* London: J. Hinton, 1764.

Inglefield, John Nicholson. *Capt. Inglefield's Narrative, concerning the Loss of His majesty's ship the Centaur.* A new edition, corrected. London for John Murray and A. Donaldson, 1783.

Isil, Olivia A. *When a Loose Cannon Flogs a Dead Horse There's the Devil to Pay: Seafaring Words in Everyday Speech.* Camden, ME: International Marine, 1996.

Jewell, J.Grey. *Among our Sailors.* New York: Harper and Brothers, 1874.

Jones, Howard, *Mutiny on the Amistad: The Saga of a Slave Revolt and its Impact on American Abolition, Law, and Diplomacy.* New York: Oxford Univ. Press, 1997.

(no author) *Journal of a Landsman, from Portsmouth to Lisbon, on board his Majesty's ship————.* London: Thomas M'Lean, 1831.

Kemp, Peter, ed. *The Oxford Companion to Ships and the Sea.* London: Oxford University Press, 1976.

King, Dean, with John Hattendorf, eds. *Every Man Will Do His Duty: An Anthology of Firsthand Accounts from the Age of Nelson.* New York: Holt, 1997.

Kverndahl, Roald. *Seamen's Missions: Their Origin and Early Growth. A Contribution to the History of the Church Maritime.* Pasadena, CA: William Carey Library, 1986.

Kynaston, A.F. (Lieut.). *Casualties Afloat with Practical Suggestions for Their Prevention and Remedy.* London: Trelawney Saunders, 1849.

Laing, Alexander. *The American Heritage History of Seafaring America.* New York: American Heritage Publishing Company, 1974.

Langley, Harold D. *Social Reform in the United States Navy, 1798-1862.* Urbana: University of Illinois, 1967.

Larabee, et al. *America and the Sea, A Maritime History.* Mystic, CT: Mystic Seaport, 1998.

Lavery, Brian. *Nelson's Navy: The Ships, Men and Organisation 1793-1815.* Annapolis: United States Naval Institute Press, 1989.

Lipman, Jean, et al. *Five Star Folk Art: One Hundred American Masterpieces.* New York: The Museum of American Folk Art and Harry N. Abrams, Inc., 1990.

Little, George. *The American Cruiser's Own Book.* New York: Richard Marshall, 1846.

Lovette, Leland P. *Naval Customs, Traditions and Usage.* Annapolis, MD: United States Naval Institute Press, 1939)

Maddocks, Melvin. *The Seafarers: The Atlantic Crossing.* Alexandria, VA: Time-Life Books, 1981.

Malloy, Mary. *African-Americans in the Maritime Trades: A guide to Resources in New England.* Kendall Whaling Museum Monograph Series #6. Sharon MA: Kendall Whaling Museum, 1990.

Malloy, Mary. 'The Sailor's Fantasy: Images of Women in the Songs of American Whalemen', *The Log of Mystic Seaport,* Autumn, 1997.

Manchester, William. *One Brief Shining Moment.* Boston: Little Brown & Co. 1983.

Markham, John. *A Naval Career During the Old War: Being a Narrative of the Life of Admiral John Markham* (Lord of the Admiralty, 1801-04, 1806-07). London: Sampson-Low, 1883.

Martin, Tyrone G. *A Most Fortunate Ship.* Rev. ed. Annapolis, MD: Naval Institute Press, 1997.

Martingale, Hawser. *Tales of the Ocean and essays for the Forecastle…* Boston: W. Cottrell, 1858.

McCarthy, Lily Lambert. *Remembering Nelson.* Greenwich, CN: Privately Printed, 1995.

McEwen, W.A. and Lewis, A.H. *Encyclopedia of Nautical Knowledge.* Centreville, MD: Cornell Maritime Press, 1953.

McGowan, Alan. *Sailor: A pictorial history – Life Aboard the World's Fighting Ships.* New York: McKay, 1977.

McKay, Earnest A. 'Privateer or Pirate', *Seaport: New York's History Magazine,* Fall 1997, pp. 16-21.

McNally, William. *Evils and Abuses in the Naval and Merchant Services Exposed with Proposals for their Remedy and Redress.* Boston: Cassady and March, 1839.

McManus, Michael. *A Treasury of American Scrimshaw A collection of the useful and decorative.* Penguin Group, Penguin, NY: 1997.

Melville, Herman, *Moby Dick.* New York: Dodd Mead & Co. 1992.

Melville, Herman. *White Jacket.* Boston: L.C. Page, 1892.

Miller, Russell. *The Seafarers: The East Indiamen.* Alexandria, VA: Time-Life Books, 1980.

Morison, Samuel Eliot. 'Old Bruin': Commodore Matthew Calbraith Perry, 1794-1858.* Boston: Little Brown, 1967.

Morison, Samuel Eliot. *The Maritime History of Massachusetts.* Boston: Houghton Mifflin Co. 1921.

National Geographic magazine *Remember the Maine?* Vol. 193, No. 2, pp.92–109.

Neider, Charles, (ed.). *Great Shipwrecks and Castaways.* New York: Harper and Brothers, 1952.

O'Connell, Robert L. *Sacred Vessels: The Cult of the Battleship and the Rise of the U.S. Navy.* New York: Oxford University Press, 1991.

Pack, James (Captain). *Nelson's Blood, The Story of Naval Rum.* Annapolis, MD: United States Naval Institute Press, 1983.

Palmer, Roy. *The Oxford Book of Sea Songs.* New York: Oxford University Press, 1986.

Petrie, Donald A. 'The Piracy Trial of Luke Ryan', *The American Neptune,* (Summer, 1995)

Petroski, Catherine. *A Bride's Passage: Susan Hathorn's Year Under Sail.* Boston, Northeastern University Press, 1997.

Phillips, James Duncan. *Pepper and Pirates: Adventures in the Sumatra Pepper Trade of Salem.* Boston: Houghton Mifflin, 1949.

Plimsoll, Samuel, MP. *Our Seamen: An Appeal.* London: Virtue and Co., 1873.

Prentice, Rina. *A Celebration of the Sea.* London: Decorative Arts Collection of the National Maritime Museum (UK), Her Majesty's Stationery Office, 1994.

Pugh, P.D. Gordon. *Naval Ceramics.* Newport: Ceramic Book Company, 1971.

Pugh, P.D. Gordon. *Staffordshire Portrait Figures of the Victorian Era.* Rev. ed. England: Antique Collectors' Club, 1987.

Randier, Jean. *Nautical Antiques for the Collector.* London: Barrie and Jenkins, 1976.

Rankin, Robert H. *Uniforms of the Sea Services: A Pictorial History*. Annapolis, MD: United States Naval Institute, 1962.

Rasor, Eugene L. *Reform in the Royal Navy, A Social History of the Lower Deck, 1850-1880*. Hamden, CT: Archon Books, 1976.

Rediker, Marcus. *Between the Devil and the Deep Blue Sea: Merchant Seamen, Pirates, and the Anglo American Maritime World, 1700-1750*. New York: Cambridge University Press, 1987.

(no author) *Revised Regulations of the Naval Academy*, Washington: A.O.P. Nicholson,

Rickover, Hyman G. *How The Battleship Maine was Destroyed*. Washington, DC: Naval History Division, 1976.

Ringle, Dennis J. *Life in Mr Lincoln's Navy*. Annapolis, MD: United States Naval Institute Press, 1998.

Robinson, Charles N. (Commander). *The British Tar in Fact and Fiction: The Poetry Pathos, Humor of the Sailor's Life*. New York: Harper and Brothers, 1909.

Rodger, N.A.M. *The Wooden World: An Anatomy of the Georgian Navy*. London: Collins, 1986.

Schaffner, Cynthia V.A. and Susan Klein. *Folk Hearts: A Celebration of the Heart Motif in American Folk Art*. New York: Knopf, 1984.

Skallerup, H.R. (ed.). *Naval Regulations Issued by Command of the President of the United States of America January 25, 1802*. Facsimile edition, Annapolis, MD: United States Naval Institute Press, 1970.

Sobel, Dava. *Longitude*. London: Fourth Estate, 1996.

Stallybrass, William Swan, ed. *Esquemeling – The Buccaneers of America*. New York: E.P. Dutton, 1923.

Starbuck, Alexander. *A History of the American Whale Fishery*. Secaucus, NJ: Castle Books, 1989 (reprint).

Stark, Suzanne. *Female Tars: Women aboard Ship in the Age of Sail*. Annapolis, MD: United States Naval Institute Press, 1996.

Starkey, David J. et al., eds: *Pirates and Privateers: New Perspectives on the War on Trade in the Eighteenth and Nineteenth Centuries*. Exeter (UK): University of Exeter Press, 1997.

Starkey, David J. *British Privateering Enterprise in the Eighteenth Century*. Exeter (UK): University of Exeter Press, 1990.

Starr, Nathan Comfort. 'Smollett's Sailors', *American Neptune*, vol. 32, 1972.

Stewart, Harris B., and Henderson, J. Welles *Challenger Sketchbook*. Philadelphia, PA: Philadelphia Maritime Museum, 1972.

Strother, Edward. *The Practical Physicians for Travellers, Whether by Sea or Land*. London, 1729.

Sumner, Thomas H. (Captain). *A New Method of Finding a Ship's Position at Sea*. Boston: Thomas Groom, 1845.

Swann, Leonard Alexander. *John Roach: Maritime Entrepreneur*. Annapolis, MD: United States Naval Institute Press, 1965.

Sweetman, Jack. *American Naval History: An Illustrated Chronology*. Annapolis, MD: United States Naval Institute Press, 1984.

Tibbles, Anthony, (ed.). *Transatlantic Slavery: Against Human Dignity*. London: Her Majesty's Stationery Office, 1994.

Tily, James C. *Uniform of the United States Navy*. New York: Thomas Yoseloff, 1964.

Uden, Grant and Cooper, Richard, eds. *A Dictionary of British Ships and Seamen*. New York: St Martins Press, 1980.

Valle, James E. *Rocks and Shoals: Order and Discipline in the Age of the Old Navy, 1800-1861*. Annapolis, MD: United States Naval Institute Press, 1980.

Vandeburgh, C.F., M.D. (Surgeon, Royal Navy). *The Mariner's Medical Guide*. London: Baldwin, Cradock, and Joy, 1819.

Ward, Edward. *The Wooden World Dissected: In the Character of a Ship of War*. 7th edn. London: 1760.

Ward, W.E.F. *The Royal Navy and the Slavers: The Suppression of the Atlantic Slave Trade*. London: Allen and Unwin, 1969. (New York: Pantheon, 1969).

Whipple, A.B.C. *The Seafarers: Fighting Sail*. Alexandria, VA: Time-Life Books, 1978.

Whipple, A.B.C. *The Seafarers: The Clipper Ships*. Alexandria, VA: Time-Life Books, 1980.

Wilmerding, John. *A History of American Marine Painting*. Boston, MA: Little Brown & Co. 1968.

Wilmerding, John. *American Marine Painting*. 2nd edn. New York: Abrams, 1987.

Wood, Peter. *The Seafarers: The Spanish Main*. Alexandria, VA: Time-Life Books, 1979.

Worden, Herbert. W., III. *In Praise of Sailors, A Nautical Anthology of Art, Poetry and Prose*. New York: Abrams, 1978.

Zogbaum, Rufus Fairchild. *All Hands*. New York: Harper & Brothers, 1897.

Zogbaum, Rufus Fairchild and James Barnes. *Ships and Sailors*. New York: Frederick Stokes Co. 1898.

Index

Page numbers in **bold** refer to illustrations or captions.